Education in Diplomacy
An Instructional Guide

The Institute for the Study of Diplomacy concentrates on the processes of conducting foreign relations abroad, in the belief that studies of diplomatic operations are useful means to teach or improve diplomatic skills and to broaden public understanding of diplomacy. Working closely with the academic program of the Georgetown University School of Foreign Service, the Institute conducts a program of publication, teaching, research, conferences and lectures. An associates program enables experienced practitioners of international relations to conduct individual research while sharing their firsthand experience with the university community. Special programs include the junior fellowships in diplomacy, the Dean and Virginia Rusk midcareer fellowship, the Edward Weintal journalism prize, the Jit Trainor diplomacy award, and the Martin F. Herz monograph prize.

◆◆ ◆◆ ◆◆

Education in Diplomacy

An Instructional Guide

Smith Simpson

Compiled and Edited with Margery R. Boichel
Foreword by Peter F. Krogh

UNIVERSITY
PRESS OF
AMERICA

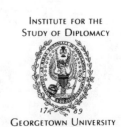

INSTITUTE FOR THE
STUDY OF DIPLOMACY

GEORGETOWN UNIVERSITY

The Institute for the Study of Diplomacy
Georgetown University
Washington, D.C. 20057

University Press of America,® Inc.
4720 Boston Way
Lanham, MD 20706

3 Henrietta Street
London WC2E 8LU England

Printed in the United States of America

Co-published by arrangement with
The Institute for the Study of Diplomacy,
Georgetown University

Library of Congress Cataloging-in-Publication Data

Simpson, Smith.
Education in diplomacy.

Bibliography: p.
1. Diplomacy—Study and teaching—United States.
I. Boichel, Margery R.   II. Title.
JX1634.S55   1987   327.2'07'073   87-23040
ISBN 0-8191-6481-X (alk. paper)
ISBN 0-8191-6482-8 (pbk. : alk. paper)

Contents

Diplomacy defined — Foreign policy and diplomacy
distinguished — Policy deciders: problems they confront
and create — The diplomat's role in his own government's policymaking — The diplomat's role in the
policymaking of host governments — Who are diplomats? — Teaching diplomacy — Urgent need to amplify
resources — Some concluding thoughts

Foreword

Peter F. Krogh

Dean, School of Foreign Service
Georgetown University

T
HE AUTHOR OF this monograph, Smith Simpson, is the
original and indefatigable advocate of teaching diplomacy. This volume distills the rationale for his advocacy
and offers a practical guide for getting on with the task. True to
Smith Simpson's penchant for the practical, it contains model
course outlines which translate the idea of teaching diplomacy
into the means to do so.

Individuals responsible for educational programs in the international field are besieged from within and without with suggestions on how to improve their programs. The tendency is to turn
a deaf ear, especially to ideas from outsiders. In this case, to do so
would be a crucial mistake. Because Smith Simpson is really on
to something, and that something is what students both want and
need—a rare combination!

Students need and want to know about how the world's work is
done. They need to know so they can face their futures realistically. They want to know because they like to have it told as it is.
Teaching diplomacy does this dual job. It illuminates the reality
of what happens when the rubber of foreign policy meets the
road of international relations. It brings the study of international affairs to life by focusing on the work of real people involved in those affairs. In the process it brings into sharp relief

the actors and terrain of international politics and the knowledge, qualities and skills required to contain and reduce international conflict.

This colorfully written volume is vintage Simpson. It is a manifesto. It gets to the heart of the matter, in this case definition, description and prescription, as follows:

Diplomacy defined: "Diplomacy is the means by which governments seek to achieve their objectives and gain support of their principles. It is the political process by which a government's foreign policies are first nurtured and then guided to their destination of influencing the policies and conduct of other governments. It thus can be defined as the process by which policies are converted from rhetoric to realities, from strategic generalities to the desired actions or inactions of other governments."

Diplomacy described: "The more onerous and demanding exercise in international politics is often not the formulation but the implementation of policy. Diplomats must operate in a diverse, complicated world community presenting conditions and nuances not confronted, nor even known to exist, by policy decision makers."

The teaching of diplomacy prescribed: Diplomacy is a liberal arts subject. "Properly conceptualized, [it] must present a synthesis of history and culture, political philosophies and systems, psychologies and ethical values, not to mention world geography and economic values and processes."

Especially arresting in the pages of this treatise are the author's argument that there is no such thing as a new diplomacy, simply new terrain on which diplomacy is practiced; his emphasis on the fundamental importance of the quality and skill of the diplomatic practitioner; his clear distinction between foreign policy formulation and implementation; and his compelling description of the proper role for the diplomat in the foreign policymaking process.

Smith Simpson is a missionary and a man of vision. His mission is to bring into prominence the key role of diplomacy in international politics. His vision is to incorporate the study of diplomacy in the general education of all Americans. As a missionary and visionary, Smith Simpson is inspired and persuasive. Read this eloquent monograph. You will see—and appreciate—what I mean.

Smith Simpson is to the study of diplomacy in international politics what George Mikan is to the execution of a hook shot in basketball. Both invented their specialties and, in the process, changed the nature of the game. The ideas advanced in this monograph will, if adopted, change the field of international studies.

Much attention has recently been paid to what is currently called the United States Institute of Peace. There has been controversy over what it should be and do. And with good reason, because there is much softheadedness among those who peddle their academic wares behind the shingle of peace. This volume could quiet the controversy because it points to what should and can be done: Study the process of diplomacy, learn what is required in human terms to make it work, and teach it in the schools and universities of the world. Thanks to this book by Smith Simpson, educators can now promptly proceed with that task.

Preface

THE RESEARCH AND editing of this volume have been made possible by a grant to the Institute for the Study of Diplomacy from the J. Howard Pew Freedom Trust. This is but one manifestation of this foundation's profound interest in the training of persons for diplomacy. The Institute is also the recipient of a Pew grant for a project in diplomatic training that seeks to adapt the case discussion method to the teaching of diplomacy and international relations. The recognition by this major charitable institution of the importance of proper preparation for those who will represent the United States abroad, as well as the many more who as citizens must understand the work of those representatives, is deeply appreciated by all practitioners and educators.

With the further support of the Pew Trust, the Institute for the Study of Diplomacy has published the essay in Part I of this volume as a separate occasional paper. Under the title *Perspectives on the Study of Diplomacy,* it is available from the Institute.

The author and the Institute acknowledge with deep appreciation the cooperation of colleagues at other universities, as well as those at Georgetown, who responded to questions and/or submitted course syllabi as part of the informal survey conducted in preparation for this volume.

Most of the works cited in part I or listed in the courses in part II have been gathered into the bibliography that concludes this volume, together with a sampling of other works appropriate to the subject. Thus a short form of citation, for the most part, is used in the course outlines. A few works are identified in full only in the course where they appear. A number of Georgetown students, including Douglas Brinkley, Deborah Smith, Jeffry Robelen, Catalino Echiverri, Nancy Frank, and Michelle Maynard, among others, assisted in compiling and checking these citations and in other ways. Their contribution is warmly appreciated.

Part I
Education in Diplomacy

Smith Simpson

Education in Diplomacy

Smith Simpson

IPLOMACY HAS BECOME a vital part of our lives, constituting as it does our principal means of tackling international problems and stabilizing a world precariously balanced between order and violence. Yet it is little understood and rarely taught. Commonly viewed as something that happens "out there," beyond the horizons of our daily cares and concerns, it appears to be remote, evanescent, and not altogether comprehensible, playing upon world affairs with fitful inconsequence, as a kind of international heat lightning. Even those citizens who band together to promote international cooperation, peace, arms reduction, a better world environment, and the like do not take it seriously, making little or no effort to understand it and the resources it requires for the success of the very causes they champion. Even more startling are university courses emerging from the 'peace studies' movement that all but ignore diplomacy. This blind spot concerning the pivotal means by which governments seek to get things done in the international community suggests the need to give thought to the place diplomacy should occupy in the education of the citizenry.

Diplomacy defined. We must begin with a clear definition of diplomacy. Diplomacy is politics, a part of that vast and intricate interplay of international activity by which national governments and international organizations seek to promote their ob-

3

jectives through diplomatic and other agents. Like all politics, diplomacy is both art and science, individual and social. As the alternative to war, it is an integral component of national and international security and central to the effective exercise of power.

As politics, diplomacy expresses the varied histories, cultures, political philosophies and systems, economic interests, and ethical values of the members of the world community. It therefore means, in some respects, different things to different societies and assumes infinitely varied forms and colorations. To some, it is a process of promoting understanding, good will, cooperation and peace; to others, of promoting deception, misunderstanding, confusion, rivalry and even conflict. To some, diplomacy is a means of generating and reinforcing international comity and law, while others view it as a means of trashing rules and undermining accepted ethical standards, and as a cover for subverting other governments.

The diplomacy of some governments thus reflects their use of politics at home as an instrumentality of deceit, repression, and domination, and accordingly becomes a means by which such governments attempt to treat other peoples and governments as they treat their own citizens. Their embassies and consular posts are converted into outposts of subversion, intimidation and espionage, inviting the periodic expulsion of their staffs in sometimes massive numbers. Now and again, terrorism and assassination are added to the repertoire of these outposts, creating a world not unlike that of the Byzantine era. While such forms of diplomacy are distasteful to civilized people, politics is politics, whether some forms of it are likeable or not. Thus, diplomacy can be civilized and civilizing, or uncivilized and decivilizing, according to its type.

The international community, however, deserves the best possible type of *politique*. As Matthew Arnold once said, "The world is forwarded by having its attention fixed on the best things." So, in the interest of "forwarding" the well-being of our planet, in this discussion we shall emphasize the best type of diplomacy.

Like all politics, diplomacy operates through strategies, tactics and techniques, as well as through the personal qualities and skills of its practitioners. These basic ingredients of all politics have characterized diplomacy throughout history. Analysis of the process reveals the significant, much overlooked fact that, when viewed in these terms, there is no need of reinventing diplomacy every few decades, with a succession of one "new diplomacy" after another. The basic ingredients are as old as the hills, although differences in their "mix" result in different types of diplomacy. If a diplomacy emerges that appears different from that of the recent past, it would be risky to call it "new" or "modern," for it is likely to be but a reincarnation of an earlier type.

The terrain on which diplomacy is deployed does change, however, and this confuses observers into inferring that the adjustment of diplomacy to such changes creates a "new diplomacy." Again, in basic terms, this is not so. In the nineteenth century, the terrain was largely one of monarchical courts and empires, dominated by Western, i.e., Judeo-Christian, values, and presented issues of limited variety. In this century, the terrain has acquired vast proportions and varied configurations through a bewildering proliferation of nation states, of international organizations, of value systems and of economic, financial, scientific, environmental, and armament issues, and of technological changes in transportation, communication, and armament. In addition, all of this has added so greatly to the personnel and equipment governments must assemble, coordinate, and deploy for the information-gathering, views-exchanging, policy-formulating, negotiating, and synthesizing functions demanded of an effective conduct of foreign affairs that it diverts attention from the continuing, basic ingredients of the diplomatic process. It is important that we keep in mind, therefore, that, despite all such changes, diplomacy remains a political process seeking to master any terrain, however complicated, over which it must operate, using for that purpose strategies, tactics, and techniques executed through the qualities and skills of its practitioners.

Foreign Policy and Diplomacy Distinguished

For analytical purposes, it is useful to distinguish between foreign policy and diplomacy. Their intimate relationship, which generates and shapes a nation's role in international politics, however, sometimes makes it difficult in practice to separate the two. This is especially true if one adopts the view that policy is what a government *does*, in accordance with the adage that deeds are more significant than words.

A government's foreign policy, properly speaking, consists of its objectives and the principles it seeks to advance in international affairs. Generally these are publicly stated or are inferable from public statements. Diplomacy is the means by which governments seek to achieve their objectives and gain support of their principles. It is the political process by which a government's foreign policies are first nurtured and then guided to their destination of influencing the policies and conduct of other governments. It thus can be defined as the process by which policies are converted from rhetoric to realities, from strategic generalities to the desired actions or inactions of other governments. Foreign policy often takes the form of an exposé, while diplomacy is the quiet, generally obscure, barely audible translation of objectives and principles into results. Foreign policy is heard, diplomacy for the most part overheard.

Unawareness of the connubial relationship between foreign policy and diplomacy has led many well-meaning people, including ardent advocates of peace, seekers of the rule of law in international affairs, proponents of the outlawry of war and of nuclear weaponry, and promoters of various kinds of international organizations, to treat foreign policy as some kind of immaculate stillbirth, having no before and no after. In this view, all one has to do to achieve a laudable objective is to create enough of a ground swell of public opinion to persuade policy deciders to think the right thoughts, with decisions, once made, having no place to go but one's own. If diplomacy is perceived at all, it is as misty, unsubstantial, and difficult to authenticate as a ghostly presence. It does not occur to promoters of these noble causes that, generally, it is diplomacy that makes things happen in the international arena and that without it, principles, proposals, and agreements, in Anthony Eden's phrase, are left flapping in the air. Little or no attention is paid to the warnings of analysts that debate over foreign policy is "little more than empty posturing unless our government and its leaders have the means to turn aspirations into action."[1]

---

[1] I. M. Destler, *Presidents, Bureaucrats, and Foreign Policy* (Princeton: Princeton University Press, 1972), p. ix.

Policy Deciders:
Problems They Confront and Create

In defining the nature and role of diplomacy, one must distinguish between "policy deciders" and "policymakers." *Policy deciders* are those who make the final decisions as to the strategic policies a government is to pursue. In the United States, this is the President. *Policymakers* are those participating in the decision-making process by which options are defined, presented to, and discussed with decision makers to facilitate the reaching of decisions. The makers of foreign policy, who generally include diplomats, are deciders of many matters on a lower than strategic level.

Next, one must not assume that foreign policy deciders are all-knowing, all-seeing, all-powerful. Often they have to leave to diplomats the function of finding out how to make a policy work—i.e., how to achieve a desired end—if, indeed, it can be made to work. In an increasingly acrimonious relationship between the United States and Mexico in which war talk erupted, President Calvin Coolidge had clearly in mind the policy he wanted to pursue—to avoid war—but found himself stumped as to how to do so. He appointed Dwight W. Morrow as the U.S. ambassador to Mexico to find the way, which Morrow did in a brilliant diplomatic performance.[2]

However wise and perceptive policy deciders may be with re spect to domestic affairs, they are especially vulnerable to error and confusion in foreign affairs, which involve other governments and societies and thus other histories, cultures, political philosophies, and experiences, other psychologies, religions, and outlooks. These factors can reduce the most nobly motivated policy to humiliating failure, as Prime Minister Neville Chamberlain discovered in his policy of appeasing Hitler, and the United States in its politico-military intervention in Vietnam. Again and again, policy deciders adopt policies or advocate proposals that go nowhere or go awry because they are not accepted by the government or governments to which they are addressed.

If the end itself is fuzzy or, due to factors abroad, does not yield a clear and practicable strategy and set of tactics, any policy

---

[2] An account of this performance will be found in Harold Nicolson, *Dwight W. Morrow* (London: Constable, 1935).

adopted to achieve that end can only be a source of confusion and ultimate failure. This is likewise true if policy deciders yield, as they sometimes do, to emotional messianic promptings to involve diplomacy in the value systems of other countries. If this involvement calls not for a single intervention, again as in the case of Vietnam, but for continuing interventions on a global scale, as in some types of human rights policies, confusion and contradictions will endlessly multiply as diplomacy tries vainly to perform the impossible task of converting the world to particular value preferences.[3] A good deal of wisdom is required of decision makers in our complex world; and it is the role of diplomats, in providing information, insights, and advice, to nurture that wisdom.

Being a political process, or, if you will, a politico-bureaucratic process, policymaking is seldom logical and tidy. It can be a messy process and lead to a messy articulation of policy, with the diplomacy required to explain and implement it correspondingly hard pressed to make clear and persuasive sense of it.

An illustration of the dilemma this poses for the diplomat is provided by William H. Sullivan, a career Foreign Service officer, who was designated U.S. ambassador to Iran in 1977 as the fateful crisis in that country mounted. During the course of a meeting with President Carter before departing for post, Ambassador Sullivan thought he had received clear policy guidance on three sensitive issues. He so reported to the under secretary of state for political affairs, who, writes Sullivan,

> was delighted to have such clear guidance from the chief executive and asked me to dictate a memorandum that he would then distribute to the appropriate offices in the bureaucracy, informing them what the policy was on these three issues and removing any further necessity for the preparation of position papers seeking a presidential decision. I . . . left feeling that the policy formulation process in this new administration seemed to be much more easily resolved than I had known on previous occasions.
>
> I discovered a few days later, however, while discussing some of the points the president had made with other members of the

---

[3]Illuminating treatment of human rights policy implementation will be found in David D. Newsom, ed., *The Diplomacy of Human Rights* (Washington, D.C.: Institute for the Study of Diplomacy and University Press of America, 1986).

Department of State at the assistant-secretary and deputy-assistant-secretary level, that they were totally unimpressed that the president had established positions on the three matters I had raised with him. They continued to grind out their position papers, some of them totally at variance with the president's position.... They took the view that the president had not really examined these matters in depth and that the bureaucracy would continue its work and then advise him more cogently on what attitudes he should take.[4]

Sullivan attributes this lack of respect on the part of subordinates for the president's major policy decisions to "the circumstance that they had been selected from members of political factions in the Democratic party who held no personal loyalties toward Carter and who felt that he, in turn, gave no particular loyalty to them."[5] This lack of respect can derive also from the feeling of seasoned operators that among policy deciders inexperienced in international politics there can be what one has called a "naive absence of knowledge."[6]

For reasons such as these, statements of policy can leave much to be desired in the way of clarity. Nor are they invariably conveyed through an identifiably authentic medium, hence a good deal of diplomatic activity is sometimes required to ascertain exactly what a government's policy is. Other governments, in Dean Acheson's words, have to "cast about like a pack of hounds searching for a scent."[7]

A nuance of this is that a decision can be made and publicized for cosmetic or propaganda purposes—to beguile the public, to placate allies, to disarm an adversary, to win votes in a parliament—with little or no intention of pursuing it. Or, as in recent U.S.-Iranian relations, a policy decider, for reasons known to himself, can covertly depart from a policy he has publicly announced, often and eloquently espoused, and pressured allies to pursue. This gives support to the view that policy can best be defined not as what a government states but as what, in fact, it does. One must take care, of course, to look behind an action to

[4]William H. Sullivan, *Mission to Iran* (New York: Norton, 1981), pp. 22–23.
[5]Ibid.
[6]Charles Naas, "Further Comments on Iran" in Newsom, *Diplomacy of Human Rights,* p. 81.
[7]Dean Acheson, *Present at the Creation: My Years in the State Department* (New York: Norton, 1969), p. 532.

discover whether it expresses the true policy of the actor or an aberration and, if the true policy, what precisely that policy is.

Even when a chief of state desires to make, and thinks he has made, a clear statement of policy, he may wind up with less than he desired. On one occasion, an American president, accepting the advice of his hard-line adviser on national security affairs, gave a speech on U.S. policy with respect to the Soviet Union that the secretary of state viewed as harsh and counterproductive. The latter had his own special adviser on Soviet affairs emphasize to the Soviet embassy in Washington some conciliatory passages the secretary had managed to get inserted in the speech and suggest that "the speech should be viewed primarily as designed for domestic consumption."[8]

In current commentary on this kind of problem, Flora Lewis, the distinguished *New York Times* correspondent, has drawn attention to the confusion characterizing Reagan administration statements with respect to arms control. "Somebody somewhere [in the administration] is busy making sure that signals are regularly crossed," she observes, citing an unnamed Soviet official who "asked seriously if Washington were determined to bewilder and disorient Mikhail Gorbachev with conflicting policy statements." She goes on to emphasize the importance of "coherent, consistent, cogent statements of American policy, so that friends and adversaries can know what to expect from the United States."[9]

While policy deciders make as many decisions as can be crowded into their days, these, like everyone else's, are limited to twenty-four hours. This necessarily results in many residual lacunae.[10] Third World governments are notable in this respect, having no declared policy on many issues, leaving their diplo-

---

[8]Reference is to a speech President Carter delivered at Wake Forest in March 1978. The quotation if from Zbigniew Brzezinski, *Power and Principle: Memoirs of the National Security Advisor, 1977–1981* (New York: Farrar Straus Giroux, 1983), p. 189. See also Richard Burt in the *New York Times,* April 17, 1978. The secretary of state, Cyrus Vance, does not refer to this in his book *Hard Choices: Critical Years in America's Foreign Policy* (New York: Simon and Schuster, 1983).

[9]"Arms Control Confusion," *Richmond* (Va.) *Times-Dispatch,* June 24, 1986.

[10]It was the opinion of Dean Acheson that these lacunae provide "room for minor officials on the spot to get us all involved in major frictions." *Present at the Creation,* p. 300.

matic representatives at the United Nations free to vote and conduct themselves according to their own judgment or caprice.

Finally to be borne in mind is that declared policies are a distillation of information, evaluations, suggestions, perspectives,
and recommendations, of which diplomats are prime providers,
and necessarily so, since policies are intended to influence the
governments to which diplomats are accredited. The process of
sorting out options and estimating their risks, likely benefits, and
probabilities of success, which is the policy-formulating process,
requires much knowledge and understanding of remote peoples
and their political leaders. This is one of the reasons diplomats
exist and why their presence among the advisers of policy
deciders is always helpful, if not indeed essential.

During a crisis that presence can be crucial. Interesting comment on Llewellyn E. Thompson's role as presidential adviser
during the Cuban missile crisis is provided by Robert F. Kennedy and Theodore C. Sorenson. Kennedy recorded that
Thompson's "advice on the Russians and predictions as to what
they would do were uncannily accurate." His "advice and recommendations were surpassed by none." Sorenson likewise attests
to the career diplomat Edwin M. Martin as "one of [President
Kennedy's] most thoughtful and steady advisers" during the
crisis. Other advisers of the president had had no service abroad
and none but Thompson had served in the Soviet Union.[11]

The Diplomat's Role in His Own Government's Policymaking

The importance of policymaking relative to diplomacy has been
grossly exaggerated in political science literature. Seats of government being distant from one another, not only geographically
but historically, culturally, and psychologically—distances not
at all overcome by sky-hovering satellites—the more onerous
and demanding exercise in international politics is often not the
formulation but the implementation of policy. Diplomats must
operate in a diverse, complicated world community presenting

---

[11]Robert F. Kennedy, *Thirteen Days: A Memoir of the Cuban Missile Crisis* (New
York: W. W. Norton, 1969), p. 116, and Theodore C. Sorenson, *Kennedy* (New
York: Harper & Row, 1965), p. 796.

conditions and nuances not confronted, nor even known to exist, by policy deciders.

In such an environment, diplomatic officers must gather information; they must report to their governments to keep them informed of what is going on, alerting them to upcoming events, decisions, and problems; they must continually advise their governments on what steps can be taken to advance their interests and improve relations with other governments; and they must clarify policies of their governments (or try to), communicating incentives to cooperation and disincentives to foot-dragging or opposition. In all of this activity, they remove doubts, allay suspicions, lubricate frictions, promote trade, protect citizens, dispense information to the public through speeches, press releases, libraries, information centers, contacts with the media, and socializing, all the while exchanging information, hints, ideas, and views through the vascular diplomatic system. What diplomacy is trying to say to us is that if governments keep themselves and one another informed of what is going on, each contributing its own little pieces to the great mosaic of truth and understanding, that mosaic will eventually triumph and provide the peace that all peoples and governments profess to desire.

For those who must deal with governments that employ a type of diplomacy designed to conceal information, intentions, and objectives, sow doubts and compound suspicions, disseminate misinformation, and promote confusion and conflict, there is all the greater need for sophisticated knowledge and experience as to what those governments are doing, as well as a thorough familiarity with available techniques and tactics for coping with the situations and crises such governments create. It is over an intricate and difficult terrain that governments must deploy their resources, and they cannot do so simply by issuing policy statements, however noble and grandiose.

This is why a long, perceptive telegram from a diplomat to his government can so electrify it as to shape its policy for decades. Such was the cable George F. Kennan dispatched from Moscow to Washington in 1946, analyzing the nature and objectives of the government to which he was accredited.[12] Acheson reports

---

[12]For Kennan's reference to this and the text of the telegram, see his *Memoirs: 1925–1950* (Boston: Little Brown, 1967), pp. 292ff and 547ff (text).

that this "truly remarkable dispatch ... had a deep effect on thinking within the Government."[13] Other memoirs of the time further suggest the profound effect of the Kennan telegram upon Washington officials.[14]

Diplomats of stature, through well-reasoned, tactfully worded analyses, can steer distant decision makers to policy decisions different from those toward which they are headed. An example of this was Ambassador David K.E. Bruce's decisive impact on U.S. policy toward the proposed European Defense Community.[15] More common are the sustained efforts of diplomats who press their views over a protracted period not only by cables but by dispatches, personal letters, and oral discussions on home visits, some of which efforts are directed to legislators, journalists and editors of the print media.

These examples of policy contribution by diplomats are from a quarter century ago. Our age of exponential technological advances in communication, migratory secretaries of state, and presidential summitry spawns a persistent skepticism of how really useful diplomats continue to be. Do they indeed still influence policy, or have they been subtly reduced to the role of transoceanic messenger boys? Obviously, in such an age, only diplomats experienced, resourceful, and courageously dedicated to their profession can succeed in preserving the role of policy contributor. In one recent case, Ronald Spiers, a career American diplomat, has demonstrated that the role can be played even to the point of reversing a policy laid down, seemingly in cement, by a two-chambered congress of 535 members. In an instructive statement of the policymaking ingredient of contemporary diplomacy, he relates the following experience:

> For almost three years during President Carter's Administration, I served as envoy to Turkey, a key NATO ally. When I went to Ankara, an arms embargo—imposed by the Congress of the United

---

[13]*Present at the Creation,* p. 15.

[14]For instance, Walter Millis and Eugene S. Duffield, eds., *The Forrestal Diaries* (New York: Viking Press, 1951), pp. 135–140. "Its significance so impressed the naval attaché in Moscow that he sent a special message to the Chief of Naval Operations recommending its study to the Navy Department." Ibid., p. 140.

[15]As set forth in Martin F. Herz, *David Bruce's "Long Telegram" of July 3, 1951* (Washington: Georgetown University Institute for the Study of Diplomacy, 1978).

States—had been in force for some time, and our relations with this important country had deteriorated badly. It quickly became clear to me that continuation of the embargo would have a very bad impact on significant U.S. interests in NATO's southern flank. . . .

I first had to make the case for a reversal of the policy to Secretary of State Vance. Vance knew what the arguments against its continuation were but initially was loath to take on the burden of challenging a policy that apparently had strong majority support in Congress. Many members of Congress had little understanding of the history of the Cyprus conflict or that the embargo policy was counterproductive, but were quite attentive to the views of ethnic Greek constituents. In time, I and others . . . prevailed on both Secretary Vance and President Carter to try to achieve a reversal of Congress' action. This meant several trips to Washington to meet with colleagues in the Departments of State and Defense to mobilize help. I also made several speeches in Turkey outlining the anti-embargo case. These angered a number of prominent senators and congressmen who felt I was stepping out of bounds in challenging a policy approved by the Congress. By that time, however, there was substantial support in the Administration for the position which I advocated.

During the spring of 1978, I returned to Washington to participate in an intensive lobbying effort in Congress. During the course of more than a month, I met with almost one hundred individual members of Congress, some of them two or three times. . . . On the day of the vote, I sat in the gallery of the Senate and watched the anti-embargo forces win by a narrow margin.[16]

As an implementing process, diplomacy shapes policy simply by the multiple interpretations involved in its explanation and application to varying environments and situations. *Si duo faciunt idem, non est idem* (if two people do the same thing, it is not the same thing) is an old Roman maxim as true as it is ancient. It is well recognized in the field of public administration that administrators shape the legislation and regulations they administer. So, too, with diplomats and the policies they explain and implement—or fail to implement. If foreign policy is what a government *does,* then the failure of one of its representatives to

---

[16]Address before the Boston Committee on Foreign Relations, February 26, 1986, in *Current Policy No. 800,* U.S. Department of State, pp. 2–3. Ambassador Spiers is currently serving as under secretary of state for management.

act when a declared policy would have him do so could be construed as making policy.

The contribution of any individual diplomat to the policymaking of his (or her) government, depends not only upon the nature and importance of his country of assignment, but also, of course, upon his standing in his government, his experience, acuity, contacts, and skills, as well as the willingness of his government to consult and listen to him. When Sir Samuel Hoare went to Spain as the British ambassador in 1940, he had had a long background in British politics: thirty-four years as a member of Parliament, four times secretary of state for air, and holder of ministerial office almost continuously from 1919 to 1940. He knew the British government intimately, and it knew him. His political experience and standing gave him access to all reaches of his government and those of the host government, enabling him as an ambassador to achieve a degree of persuasiveness at home and at post that would otherwise have been difficult, if indeed possible.[17]

The literature dealing with the activities of diplomats within their own countries is sparse. One may note, however, that the United States has formalized one of these activities by appointing Diplomats in Residence at American colleges and universities.[18] It might be added that in the United States, more and more retired diplomats are becoming faculty members in institutions of higher learning and thus in a position to convey to students, the academic community generally, and the public a clearer understanding of diplomacy, foreign policies, and policymaking.

The timing of policies and moves, the choices that must be made, and which governments should be consulted in advance are important factors in the success of any policy, and give to the experienced diplomat, who is generally a good judge of these things, a correspondingly important role in both the shaping and implementation of policies. For this reason, he and his collegial

---

[17]Sir Samuel Hoare has left an account of his mission to Spain in *Complacent Dictator* (New York: Knopf, 1946), originally published in Great Britain under the title *Ambassador on Special Mission* (London: William Collins, 1946).

[18]One of the few treatments of these activities will be found in Smith Simpson, *Anatomy of the State Department* (Boston: Houghton Mifflin, 1967), chapter 10 and pp. 229-32.

network, extending around the globe, provide an invaluable guidance system for the world community's foreign policy missiles. Any time it appears that diplomats are only messengers at the end of transoceanic communications systems, it is a clear indication they have been consigned to the ranks of the dangerously underemployed, with the possibilities of international understanding and peace correspondingly jeopardized.

The Diplomat's Role in the Policymaking of Host Governments

What role does the diplomat play in the formulation of policy by other governments? Space permits but a few suggestive illustrations. One is that of Jean Jules Jusserand, the French ambassador to the United States from 1903 to 1915. He became a close friend and trusted adviser of Theodore Roosevelt, a president so ebulliently self-confident he was not generally considered to be in the market for much advice. But Roosevelt was a savvy statesman; when he had a particularly difficult question to resolve, whether domestic or foreign, he sought the counsel of the broadly experienced, sagacious and personable French ambassador. When Secretary of State John Hay fell ill and the president wished the best advice he could get on some international question, he turned not to the acting secretary of state or to some member of his cabinet or White House staff, but to this perceptive emissary of a foreign government.

Remarkable indeed was this relationship, and it could not have evolved from anything the French government could have done save post such a representative in Washington. The influence Jusserand acquired in the shaping of American policy and tactics could not have been exerted either by the president of France, by its premier, or by its minister of foreign affairs, and any attempt on their part to have done so would have been brusquely rejected as "intervention" in American affairs. It could only have been developed in the American capital by an erudite, sensible, empathetic ambassador, fully cognizant of the local scene and the possibilities it offered, acting quietly, out of the limelight. Here lies the subtle secret of influence and diplomatic leadership in world affairs.[19]

With dictatorships numerous these days, a second example which might usefully be cited is that of David Eugene Thompson, who was appointed American ambassador to Mexico at a critical time in the history of that country. He was described by a colleague in his embassy as

> a man of powerful personality, of large intelligence and shrewd judgment, and of sharp and forthright tongue. . . . By the lifelong exercise of a naturally strong intellect on a vast number and wide variety of books, he had, for all his lack of formal schooling, made himself into an unusually well-educated man. . . . His great value to his country lay in the fact that he possessed, as no other man possessed, the absolute confidence of the aging Mexican dictator, Don Porfirio Diaz . . . and the friendship between them illustrates the great and beneficent power a North American diplomat could, if he were trusted and well-liked, exercise unofficially in Spanish-American capitals.[20]

Observe what this produced. As the same colleague goes on to report: "Aware of the relationship between the President and the Ambassador, state governors, generals, police officials, federal judges and even judges of the supreme court would drop by the Embassy to consult him about any case that might happen to in-

---

[19]Jusserand's relations with President Theodore Roosevelt were so highly personal and intimate that neither of them evidently deemed it prudent to refer to them *in extenso*. Suggestive references may, however, be found in *Letters of Theodore Roosevelt*, selected and edited by Elting E. Morison (Cambridge: Harvard University Press, 1951, volumes IV and V), and in Jusserand's discreet autobiography, *What Me Befell* (Boston: Houghton Mifflin, 1933). The French ambassador justly deemed himself "not considered to be really a foreigner," not only by the president but by many private citizens and groups in the United States (ibid., p. 282). He says of the period of John Hay's illness and later: "During the brief interval between the cessation of Mr. Hay's functions and the assuming of them by Mr. Root, the President continued to use me as a friendly adviser *amicus curiae,* calling me John Hay. Some time afterwards, as he was discussing confidential matters with a senator, he thought he noticed a little surprise on his visitor's face at the presence, among a few intimate friends, of the French Ambassador. 'Never mind,' said the President, 'he has taken the oath of Secretary of State.'" (Ibid., pp. 302-3.)

[20]William Franklin Sands, *Our Jungle Diplomacy* (Chapel Hill: University of North Carolina Press, 1944), pp. 123, 133.

volve Americans or American interests."[21] Here again is diplomatic leadership—indirect, indeed, but effective all the same,
because it was sought, not imposed, and carried no taint of
intervention.

Important, also, is the indirect influence exerted upon governments and their decisions by the skillful work of diplomatic
officers in influencing public opinion both abroad and at home.
One might recall John Moors Cabot, who held question-and-
answer sessions with university students and representative
citizens, both in his office and in various parts of the host countries in which he served, so as to cultivate greater understanding
of the United States and its policies.[22]

Geri Joseph, appointed by President Carter as the U.S. ambassador at The Hague, was confronted by the divisive controversy created by the NATO plan to deploy nuclear weapons in
The Netherlands and four other West European countries. She
has recalled her role in this situation:

> The coalition government, clinging to a slim and unpredictable
> margin of support, kept hoping the opposition would just go
> away, even as the peace movement grew stronger. It was impos-
> sible to persuade government officials to discuss the subject
> openly and present their position in a constructive way. While the
> prime minister assured me of the government's support, he and
> other government officials kept silent and wanted us to do the
> same.
>
> It was my job to inform them that they were asking the impossible
> and that we intended to hold forums and interviews and generally
> speak out on the subject. We found a number of Dutch leaders
> outside of government who joined us. The issue was profoundly

---

[21]Ibid., pp. 133-34. If a reader suggests that Thompson was participating not
so much in policymaking as in the implementation of policy, I would point out
that in fact the character, personality, intellectual ability, and good sense of the
ambassador led the Mexican dictator to adopt (or countenance) the practice of
consulting the ambassador on any matter affecting his country. This, indeed, is
shaping policy—basic policy.

[22]A career U.S. Foreign Service officer, Cabot was the United States minister
to Finland in 1950-52 and ambassador to Pakistan, 1952-54, Sweden 1954-57,
Colombia 1957-59, Brazil 1959-61, and Poland 1962-64. See his *First Line of
Defense: Forty Years' Experiences of a Career Diplomat* (Washington: School of
Foreign Service, Georgetown University, 1979) and Robert Shaplen, "Profiles:
Ambassador," *The New Yorker,* March 4, 1961, pp. 39 ff.

emotional, making it difficult to discuss with opponents, but we tried with members of parliament and various representatives of the peace movement. It was a hard test for my patience as well as for the remnants of my high school debating skills. If we didn't change many minds, at least we earned their respect.[23]

The same ambassador provides an interesting example of diplomatic performance on an issue involving not a governmental decision but currents of public opinion. She reports how she took on two of these:

... [A]t the time of the Soviet invasion of Afghanistan—a human rights violation of gigantic proportions—a story appeared in a Dutch newspaper about our immigration policy toward homosexuals. While we were strongly urging the Dutch government to condemn the Soviet action, 132 of the 150 members of parliament debated our [immigration] policy and signed a petition condemning it. Some 500 demonstrators paraded in front of our embassy one afternoon. We received scores of bomb threats. Our Amsterdam consulate was picketed and had windows broken and paint thrown on the building. Several weeks later, when the Dutch government finally responded to the Soviet invasion, the demonstration before the Soviet residence was a pale, unemotional affair compared with the spectacular one we had merited.

Several party members asked to meet with me at the time, but I was so angry I put the appointments off for a few weeks. When they finally came to the office, they were appropriately uncomfortable. It's rare that I lose my temper, but even after two weeks' wait, I felt they deserved a tongue-lashing. I reminded them the law is rarely enforced and there are ways for homosexuals to ensure they will not be turned back from entry ports. I also mentioned that the United States has large and active organizations working for gay rights and that homosexuals hold public office and are an influential pressure group. "How could you possibly give us priority criticism over the Soviet Union?" I demanded. They didn't have an answer and, several days later, they told my political attaché that I was right to have been so angry. Sometimes losing your temper at the right time can be useful, but it ought not to become habit-forming.[24]

[23]Geri Joseph, "Learning to Lead," *Foreign Service Journal,* Vol. 62, No. 5 (May 1985):36.
[24]Ibid., pp. 36-37.

This indirect influence is brought into play not only by ambassadors, but by diplomatic officers of all ranks—including informational, cultural, and labor attachés, along with consular officers—and their intelligent and skillful spouses.[25]

If a government wishes its diplomats to acquire this kind of indirect influence, it must keep them fully informed on matters relating not only to their host government but to developments domestic and international that touch upon their assignment, bearing in mind that the better informed they are on strategic and tactical developments in the world community, the better are they positioned to offer shrewd advice to their own and host governments. An individual must be not only cultured, discerning, and articulate, but also currently well-informed, to play the role of a Jusserand or David Eugene Thompson, a John Moors Cabot, Ronald Spiers, or Geri Joseph. In these days of fast-paced events, it is a role by no means as easy to play as it was eighty years ago. With diplomats engaged in a highly competitive business, any government desiring its overseas representatives to meet the competition creditably and be influential with other governments must keep them better informed than their competitors.

From all this it must be clear that diplomacy is not simply an implementing process. Nor is it simply the projection abroad of a government's policies, values, and influence. It is also a process by which the policies, values, and influence of other governments are relayed to a diplomat's home capital to become a part of the policymaking process there. In other words, diplomacy is not simply one government's "outreach" or "output," but is also an input into its thinking about what its own policies should be. No government could act intelligently in the world community without this internalizing of the conditions and views of other countries.

---

[25]The much overlooked contribution of consular officers to diplomacy has been analyzed in Martin F. Herz, ed., *The Consular Dimension of Diplomacy* (Washington: Georgetown University, Institute for the Study of Diplomacy, 1983). For useful discussions of the role of diplomats' wives, see Martin F. Herz, ed., *Diplomacy: The Role of the Wife* (Washington, DC: Institute for the Study of Diplomacy, Georgetown University, 1981), and Richard Fyfe Boyce, *The Diplomat's Wife*, (New York: Harpers, 1956). Jane Ewart-Biggs, *Pay, Pack and Follow* (Chicago: Academy Chicago, 1986) provides a graphic account of the experiences of the wife of a British diplomat whose life was ended by terrorists.

Who Are Diplomats?

"Certain subjects," Fred Charles Iklé has observed, "seem quite clear as long as we leave them alone."[26] Who constitutes a diplomat is one of these. It presents a prickly issue, invested with all the distaste of democratic peoples for an elite class or group. Still, the requirements of systematic study call for precise distinctions.

Since diplomacy is an integral part of international politics, the diplomat is a political operator, albeit only one of a number of operators in international politics; and what he practices— diplomacy—is only one segment of international politics. Diplomacy at the highest levels is practiced by those occupying positions recognized by the international community as conferring, *ipso facto,* a representative capacity, such as heads of state and prime ministers. The designation 'diplomat' is commonly applied, however, to those holding a special commission from a head of state conferring authority to speak and act in his or her behalf, with the foreign minister accorded the status of chief diplomat.

The distinction between such diplomats and others engaged in international politics is not one based on relative importance. It is an observable distinction that is needed if international politics is indeed to be reduced to sufficient precision to qualify as a subject of scientific study. It does not suggest that diplomacy is some mysterious activity carried on as a rite reserved to the specially anointed and in ways known only to them. The distinction certainly does not exclude from international politics other officials of a national government or those of international organizations. It simply points out that specially marked people called diplomats engage in international politics, and their activity is designated, for the sake of precision, diplomacy.

To clarify the point, let us borrow, in Aristotelian spirit, an analogy from another science. Ornithology, say. All birds engage in much the same activity, but this does not mean they are indistinguishable. All do not fly alike, sing or call alike, eat the same things or in the same way, have the same migratory habits, nest alike, or lay eggs of the same size and color. In addition, they are

---

[26]Fred C. Iklé, *How Nations Negotiate* (New York: Harper & Row, 1964), p. 1. [Republished by the Institute for the Study of Diplomacy, 1979.]

of distinctive shapes, sizes, and markings. Not only is classification possible but scientific precision decrees it. So, in the study of international politics, if we are to be scientific, we must recognize obvious distinctions among those who engage in it.[27]

Other terms needing definition. Diplomacy being politics and therefore requiring analysis in terms of strategies and tactics, techniques, personal qualities, and skills, definitions of these terms are needed. While recourse to the concepts of "strategy" and "tactics" has increasingly characterized the diction of commentators on diplomacy since Henry Kissinger became an articulate practitioner, there has been a notable diffidence among both practitioners and academicians about trying to define them. I have had a go at this,[28] but there is plainly needed some collegial effort. If we are to employ these terms, we must define them in a manner that meets instructional requirements.

Teaching Diplomacy

Having become a vital part of our lives and an integral ingredient of our national security, diplomacy constitutes a challenge to which our educational system must give a high priority.

As the model course syllabi included in this monograph suggest, one of the issues confronting instructors is that of methodology. How does one design a course in diplomacy? We are talking about the basic, introductory course, dealing with the overall process of diplomacy. Obviously, once a basic conceptualization of diplomacy has crystallized and courses emerge, the task of designing supplementary instruction becomes more complex, for the social sciences are providing insights into the nature of all political processes.

---

[27]In distinguishing between diplomats and other operators in international politics I am aware I risk the dissatisfaction of those who consider the distinction élitist and "unrealistic," as I did myself for many years, preferring to conceptualize all international activity as "diplomacy" and similar activity by private individuals as "private diplomacy," "business diplomacy," and the like. Since I once belonged to this school of thought, I understand it; but mature consideration of the problem it poses for scientific study has persuaded me to reject it.

[28]In *The Crisis in American Diplomacy* (North Quincy, MA: Christopher, 1980), pp. 10-11.

We know from our experience in innovating and developing instruction in international relations that there is no single way to approach that field. No dominant school of thought or even a commanding style of research has emerged. Some analysts, such as Hans J. Morgenthau (in *Politics Among Nations*) and Raymond Aron (in *Peace and War*) have been inspired by "power theory." Others view state actions as the outcome of a decision process in which the more important variables are the decision maker's sphere of competence, his role in the decision structure and his motivations. "Strategy theorists," such as Thomas Schelling (in *Arms and Influence*) and Philip Greene (in *Deadly Logic: The Theory of Nuclear Deterrence*), combine these two perspectives, at the same time resorting to game theory, which results in an approach emphasizing explicit as well as tacit processes of bargaining and the evaluation of competing policies and actions in terms of alternative payoffs and cost-risk calculations. Another group of scholars has taken root in systems theory.

Similarly, there can be more than one theoretical approach to diplomacy; but it will be observed from the outlines and syllabi we are presenting that the approach at our present stage of education in diplomacy is almost exclusively a practical one. Instructors are trying to set forth the realities of diplomacy—what *in fact* it is, as practiced by governments; the myriad functions it discharges; what qualities and skills it requires; through what systems it works; what impact it has upon policymaking; what are its resources and problems, its strengths and weaknesses, its limitations and potentialities. In a word, how it works, what it achieves, and what it fails to achieve.

The fact that we live in an age in which global peace seems to rest precariously on the relationship of two superpowers, each with the capacity to pulverize the world, may explain, at least in part, the reported enthusiasm of students for such courses as these. But this response appears to be due, also, to a dissatisfaction with what students consider an overdose of "theoretical courses" and a craving for "practical," "down-to-earth" explanations of international politics. Those whose outlines and syllabi are presented herewith advise that, far from having had to cancel their courses at any time for insufficient enrollment, they are obliged to turn students away.

How does one set forth "the facts" of the diplomatic process and the global system it has created, in a "practical," "down-to-earth" manner which will at the same time satisfy academic requirements? In my own case, when invited in 1973 to pioneer a course at Georgetown University to present diplomacy as political science and art, I felt—perhaps inspired by my legal education—that actual cases would effect the desired fusion, and at the same time shift learning from a passive to an active mode. Properly chosen, cases can provide the detail needed to enable students to grasp quite precisely what a situation was, the strategic and tactical problems it posed, and with what resources the diplomats tackled them. Except for our nation-building exercise in Vietnam, which I considered essential to deal with and on which I prepared a study, cases were readily available, mainly in memoirs.

Those I chose illustrated both bilateral and multilateral diplomacy and their interplay, conducted by both career and non-career diplomats, on binational, regional, and global scales, involving both developed and developing nations, and thus a wide range of histories, cultures, psychologies, political, economic and value systems, along with domestic pressures. They thus illustrated a variety of national and personal types of diplomacy. While diplomatic memoirs are almost universally those of ambassadors, instructors experienced in diplomacy can easily find in them useful references that suggest the contributions of all diplomatic officers. If there is one thing that any course on diplomacy must take care to convey, it is that diplomatic officers of every rank and specialty, and their spouses, contribute significantly to making the process and system work.

Indeed, it is this totality of resources and results of the diplomatic system that any methodology must keep in focus. In another place, I have likened the political life-support system that diplomacy provides the international community with a phenomenon of the physical world. A full quarter of the oxygen we breathe on this planet is produced by infinitesimal, free-floating aquatic plants, known as phytoplankton, lying on the surface of the oceans where air and water meet. Our planet is habitable only because so much of its surface consists of water and this minuscule plant is so widely distributed. Similarly, our planet has achieved as much peace as it has because of the

widespread diffusion of diplomatic and consular officers—
officers of all ranks, all specialties, all nations—and their
spouses. Their multiple, quiet, often subtle efforts around the
globe, day in and day out, get much of the world's business
rationally done, suspicions allayed, doubts removed, infinite
questions answered, ideas and suggestions sown, advice im-
parted, mistakes headed off, frictions lubricated, negotiations
inched forward, problems large and small resolved—and thereby contribute much of the progress made toward a world more
habitable, more just, more responsive to human needs. If this
perspective is not kept in mind and instructors focus only on
crises, "crisis management," "conflict resolution," and the like, or
on the role of ambassadors, one can miss the essence of
diplomacy.

Increasingly, college courses are being offered by diplomatic
practitioners, who have the advantage of providing not only a
grasp of reality but a personal authenticity to class discussion.
These ingredients can also be introduced or amplified by bringing guest diplomats into class discussions; or, if instruction occurs in a community of active or retired diplomats, by obtaining
their consent to be interviewed by students on their experience
with the subjects of the students' research. Burlington, Vermont,
may seem to be distant from such resources, but Professor James
Pacy, of the University of Vermont, reports:

> I call upon alumni and parents of my students who are diplomats.
> I have used retired diplomats who summer in Vermont well into
> October. I have used people from Embassy Ottawa and con-
> sulates in Montreal. Given our large Canadian studies program I
> have been able to have Canadian diplomats from Ottawa, the
> Canadian U.N. Mission in New York, consulates in Boston and
> New York, and the embassy in Washington. I have called upon
> personal friends—American, Italian, Japanese, etc. I have had
> diplomats-in-residence either on this campus or those nearby.[29]

Admirable surrogates for living diplomats reside in their
memoirs. Only a trickle until well after World War II, these have
now become a sizeable rivulet, providing abundant material on
the dynamics of diplomacy, including what James Rosenau calls

---

[29]Response to author's questionnaire (n.d.).

the "I (idiosyncratic) factor." Imaginative use of memoirs is made in several of the courses presented in this volume.

All of this brings specific, firsthand experience to bear on what has been viewed as a remote, nebulous, hard-to-describe process. It also frees diplomacy from the mystifying jargon that has come to characterize some political science literature. A diplomatic historian confided to me several years ago that he had given up trying to read political science journals because he found them unintelligible. On the other hand,

> political scientists often accuse their historian colleagues of simply "scratching around" and lacking any rigorous methodology at all, failing to be concerned with contemporary problems, and being "mere chroniclers" of an "embalmed past." Historians, not to be outdone, frequently criticize the theorists for erecting artificial models *ex nihilo,* creating smoke screens of jargon, and becoming infatuated with computer paraphernalia instead of human beings.[30]

The last thing that is needed in offering instruction in diplomacy is to render the subject unintelligible, substituting esoteric vocabulary for clearly articulated reality.

At the same time, practitioners must not fail diplomacy by being so down-to-earth as to miss its central, long-term role in the development of the international community. Practitioners and scholars alike must recognize that diplomacy encapsulates the core elements of undergraduate education in the development and meaning of civilization. The nature, functions, and processes of diplomacy are not simply a segment of political science. By setting forth how nations view and conduct their relationships, address their problems, attempt to resolve (or promote) conflicts and exchange (or refuse to exchange) information and views, any course in diplomacy, properly conceptualized, must present a synthesis of history and culture, political philosophies and systems, psychologies and ethical values, not to mention world geography and economic values and processes.

---

[30]Paul Gordon Lauren, *Diplomacy: New Approaches in History, Theory, and Policy* (New York: Free Press, 1979), p. 4. Lauren's book is an attempt to effect an understanding between diplomatic historians and political scientists as to the nature of diplomacy.

It is, therefore, one of the basic subjects with which any intelligent resident of this planet must seek to become familiar. No introductory course can hope to do more than suggest this synthesis, but a more advanced, year-long course could essay a thoroughly interdisciplinary approach.

Such an approach—focusing on diplomacy the resources of history, economics, psychology, sociology, socio-psychology, law, and the like—is becoming increasingly urgent. Achieving this, however, depends in part upon the interest in diplomacy that these other disciplines have or can be nudged into taking and their willingness to employ comprehensible terminology. In this compilation, a general historical perspective is incorporated into several of the outlines and syllabi, while a multidisciplinary approach is, necessarily, used in such cases as those involving U.S. diplomacy in Southeast Asia.

Historical perspective is not enough. "Scratching around," in Paul Gordon Lauren's phrase, will not suffice. Needed is analysis of diplomacy in other times in terms of strategies and tactics, techniques, personal qualities, and skills. This requires a particular kind of research which has yet to emerge. For this we need a clear-cut definition of the nature of diplomacy, which we have endeavored to provide here, so that researchers know what to look for.

Urgent Need to Amplify Resources

As our outlines and syllabi (and the nationality of the instructors) suggest, the approach to education in diplomacy in this country has so far been largely confined to American experience and viewpoints. Since the Stephen D. Kerteszes and Michael Flacks have retired from the scene,[31] this has become so pre-

---

[31]Stephen D. Kertesz, who resigned from the Hungarian diplomatic service when serving as Minister to Italy in 1947, joined the Notre Dame faculty two years later. There, among other things, he taught diplomacy until his retirement in 1975. Michael Flack, a former official of the Czechoslovakian Ministry of Foreign Affairs, taught diplomacy at the University of Pittsburgh until his retirement in 1983. See Kenneth W. Thompson, ed., *Diplomacy and Its Values: The Life and Works of Stephen D. Kertesz in Europe and America* (Lanham: University Press of America, 1984). For one stage of Kertesz's diplomatic experience, see his *Between Russia and the West: Hungary and the Illusions of Peace Making, 1945-1947* (Notre Dame: University of Notre Dame Press, 1984).

dominantly the situation that one fears it may reinforce a parochial view that American diplomats may be presumed to be best, or at least typical, and that their experience can therefore predominate in the educational process. Special steps need to be taken also to avoid any misleading conception by Americans of diplomacy as simply or mainly the projection of U.S. policies, values, and experiences abroad. One sees here again the usefulness of real-life case studies as a means of avoiding tunnel vision, for they clearly depict the interactions of various types of diplomacy, including the mutual, reciprocating efforts of all governments to influence the behavior of other governments. A serious limitation of many artificial constructs is that they are limited by the nationality of the constructors and the class discussants.

A comparative approach is essential to any realistic education in diplomacy, and there is a corresponding urgency to the development of comparative materials. A relatively few studies have begun to contest the *cordon national* which invests so much of American thinking about diplomacy and to produce the materials needed for a more satisfactory comparative methodology.[32] Such efforts need encouragement and amplification, with scholars and practitioners of other countries enlisted for the task.

Apart from certain basic requirements, perhaps one can say that approach is best with which the instructor feels most comfortable. I felt most comfortable with a case study approach, with its specific reality and comparative insights; Armin Meyer, with a structured approach well fortified by personal experience; and Charles Cross, with systematic class discussions underpinned by

---

[32]Among these few studies are Michael Blaker's *Japanese International Negotiating Style* (New York: Columbia University Press, 1977) and the earlier, pioneering work of R. Dennet and Joseph E. Johnson (eds.), *Negotiating with the Russians* (New York: World Peace Foundation, 1951). Studies in the field of negotiation are reaching out for comparative insights, as, for example, I. William Zartman and Maureen R. Berman, *The Practical Negotiator* (New Haven: Yale University Press, 1982). From abroad have come a few similar studies, such as Christer Jonsson's *Soviet Bargaining Behavior: The Nuclear Test Ban Case* (New York: Columbia University Press, 1979). Among bibliographers who have sought to shatter the *cordon national* one must mention Robert B. Harmon, *The Art and Practice of Diplomacy: A Selected and Annotated Guide* (Metuchen: Scarecrow Press, 1971).

textbook assignments. James Pacy uses an unstructured approach based upon student reports on diplomatic memoirs (which, incidentally, provide comparative insights) and upon exploiting questions raised by class discussions to wedge in basic, integrating concepts. David Newsom makes extensive use of 'real world' exercises and simulations involving situations he has experienced; Paul Kattenburg follows a theoretical approach that uses memoirs extensively; and others evolve their own combinations of these. Student response to each of these methods has been such as to suggest that method is subordinate to the instructor's insights into diplomacy and ability to convey these in intelligible, stimulating, down-to-earth terms.

History is important because it cannot be escaped and provides insights into constants of human behavior. It also offers lessons through the repetition of human relationships and situations that are comparable or similar in basic elements—of plots, so to speak, as old as humanity. We will find this true of diplomacy as we explore its history more systematically, with its fundamental elements clearly in mind. The diplomacy of Philip of Macedon, for example, by which he brought the Greek City States within his sphere of influence, was replete with basic elements that totalitarian regimes employ today—the tactics of subversion, bribery, intimidation, deceptive propaganda, organizing local groups favoring the aggressor's policies, and the like, along with techniques, personal qualities, and skills to match. One of the resources urgently needed for a realistic understanding of diplomacy is that of politico-historical studies pointing out the similarities and differences between past and current diplomatic situations—again, the strategies, tactics, and techniques, the personal qualities, and skills employed, as well as the outcomes and the lessons or insights to be extracted.

Oral history is an invaluable tool for research and instruction much neglected in the field of diplomacy. This is not to say that diplomats have not been interviewed for the various oral history libraries that have sprung up around the country; rather, that diplomats interviewed have been asked too few of the right questions for the development of materials on the processes and basic elements of diplomacy, and therefore a rich resource has been far from adequately tapped. Among those conducting interviews should be practitioners fully aware of the dynamics of diplomacy and therefore certain to press the analysis of situations in terms of diplomacy's basic ingredients. An oral history library specifically on diplomacy is one of the items that should be high on our agenda if we are to move research and instruction now being undertaken from a slow walk to a canter.[33]

This inquiry into education in diplomacy raises some larger perspectives. I have suggested on an earlier occasion that diplomacy should be taught in secondary and even elementary schools.[34] I think this deserves serious and urgent consideration. In a world as hazardous as ours and dependent in free societies upon popular understanding of the processes of peace, an understanding of diplomacy should not be deferred to higher education. Earlier exposure would have the additional benefit of generating greater popular interest in all efforts to preserve the peace, greater popular restraint in times of crisis, and greater popular support of efforts to improve the quality of diplomacy.

For increased educational reach, we must resort to a medium that has lain beyond our customary consideration of this question, namely, television. A television documentary on diplomacy similar to that brilliant exposé of "civilisation" by the late Sir Kenneth Clark would constitute an immense step forward not only in the education of the public but, as an audio-visual aid in the classroom, in putting diplomacy in a profound historical context such as few American instructors are presently equipped to do.

If this could be supplemented by a successful television serial on the life of a typical diplomatic family, this would further help to popularize what diplomats do, how they interact with other peoples on the globe, the problems they face, and how they cope with them. Television serials have proliferated on doctors, nurses, lawyers, policemen, detectives, waitresses, veterinarians, high school teachers, wheeling and dealing businessmen. Why should we not experiment with diplomats, whose varied experiences and challenges provide an almost inexhaustible source of interesting material?

---

[33] A Foreign Service oral history project has recently been launched at the George Washington University in Washington, D.C. by career diplomats Charles S. Kennedy and Victor Wolf, Jr. To what extent this will be developed along the lines recommended here remains to be seen.

[34] See Smith Simpson, ed., *Instruction in Diplomacy: The Liberal Arts Approach* (Philadelphia: American Academy of Political and Social Science, 1972). For more along this line, see Gilbert J. Donahue, "Diplomacy in the Schools: Creating Understanding," *Foreign Service Journal* 62 (December 1985): 26-28.

Some Concluding Thoughts

We must not underestimate the task confronting educators in the satisfactory definition, analysis, and articulation of a political process that takes on the nuances and inflections of human relationships throughout our planet, through endlessly varied cultural, historical, psychological, political and economic experiences. This enormous task is all the more complex now that diplomacy is once again beset by challenges to the civilized behavior and legal norms to which the Western world has long been habituated and on which the Western type of diplomacy—once pervasive—has rested. That task has only begun to be tackled. As was strongly emphasized at the Philadelphia conference on "Instruction in Diplomacy" sponsored by the Academy of Political and Social Sciences in 1970, "a center of research and publication could be an expediting agency."[35] One such center, the Institute for the Study of Diplomacy, has materialized at the Georgetown University School of Foreign Service; but not only are its resources limited—relative to the magnitude of the task—but a multiplication of such centers is needed if so many-faceted a subject is to be as fully and rapidly explored as its importance demands.

Let me close with the thought that brought to an end the monograph of the 1970 conference. It picked up the observation of Oliver Wendell Holmes that when he thought of the law, he saw "a princess mightier than she who once wrought at Bayeux, eternally weaving into her web dim figures of the ever-lengthening past—figures too dim to be noticed by the idle, too symbolic to be interpreted except by her pupils, but to the discerning eye disclosing every painful step and every world-shaking contest by which mankind has worked and fought its way from savage isolation to organic life." So, too, I suggest, should one think of diplomacy, a political process that eternally weaves into its tapestry the strategies, tactics, techniques, personal qualities, and skills of its actors in an ever-lengthening past—too dimly to be observed by the idle or the superficial or by those mesmerized with close-at-hand affairs or by minds cluttered with the images and glamour of military power; too symbolic of man's ingenious efforts to seek peace to be interpreted by any save its truly dis-

---

[35]Ibid., pp. 272, 289.

cerning students; yet to these few disclosing every painful step and every world-shaking contest by which mankind has fought, negotiated, and, by minuscule advances, edged its way from savage isolation to an increasingly organic international life.

This is the subject that we must somehow be imaginative and resourceful enough to analyze and describe. It demands the concerted efforts of both the learned and the practiced, of many disciplines, and of many alert and generous funders in many countries.

Part II

A Guide to Instruction on Diplomacy

Selected Course Syllabi

1
Techniques and Practices of Modern Diplomacy

Charles T. Cross

THIS OVERVIEW COURSE, taught by a diplomatic practitioner of broad experience, searchingly examines the diplomatic process in both its historical and contemporary milieus. Through readings, lectures, class discussion, and a term-long simulation exercise, Ambassador Cross aims to develop understanding of the vital role of diplomacy and how it is conducted. He raises the issue of whether the quality of diplomacy can be improved and, if so, how.

After an introductory three weeks of analyzing "the atmosphere of modern diplomacy," diplomatic operations are explored in discussions of the overseas mission as a cluster of power centers à la John Esterline; protocol; reporting; conference diplomacy; problems with the home office; and "the indirect understandings and expectations that condition the diplomatic world." A section on "influencing" includes clandestine operations, economic development assistance, cultural exchange, military assistance programs, propaganda, and trade policies.

Organization of syllabus:

Techniques and Practices of Modern Diplomacy

Charles T. Cross

University of Washington
School of International Studies
Spring 1983

War, it was said, was the extension of diplomacy by other means.
Modern weapons make recourse to war suicidal. It is thus not a
question of giving diplomacy a chance. Diplomacy is the only
chance we have.

—Drew Middleton

Aims of the course

The purpose of the course is to provide some insights into the ways of
contemporary, especially American, diplomacy. As such, it should
complement studies in modern history, American government, and
national security policy, among others. The stress will be on the day-to-
day conduct of relations between nations, how things actually work—
or don't work—with some suggestions as to why in both cases. By the
end of the course, the student should have an appreciation of how the
customs and practices of diplomacy—built up over the centuries—
enable nations to pursue their national interests peacefully and an understanding of the effects of the erosion of some of these traditions
under modern conditions.

Requirements

Since we will be using broad definitions of diplomats and diplomacy, the pace will have to be fast to cover all the areas. You will need to take good notes and keep up with the suggested readings.

The classics, Nicolson's *Diplomacy* and Calliére's *On the Manner of Negotiating with Princes,* should be read entirely as soon as possible. A modern work, not a classic but useful for the course and later, is Smith Simpson's *The Crisis in American Diplomacy: Shots Across the Bow of the State Department.*

Class Exercise. The exercise has several aims: 1) to acquaint the student with the kinds of problems faced by an active American mission to a middle-sized Third World country (located in the Southeast Asian part of Latin America); 2) to show what Washington's instructions to such a mission would be like and how the mission would reply; 3) to show the interaction of U.S. government agencies in foreign affairs, their separate interests and objectives, and the difficulties of coordination and control; and 4) to give each student the experience of playing the role of a senior mission officer on a sustained basis—i.e., each participant will have the same job and be a member of the same mission throughout. The exercise will begin in Week 4 and, depending upon the size of the class, will be in two or three stages, concluding in Week 9 or 10.

Reading list

1. Briggs, Ellis. *The Anatomy of Diplomacy*
2. Calliéres, F. de. *On the Manner of Negotiating with Princes*
3. Clark, Eric. *Corps Diplomatique*
4. Esterline, John H., and Robert B. Black. *Inside Foreign Policy*
5. Greene, Graham. *The Quiet American*
6. Halperin, Morton H., et al. *Bureaucratic Politics and Foreign Policy*
7. Hayter, Sir William. *The Diplomacy of the Great Powers*
8. Harmon, Robert B. *The Art and Practice of Diplomacy*
9. Johnson, E. A. J., ed. *Dimensions of Diplomacy*
10. Kertesz, Stephen D., and M.A. Fitzsimmons, eds. *Diplomacy in a Changing World*
11. Lansdale, Edward G. *In the Midst of Wars: An American's Mission to Southeast Asia*
12. Lederer, William J., and Eugene Burdick. *The Ugly American*
13. Macomber, William B. *The Angels' Game*
14. Nicolson, Sir Harold. *Diplomacy*
15. Plischke, Elmer, ed. *Modern Diplomacy*
16. Roetter, Charles. *The Diplomatic Art*

17. Satow, Sir Ernest. *A Guide to Diplomatic Practise*
18. Simpson, Smith. *The Crisis in American Diplomacy*
19. Strang, William [Lord]. *The Diplomatic Career*
20. Thayer, Charles. *Diplomat*
21. U.S. Department of State. *Diplomacy for the '70s*
22. Watson, Adam. *Diplomacy*

Course organization

Although there will be considerable flexibility, and some aspects will be covered from different angles throughout the course, the lectures and suggested readings have been roughly grouped as follows:

WEEKS 1–3—The Atmosphere of Modern Diplomacy

Viscount Castlereagh: "There is nothing dramatic in the success of a diplomatist. His victories are made up of a series of microscopic advantages, of a judicious suggestion here, of an opportune civility there, of a wise concession at one moment, and a far-sighted persistence at another; of sleepless tact, immovable calmness and patience that no folly, no provocation, no blunders can shake."

Three weeks of tightly compressed lectures with time out for discussion covering: the institutions of diplomacy; the diplomats; the kinds of jobs they have and how they deal with each other; what they expect from each other; the agreed procedures for conducting business; the indirect understandings and expectations among diplomats that condition the diplomatic world; different diplomatic styles. Some time will be spent in comparing traditional with contemporary diplomacy.

Reading
1. As much as possible of both Nicolson and Callières. Read, with Nicolson, from Plischke—pp. 43–53 on transition from "old" to "new" diplomacy.
2. Simpson—Ch. 1: "The Nature and Dimensions of Diplomacy." Ch. 3: "Reflections on 20th Century Diplomacy."
3. Strang—Ch. 1: Read with Nicolson. Excellent description of practical diplomacy.
   Ch. 3: More on requirements for a diplomat.
   Ch. 4: On language in diplomacy—good on phrases—style of talking.
   Ch. 5: Rather good on the actual practice of diplomacy; p. 79—excellent statement of traditional diplomacy; applied to Castlereagh.

4. Hayter—Should be read in its entirety. Not-yet-out-of-date comparisons of different diplomatic styles.
5. Roetter—Ch. 9: A little bit out-of-date on Moscow's militant diplomats but certain characteristics remain.
   Ch. 11: Not-so-gentle art of spying; sneaks in a little personal knowledge.
   Chs. 12 & 13: Diplomatic behavior and immunity.
6. Esterline—Ch. 4 (pp. 65–105): A description of a field mission as a cluster of power centers. Useful for understanding motivations of different members of a "country team," how they interact.
7. Clark—Ch. 1: Again, differences between traditional and con temporary diplomacy.
8. Thayer—Good foreword by Nicolson.
   Chs. 4 & 5: Quick historic run-through. Background on Soviet diplomatic practice.
   Ch. 6: History of U.S. diplomatic service.
   Ch. 10–17: Operations of an embassy and diplomatic life.
   Ch. 20: On protocol.
9. Johnson—Ch. 6: Essay by Livingston Merchant on new techniques in diplomacy.
10. Kertesz/Fitzsimmons—Ch. 7: Essay by George Kennan. Discussion of history from a professional viewpoint; a little world-weary.
11. Satow—Ch. 20: Even now the world is still organized this way for diplomacy. Uniforms yet!

WEEKS 4–5—Influencing

Ellis Briggs: "It should be noted that influencing *institutions* (which includes influencing ideology) is a different proposition from influencing *foreign policy*. Influencing policy is an objective of traditional diplomacy, whereas influencing foreign institutions is a postwar extension of governmental activity. It is at this point that the paths of traditional diplomacy and of the so-called New Diplomacy most often diverge."

This section probably would not have been allowed in a class on diplomacy prior to World War II because we will be talking quite frankly about how governments (including especially our own) try to affect the internal affairs of other countries. We will cover, in order: clandestine operations, military assistance, economic/developmental assistance, propaganda, certain trade policies, and cultural exchange. We will discuss the incentives for governments to undertake such operations and the factors that influence their choices of techniques to use.

Reading

1. Greene, *The Quiet American:* An important novel of the mid-fifties. The dangers of innocence and purity combined with self-righteousness.
2. Lederer & Burdick, *The Ugly American:* A very influential book for the sixties, despite its not being very well-written. It created some of the mystique of counterinsurgency.
3. Lansdale—An operator's story.
4. Esterline—Ch. 7: On USIA.
    Ch. 8: On the evolution of foreign assistance programs.
    Ch. 9: The politics of economic assistance; what aid is really about.
5. Macomber—Ch. 14: On CIA, USIA and AID.
6. Briggs—Ch. 6: The difference between influencing *institutions* and influencing *foreign policy.*

WEEK 6—Diplomatic Reporting

Describing developments abroad for the use of policymaking at home is one of the traditional diplomatic skills and still highly prized. We will go into the differences between scholarly or journalistic writing and diplomatic reporting, with some attention to the role of intelligence (the espionage variety not the intellectual) in reporting. We will discuss the pressures on reporting officers, how they cope, and what happens to reports, thereby forming some judgments on the integrity of the American reporting system. Plenty of examples.

Reading. Almost all the readings have something on this vital subject, but of particular note are:

1. Thayer—Chs. 21 & 22, which talk about the role of the ambassador and say some things about biased or inaccurate reporting and other forms of intellectual dishonesty in reporting.
2. Clark—Ch. 4, pp. 69-74.

WEEK 7—Negotiation and Conference Diplomacy

We will not be covering the theories of negotiation, a huge subject by itself, but will discuss some of the attitudes and weaknesses of American and other negotiators, plus some useful general rules. There will be a three-lecture series on the fourteen-nation conference on Laos held in Geneva 1961-62. This will afford opportunity for some observations on conference diplomacy, as well as a highly personalized account of a fascinating piece of modern diplomatic history.

Reading. No special readings suggested for this broad subject, which we will cover in condensed fashion.

WEEKS 8-9—Home Office and Decision Making

We will be talking about the other end of the line—the home office, the headquarters, the receiver of reports and the sender of instructions. Mostly about the State Department just below the top—the interplay between the field and Washington; the interagency push and pull in Washington; the intriguing question of who really decides what; the planning process; the Washington merry-go-round.

Reading
1. Halperin—Very useful.
    Part I, Ch. 3: Dealing with organizational interests in Washington. What the various agencies and departments are after.
    Ch. 5: Viewpoints of individuals as career officials. Political appointees.
    Part II, Ch. 7: How to get the decisions you want.
    Ch. 10: Uses of the press. Leaks.
    Part III, Ch. 13: Gaps between decisions and implementation.
    Ch. 14: How to avoid doing what you don't like.
    Ch. 15: Presidential control. The President isn't totally helpless.
    Ch. 17: "A Complicated Reality"—a key to understanding this course.
2. Johnson—Ch. III: Rostow essay on foreign policy planning.
3. Plischke—Ch. IV: Harlan Cleveland discussion of crisis management.

WEEK 10—Can We Do It Better?

Elmer Plischke: The true test of statesmanship is "molding the process of diplomacy to blend the best of both the old and the new to produce the better—or at least the most liveable results."

What can the United States do to improve the ways countries conduct their day-to-day relationships? This is a vital question which goes to the heart of whether or not we will have a more peaceful, more civilized world in the future. The student is expected to have been forming opinions on the subject throughout the course.

Callières: "Disappointment awaits us in all walks of life, but in no profession are disappointments so amply outweighed by rich opportunities as in the practice of diplomacy."

Reading
1. Diplomacy for the '70s—Part I: The latest in-house, determined effort to reform the American system.
2. Simpson—Chs. 11, 12 and 13.

2
The Craft
of Diplomacy

James S. Pacy

PROFESSOR PACY HAS been one of the pioneer instructors in diplomacy in the United States, having innovated "The Craft of Diplomacy," an undergraduate course, in 1971. In contrast with other courses, it has been over the years largely unstructured, depending much upon class discussion of students' oral book reports to raise basic concepts, diplomatic procedures, issues, and problems. As the current syllabus shows, however, three textbooks are now used for underpinning. The syllabus is accompanied by a list of diplomatic terms and a general format for the oral book reports.

It will be noted that the books from which students are to make their selections for oral reports include memoirs of other than American diplomats, an option that nudges students to keep in mind that diplomacy is an interaction of different types of diplomacy arising from different histories, cultures, political systems and psychologies. Also on the reading list are memoirs of ambassadors' wives, suggestive of a dimension generally overlooked in courses on diplomacy. Additional interesting features are the instructor's systematic involvement of students in building up files for future enrichment of the courses and his use of guest speakers.

Organization of syllabus:
- Purpose   45
- Texts   45
- Term paper   46
- Book reports   46
- Expansion of files on diplomats   47

The Craft of Diplomacy

James S. Pacy

University of Vermont
Department of Political Science
Fall 1984

The purpose of this course is to explore the world of diplomats and diplomacy. Among other areas, the course will concern itself with the terminology of diplomacy; with diplomatic privileges and immunities; with the recruitment, selection, and training of diplomats; with subjects such as career vs. political appointments, language competence, foreign service organization and embassy organization—all with emphasis on American practice. In short, the course treats the subject of *diplomats*: how they have evolved and developed, what they do, and how they do it.

Texts

There are three texts for this course.
1. *Diplomatic List*
2. Martin F. Herz, *215 Days in the Life of an American Ambassador*
3. Martin Mayer, *The Diplomats*

Each student must bring his own *Diplomatic List* to each and every class. Assorted materials distributed from time to time must also be brought to every class. All such items must be read, and graphic items understood through study.

Term paper

The term paper must reflect a *semester's* serious endeavor. The paper must be at least twenty (20) double-spaced typewritten pages in length inclusive of proper *footnotes* and *bibliography*. Footnotes can be at the end of the paper or at the bottom of the page. There is no limit on the maximum number of pages for the paper, but it is quality, not quantity, that is desired. Some suggested topics are:

Women Diplomats
Minority Diplomats
Canadian Diplomats
Career vs. Political Ambassadorial Appointments
Is Diplomacy a Profession?
The Russian Foreign Service
Diplomatic Privileges and Immunities
Vatican Diplomacy

Consult the instructor regarding your topic.

Familiarize yourself with, and consult, the magazine of our Foreign Service, the *Foreign Service Journal.*

Investigate our library holdings under subject categories such as:

Diplomacy
Diplomat(s)
Foreign Service
United States: Diplomacy; Diplomats; Foreign Service
[Other countries]: Diplomacy; Diplomats; Foreign Service

Other key words for you to consider: Ambassador(s); Consular; Consuls; Diplomatic Service; Embassy(ies), Envoys; Legation(s); Ministers; etc.

Book reports

Each student will deliver two oral presentations in class. These presentations will be made according to a format which will be provided immediately after enrollment stabilizes. [See appendix 2 of this syllabus. —Ed.] Times, dates, and book assignments will be announced at that point. The books for this semester are as follows:

Allison, John. *Ambassador from the Prairie, or Allison Wonderland*
Bazna, Elyesa. *I Was Cicero*
Beaulac, Willard. *Career Diplomat: A Career in the Foreign Service of the United States*
Bowers, Claude. *Chile through Embassy Windows*
Bowles, Chester. *Ambassador's Report*
Briggs, Ellis. *Farewell to Foggy Bottom: The Recollections of a Career Diplomat*

Buchanan, Wiley. *Red Carpet at the White House*
Cerruti, Elisabeth. *Ambassador's Wife*
François-Poncet, André. *The Fateful Years: Memoirs of a French Ambassador in Berlin, 1931–38*
Griffis, Stanton. *Lying in State*
Griscom, Lloyd. *Diplomatically Speaking*
Henderson, Sir Neville. *Water under the Bridges*
Kirk, Lydia. *Postmarked Moscow*
Knatchbull-Hugessen, Sir Hugh. *Diplomat in Peace and War*
Lombard, Helen. *Washington Waltz*
Marye, George. *Nearing the End in Imperial Russia*
Miller, Hope. *Embassy Row: The Life and Times of Diplomatic Washington*
Morrow, John. *First American Ambassador to Guinea*
Moyzisch, L. C. *Operation Cicero*
Peterson, Sir Maurice. *Both Sides of the Curtain: An Autobiography*
Phillips, William. *Ventures in Diplomacy* (North Beverly, MA: Private printing, 1952)
Quaroni, Pietro. *Diplomatic Bags: An Ambassador's Memoirs*
Simpson, Smith. *The Crisis in American Diplomacy*
Smith, Walter Bedell. *My Three Years in Moscow*
Symington, James. *The Stately Game*
Thayer, Charles. *Diplomat*
Tilley, John. *London to Tokyo*
Trautman, Kathleen. *Spies behind the Pillars, Bandits at the Pass*
Trevelyan, Humphrey. *Diplomatic Channels*
Varé, Daniele. *Laughing Diplomat*
Villard, Henry. *Affairs of State*
von Dirksen, Herbert. *Moscow Tokyo London*
West, Rachel. *The Department of State on the Eve of World War I*

Expansion of files on diplomats

The files of the following diplomats have been selected for additional research this semester. Expansion will be made according to a format to be provided immediately after enrollment stabilizes. [See appendix 3 of this syllabus.—Ed.]

Ageton, Arthur Ainslie
Berle, Adolf Augustus, Jr.
Biddle, Anthony Joseph Drexel, Jr.
Bingham, Robert Worth
Braden, Spruille
Brentano, Theodore

Brown, Neill Smith
Crane, Richard
Cudahy, John Clarence
Houghton, Alanson Bigelow
Owsley, Alvin Mansfield
Philip, Hoffman
Sackett, Frederic Mosley
Steinhardt, Laurence Adolph
Stetson, John Batterson, Jr.
White, Andrew Dickson

Class schedule

Class 1: Diplomatic terms; Diplomatic List
       2: Diplomatic terms; Diplomatic List
       3: Diplomatic terms; Diplomatic List; topic cards due
       4: First half of Herz; presentations
       5: Second half of Herz; presentations
       6: First third of Mayer; presentations
       7: Second third of Mayer; presentations
       8: Last third of Mayer; presentations
       9: Report by each student on his term paper
      10: Quiz
      11: Speaker
      12: Speaker
      13: Speaker; term papers due

Course outline

Although this seminar is essentially unstructured, as the tentative schedule above illustrates, the subject matter covered can be placed within seven broad categories:
    Introductory
    Organization for the Conduct of Foreign Affairs
    The Department of State
    The Foreign Service
    Overseas Missions
    The Ambassador
    The Diplomatic Corps
These seven categories and the subjects listed within them are not discussed in the order presented here. Rather, these subjects are treated as they arise in our discussions of (1) diplomatic terms; (2) the texts; (3) the oral book reports; (4) disseminated materials (charts, graphs, pictorials,

article reprints, clippings, excerpts of printed items, etc.); (5) the showing of slides; and as discussion of the subjects is generated by (6) visiting speakers and by (7) course-requirement research. Nothing, however, is left to chance. All subjects are treated. Thus, by semester's end students will have become knowledgeable in all categories and subjects.

Introductory
Development of Diplomatic Practice
Development of Consular Practice
François de Callières and Harold Nicolson
The Italian City States
Changing Diplomatic Practice: Is There Really a "New" Diplomacy?
Deans of the Diplomatic Corps; Deans of Yore: China and the Ottoman Empire; Anatoly F. Dobrynin; The Dean in Tehran during the Hostage Crisis
Is There a Diplomatic Culture?
Elites in Foreign Services: What about the Ivy League, "Cookie-Pushers," "A Pretty Good Club," Nobility, Titles, etc.?
Foreign Service Journal, State, Key Officers of Foreign Service Posts, Washington Dossier, and Other Publications
The Defunct *Biographic Register of the Department of State*
The Basic Literature of the Craft; Archives; Personal Papers

Organization for the Conduct of Foreign Affairs
The President
The Secretary of State
Congress
National Security Council
Foreign Aid Agencies
Information and Cultural Programs of USIA
Department of State Relations with Other Government Agencies
Foreign Agents of Other Departments and Agencies
CIA

The Department of State
Origin and Development
Alvey A. Adee, Wilbur J. Carr and Others
Organization of the Department as Seen through the Department's Telephone Book and the Organization Charts Therein
Functional and Geographic Bureaus
Country Officers
The Foreign Service Officer on Washington Assignment

The Foreign Service
Origin and Development
Written Examination, Sample Test Questions, Oral Assessment,
    Medical Requirements
Selection, Appointment, and Training; Cones; Assignment
The Foreign Service Institute
The Vienna *Diplomatische Akademie* and Other Such Institutions
Georgetown, Fletcher, Johns Hopkins SAIS, and such
Foreign Languages and the Diplomat
Salaries
The Rogers Act
Lateral Entry; Wristonization
The Foreign Service Act of 1980
Career Development
Generalists vs. Specialists
Special Recruitment Programs
Foreign Service Specialists
Generals and Admirals as Ambassadors and Ministers
Women Diplomats
Minority Diplomats
Ethnic Appointments

Overseas Missions
The Diplomatic Mission
Consulates: Immigration, Visas, Passports, Nationality Law, Over-
    seas Citizens Services
Jerusalem: A Special Case
Organization Chart: Embassy Caracas as a Case Study
The Country Team
Daily Embassy Routine: Herz and Others
The Relationship between the Foreign Service and the Department
    of State
Reporting
Some British Reporting: Heads of Mission Reports; Leading Per-
    sonalities Reports; Annual Country Reports
Who Reads Embassy Reports?
Codes
Bugging, e.g., George F. Kennan as a Soviet Recording Artist
The Defense Attachés
Visiting Congressmen
How Long in a Post?
The Dreaded Diplomatic Diseases: Clientitis and Localitis

How Far Should One Go in Contacts with the Political Opposition in a Host Country?
On Diplomatic Assignment in the Communist World
Foreign Service National Employees
The British, Canadians, Hungarians, Russians, and Others as Diplomats
The Latin American Employment of Literati Such as Pablo Neruda and Carlos Fuentes as Diplomats
FBIS (Foreign Broadcast Information Service)
The Foreign Service Family Overseas

The Ambassador
Are Ambassadors Out-of-date?
Political vs. Career Appointments
If Anyone Can Do It, Is It a Profession?
A Quota System for Political Appointments?
Ambassadorial Qualities; Vermont's Own Ellsworth Bunker
Ambassador Richard N. Viets, Political Science, Class of 1955, University of Vermont
Ambassadorial Duties
Some Typical Ambassadorial Days: Herz and Mayer
Do Ambassadors Execute Policy Only or Also Help to Make It?
The Permanent Representative to the United Nations
The U.S. Mission to the U.N.: The Other State Department? Is Cabinet Status for the Permanent Representative Necessary?
President Carter's Advisory Committee on Ambassadorial Appointments
An American Academy of Diplomacy to Judge Ambassadorial Appointments

Diplomatic Corps
Vienna Convention
Privileges and Immunities
Protocol
Presentation of Credentials
Entertainment
Representation Allowances; the Spirit of Congressman Rooney
Foreign Missions Act: Office of Foreign Missions
Security for Foreign Diplomats Here and American Diplomats Abroad
Diplomatic Terrorism
Soviets, Cubans, Turks, etc. in the U.S.
Tehran and Beirut

Appendix 1
Diplomatic Terms and Ranks

Agrément
Aide Mémoire
A.E.P./Ambassador Extraordinary and Plenipotentiary
Apostolic Delegate
Apostolic Nunciature
Attaché
Bag
Chancery
Chargé d'affaires
Chief of Mission
Consul
Consular Agent
Consular Corps
Consulate
Consul General
Consulate General
Country Team
Dean
DCM/Deputy Chief of Mission
Diplomatic Corps
Diplomatic List
Diplomatic Service
Doyen/Doyenne
Embassy
Envoy
E.E.M.P./Envoy Extraordinary and Minister Plenipotentiary
Exequator
Foggy Bottom
FSO/Foreign Service Officer
Head of Mission
High Commissioner
Holy See
Honorary Consul
Interests Section
Internuncio
Letter of credence
Letter of recall
Nunciature
Nuncio
Persona non Grata
PNG

Permanent Representative (U.N.)
Pouch
Pro-Nuncio
Protecting Power
Vice-Consul
Vienna Convention
Visa

U.S. Foreign Service Ranks

Senior Foreign Service:
 Career Minister
 Minister-Counselor
 Counselor
 FS 1, FS 2, FS 3, FS 4, FS 5, FS 6

Appendix 2
General Format for Oral Book Reports

1. Who is the author? What is his background? If a diplomat, how did he enter the diplomatic service? When and where did he serve as a diplomat?

2. What was his purpose in writing the book?

3. What qualities does he suggest as essential for an effective diplomat? What kind of qualities did he possess that make for an effective diplomat? Does he suggest and/or have any special education or in-service training?

4. What advice does he offer for a diplomat, or what advice can you derive from his experiences?

5. What were the major problems he faced as a diplomat? With his own foreign office? With the host government(s)? With other diplomats in the country(ies) in which he served? With languages?

6. How does he regard relationships between embassies and their foreign offices? Does he think there should be an improvement in their relationships?

7. How did he work with other members of the diplomatic community on common problems with the host government(s)?

8. What criticisms does he make of the organization of the foreign service? Does he suggest reforms and if so, what are his sugges-

tions? Does he feel that the organization of the foreign service is outmoded? Why?

9. What does he have to say about personnel policies in foreign offices and in foreign services?

10. What was his social life like? Did he find social functions profitable for achieving his objectives? What are his views about protocol?

11. What about the spouse? Family life and problems? Pets?

12. Does he look upon diplomacy as an element of national power? What conclusion, on the basis of your reading, do you draw as to diplomacy as an element of national power?

13. How successful a diplomat was he?

14. Did he say anything to allow you to comment on whether diplomacy is a profession, i.e., in the sense that medicine or the military is a distinct profession?

Naturally, not all books read for this seminar will fit the above reporting format. Every student, however, will report on one book which will fit.

Keep in mind, regardless of fit, that we want to learn as much as we can about the diplomatic career, the problems, what diplomats do, and how they do it.

Appendix 3
Sources to Be Examined for Expansion of Files on Diplomats

1. *Biography and Genealogy: Master Index*

2. *The National Cyclopedia of American Biography*

3. *Current Biography*

4. *Who's Who* or *Who Was Who*

5. *The New York Times* (obituary)

6. *Library of Congress: National Union Catalog*

7. Vermont Card Catalog, author or subject

8. *National Union Catalog of Manuscripts*

3

Practicing Diplomacy Abroad

Armin H. Meyer

ARMIN MEYER'S UNIQUE undergraduate course focuses on the ambience, perspectives, and problems of the diplomat in his overseas service and emphasizes written exercises. Students are required to produce a diplomatic case study that involves them in collaboration with a U.S. ambassador, with the further requirement of writing formal memoranda of interview conversations. To assist them in these assignments, supplementary "tabs" provide guidance on course projects, "Suggestions for Contacts with Ambassadors," a model "memcon," and a directive on "Drafting Memoranda for Senior U.S. Officials."

Included with the syllabus are Ambassador Meyer's lecture notes, designed for his own guidance, mapping the terrain he wished to cover in class discussion. The reader may thus find portions of the notes somewhat cryptic.

Organization of syllabus:

Practicing Diplomacy Abroad

Armin H. Meyer

Georgetown University
School of Foreign Service
1985

Purpose

At Georgetown and other schools of foreign service, curricula feature subjects such as international relations theory, the formulation of foreign policy, decision making in Washington, etc. The purpose of *Practicing Diplomacy Abroad* is to study, as an added dimension, the actual execution of foreign policy, notably the role of diplomatic missions. For this purpose, Georgetown enjoys a unique location, there being a virtual gold mine of human resources in the form of distinguished diplomats, both retired and still active.

Weekly seminar topics

Discussions in the weekly class seminars focus on the following topics:
  I. Diplomacy and Its Changing Nature (history and evolution)
  II. Framing Foreign Policy versus Implementation
  III. Functions of an Embassy (classic and contemporary)
  IV. Structure and Control of a Modern American Mission
  V. Locus for Implementation (including summitry/shuttle diplomacy)

VI. Perspectives (specialization/localities)
VII. Need for Adequate Guidance
VIII. Policy Input
IX. Initiatives and Techniques
X. Diplomacy (conference diplomacy, UN, etc.)
XI. Comparative Diplomacy (European, Soviet, Third World, etc.)

The case study

As a major project, each student will undertake the study of a single diplomatic issue, the historical environment in which it occurred, how it developed, and how it was resolved. Primary attention will be given to the role of the diplomatic mission, e.g., what contribution it made to the formulation of policy, what the options were, what guidance it received, and how the mission's role could have been improved. The object of the exercise is to demonstrate to what extent the implementation of American foreign policy may be dependent upon the performance of the American representation in the country concerned. For grading purposes, analysis will be given much greater weight than mere reportage. A variety of resources should be tapped, including officials directly involved, contemporary documents, newspapers, journals, etc.

In the development of the case study, each student will be assigned to an experienced American ambassador who will serve as a primary source. Soon after the assignment has been made (taking the student's preferential interests into account), the student will be expected to communicate his or her appreciation to the ambassador and make arrangements for an interview which will concentrate on: a) the ambassador's views in general about the role of ambassadors and embassies, and b) a review of various issues handled any time during the ambassador's diplomatic career, with a view to choosing a subject for the case study. Suggestions will be invited as to other sources to be tapped. Later on, in a second interview, the case study subject will be discussed with the ambassador in greater detail. Students are advised to respect confidences when off-the-record or not-for-attribution observations are made. Following each interview the student undertakes during the semester, he will prepare a memorandum of conversation. The aim is to develop drafting skills and an awareness of the need for registering thoughts while they are still fresh.

Reading list

Briggs, Ellis. *Farewell to Foggy Bottom*
Commission on the Organization of Government for the Conduct of Foreign Policy (Murphy Commission). *Report of the Commission on*

the Organization of Government for the Conduct of Foreign Policy, June 1975
Department of State. "Diplomacy for the Seventies," Publication 8560, December 1970
Destler, I.M. (I). *Presidents, Bureaucrats and Foreign Policy*
___(II). *The Textile Wrangle*
Esterline, John H., and Robert B. Black. *Inside Foreign Policy*
Galbraith, John Kenneth. *Ambassador's Journal*
Halperin, Mortin H. *Bureaucratic Politics and Foreign Policy*
Kennan, George F. *Memoirs*
Macomber, William. *The Angels' Game*
Meyer, Armin H. *Assignment Tokyo: An Ambassador's Journal*
Murphy, Robert. *Diplomat Among Warriors*
Nicolson, Harold. *Diplomacy*
Plischke, Elmer. *Modern Diplomacy, the Art and the Artisans*
Thayer, Charles. *Diplomat*
Yost, Charles. *The Conduct and Misconduct of Foreign Affairs*

Course organization

Overview [first class]: Course and projects (see Tab A)

Unit

I. **Diplomacy and Its Changing Nature**
   Reading: Nicolson I-IV; Macomber I, XV; Thayer IV, VI
   Due: Student's résumé, 3 copies (see Tab A)

   A. Definitions—protection of national interests via negotiations

   B. Historic evolution: Greece, Rome, Byzantium, Italy, Vienna, "boudoir"

   C. U.S. "democratic diplomacy"—from isolationism through Wilsonian idealism; cf. restraints, e.g., ratification, public support, 1924 Rogers Act

   D. Postwar expansion: globalization of interests, problems, challenges

II. **Framing Foreign Policy vs. Implementation** (two weeks)
   Reading: Esterline II, III; Halperin XIV; Destler (I) V; Plischke (Rusk) pp. 381-87; Yost pp. 62-68
   Due: 1st week—Ambassadorial preferences (see Tab A)
       2nd week—Ambassadorial assignments to be negotiated

   A. Decision making: 1) Substance, 2) Process: President, State Department, many actors

   B. Presidential styles: from Roosevelt to Reagan

C. Implementation: unlike army, strategy/tactics, planning, effectiveness; cf. NSC, OCB, Task Forces, SIGs [Senior Interdepartmental Groups], "options," collegialism, boardroom
D. Perils: uncertainties, difficulties, resistance
E. Field indispensability; professionalism; fateful errors, horseshoe nail

III. **The Functions of an Embassy**
Reading: Macomber IV–VI, IX, X; Plischke (Gordon/Swayne) pp. 346–63; Thayer VII, VIII; Murphy Commission Report IX
Due: Pre-ambassadorial meeting position paper (Tab A)

A. Classic: reporting, representation, negotiation, interests protection
B. Postwar: classic four upgraded + operations and can-do spirit
C. Art of possible: persuasion. Warrior/shopkeeper, Old Testament (eye for an eye) vs. New Testament (Golden Rule), stick/carrot
D. Sense of mission: actor vs. messenger; quiet diplomacy; accomplishment

IV. **Structure and Control of a Modern American Mission**
Reading: Macomber XIII, XIV; Thayer X–XVII; Plischke (Thayer/Briggs) pp. 323–45; Esterline IV; State Dept. FSO brochure, Meyer VII
Due: Contact with ambassador for appointment (Tab B)

A. Ambassador: his authority, style. Selection: career vs. non-career
B. State: DCM (deputy chief of mission), Political Section, Economic Section, Political-Military Affairs, Consular Section, Administrative Section (for whole mission)
C. Other agencies: FCS, USIA, CIA, AID, DOD plus others
D. Control, especially other agencies; JFK's landmark directive: ambassador is boss
E. Typical format: daily "command post," weekly "country team" meetings
F. Size of mission, tiny to large; typical day

V. **Loci of Implementation**
Reading: Meyer II, III, VI; Plischke pp. 169–87; Destler II, XIII
Due: Job preference paper (Tab A)

A. Changing nature: Classic Embassy X to Country Y. New conditioning factors
B. Washington venue. Pros/cons, e.g., expeditious but domestic influences
C. Field venue. Pros/cons, e.g., thorough but time-consuming
D. Personal diplomacy: 1) summitry; cf Camp David; 2) shuttle diplomacy. Like summitry, not without value on occasion; importance of preparations; virtuoso good, orchestra better
E. Role of embassy: provide information, missionary work, follow-up. Maintain embassy credentials, assure coordination

VI. **Perspectives** (half-week)
Reading: Macomber VIII, Meyer V, Galbraith at random

A. Expertise: its value, role of Foreign Service Institute (FSI), drawbacks
B. "Localitis": occupational hazard, various degrees, Kissinger's GLOP (Global Outlook Program), mandatory assignment outside one's area of expertise
C. Washington insensitivities. Domestic forces, need for "victories"
D. Need for balance: interests-sensitivities, sympathy-cynicism

VII. **Need for Adequate Guidance** (half-week)
Reading: Murphy report pp. 125–27, Macomber IX, X; Halperin XIV
Deadline: First ambassadorial interview completed

A. "Linkage" improvements recommended by Murphy to achieve home-field understanding
B. General directives/past precedents: provide main objectives and safety
C. Policy planning. Common understanding but unpredictabilities always possible
D. Instructions from Washington: Specific issue, but language often vague
E. Blackout of information; distrust of bureaucracy; "need to know" best
F. Deductive reasoning; determining policy overseas from a variety of sources

VIII. **Policy Input**
   Reading: Macomber VII, Galbraith at random, e.g., p. 556
   Due: First ambassadorial interview memcon(s) (Tabs A & C)

   A. President has ultimate responsibility; can use Foreign Service advice; cf. JFK and Cuba.
   B. "Man in the field"; advice often welcome when Washington in quandary
   C. Seldom acknowledged; clearance problems, preoccupations of top officials
   D. Often ignored; incompatible with domestic influences, preconceptions
   E. Indirect maneuvers; use of press, congressional and other visitors, third countries
   F. Direct appeals to top: by letter or home consultations
   G. Problems of loyalty and dissent; from within better than resignation

IX. **Initiatives and Techniques**
   Reading: Thayer I–III, Nicolson X

   A. Decision making on the scene overseas
      1) Routine, e.g., handling visa problems
      2) Crisis situations: a) protection/evacuation, b) political role: fostering U.S. interests
      3) Taboo issues: quiet, informal behind-scenes coaching
   B. Techniques
      1) Direct to centers of power, bridge-building, quiet diplomacy
      2) Indirect: via close confidants of rulers, opposition, scholars, visitors
   C. Public Diplomacy: USIA; useful but careful deployment
   D. Importance of timing; Dulles: "Knowing when to go to the brink is the necessary art."

X. **Multilateral Diplomacy**
   Reading: Yost pp. 180–210; Plischke (Claude) pp. 188–98; Thayer IX; Murphy Report
   Due: Work outline (Tab A)

   A. Community of interests (Nicolson's theory)
      1) Expanded bilateralism—political, economic, security issues
      2) Nontraditional issues: shrinkage of planet, global chal-

lenges, cf. food, energy, seas, space, environment—specialists needed
B. Conference diplomacy: on increase, various types, logistical considerations, e.g., membership, delegations, nose counting, corridor work
C. Above all, importance of preparations and realistic expectations
D. UN: what it can and cannot do, value of auxiliary agencies; tendency to herd instinct, play to gallery, logrolling; redeeming value
E. Embassy backstopping no less important, front line in vote influencing

XI. **Personal Qualities and Skills**
Reading: Nicolson V; Macomber II, III, XI, XII; Plischke (Bailey/Kennan/Briggs) pp. 211–22/286–96; Thayer XX

A. Qualities: integrity, energy, elasticity, self-control, modesty, loyalty
B. Skills: assessment, persuasion, management
C. U.S. Foreign Service: entrance requirements—formalities; career
D. Diplomatic life: protocol, amenities, immunities, hardships, satisfactions

XII. **Quiz**

XIII. **Class Discussion:** Foreign Service exams with State Department representative

XIV. **Last class:** Case Study due, 2 copies

Tab A
Student projects

1. *Résumé.* A personal résumé will be due on [the date of the second class]. The purpose is to acquaint the instructor with each student's background and to facilitate quick communication. The résumé should be articulate. It should include: full name, present address, permanent address, telephone numbers, date and place of birth, educational background, extracurricular activities, awards, work experience if any, travel, languages, and career objective, including whether the student expects to take the Foreign Service examinations.

2. *Ambassadorial Preferences.* The student should study the biographic sketches of cooperating ambassadors and list all of them in order of preferred interest. With respect to the student's top five choices, a short paragraph should be written explaining the reason for wanting to work with each. This list is due by the third week's class. Since there are bound to be conflicting top choices, assignments will be determined during the fourth class.

3. *Pre-ambassadorial–meeting Preference Paper.* Prior to meeting with the assigned ambassador, the student will prepare and submit a paper outlining the subjects to be explored during the interview. This paper will be due by the fifth class. See also Tab B.

4. *Job Preference Paper.* Following class discussions regarding the functions and structure of a diplomatic mission (syllabus units III and IV), the student will submit a paper, due by the seventh class, stating what type of non-ambassadorial position at a diplomatic mission he or she would prefer and why.

5. *Memoranda of Conversation (Memcons).* In connection with the case study, the student will be conducting interviews with his or her assigned ambassador and other useful sources. After each of these conversations, a memorandum should be written, succinctly reporting the highlights. A key purpose is to develop competence in producing useful and readable materials. While a minimum of two "memcons" will be required, the student's semester grade will be improved by the amount of initiative displayed via interviews and memcons with additional sources. A sample memcon is included as Tab C. Observe especially the "summary" and the subcaptions. The summary should *not* merely report that a discussion took place but should try to convey the *gist* in at most two sentences. The subcaptions assist in articulation. Of pertinent interest is the circular (Tab D) once sent to all officers in the State Department's Bureau of Near Eastern and South Asian Affairs (NEA). It emphasizes the importance of keeping the needs of busy readers in mind.

6. *Work Outline.* Following the first interview with the ambassador and determination of the subject for the case study, the student should organize his approach and describe it as specifically as possible. This brief paper will be due by the tenth class. The work plan should include contacts with other individuals knowledgeable on the subject plus research of documentary and other literature.

7. *The Case Study.* The major project for the semester will be the case study. It will center on a diplomatic issue that was well (or poorly) handled at any time during the career of the ambassador with whom the

student is paired. The student will be expected to study the historical environment at the time the issue occurred, how the issue developed, and how it was resolved. Primary attention should be given to the role of the diplomatic mission, e.g., what initiatives it took, what its options were, how much guidance it received, and how the mission's role could have been improved. The object of the exercise is to demonstrate to what extent the implementation of American foreign policy may be dependent upon the performance of the American representation in the country concerned. The value of the case study will depend not only on the ambassadorial interviews, but also on interviews with others involved in the issue selected, and in a thorough research of contemporary documents, newspapers, journals, magazines, books, and other literary sources. It should be stressed that, in the grading, *analysis* will be given much greater weight than the mere reportage of events. The case study should be less newsreel than editorial. It should also be stressed that students should get started early. Often the ambassadors have other preoccupations and procrastination can be fatal. The various deadlines set forth in the program for the course should be scrupulously observed, so that the case study will be delivered without fail on the due date, i.e., [the last class].

Tab B
Suggestions for contacts with ambassadors

1. Obtain full biographic information, e.g. *Who's Who,* State Department Biographic Register, ambassador's own biographic sketch.

2. Send a handwritten note identifying yourself and expressing appreciation for the opportunity of benefitting from the ambassador's wisdom. An indication should be given as to subjects in which you will be interested. Also note that you will be telephoning with the hope of arranging an appointment (via a secretary in cases where the ambassador has an office). Make contact no later than by [the sixth class].

3. Begin preparations immediately by researching other sources for background on issues with which the ambassador dealt in his various assignments during his career.

4. Write up a pre-interview position paper outlining the subjects to be explored. This paper is a must. A copy should be turned in at the fifth class session.

5. After having made an appointment, proceed with the first interview. It should concentrate on two objectives: a) the ambassador's views in general about the role of ambassadors and embassies, and b) reviewing with the ambassador various interesting issues that were handled during his career. With regard to the latter, try to narrow the field to one subject that will be worth a case study. Once one or two subjects are selected, seek information as to other sources that might be tapped, e.g., other officials in the State Department or in the embassy who were involved, documentary materials, etc. NOTE: As with senators, governors, and judges, it is appropriate to address former ambassadors, whether retired or still on official duty, as "Mr. Ambassador."

6. During the interview, it is permissible to take notes. However, it is best not to be too ostentatious about it, perhaps even inquiring if the ambassador does not object to a note or two to refresh your memory later. The ambassadors have been informed that confidences will be respected. So there may be times when the conversation may be "off-the-record," i.e., no notes taken. The case study, incidentally, should be a synthesis of all your efforts, not a series of quotes from your ambassador. Often it is preferable to use non-attributable sources, e.g., "an official involved," etc.

7. As soon as feasible after the interview, one or more memoranda of conversation should be written. One memorandum, for example, might center on the ambassador's general observations about the conduct of diplomacy abroad, while the second might focus on the issues considered as possible subjects for the case study. Write the memcons while the memory is fresh.

8. Above all, it is suggested that good manners be observed. Before departure, the hope should be expressed to have an opportunity for another meeting to discuss in detail the issue that will be chosen for the case study.

Tab C
Memorandum of conversation (Memcon)

Participants: Hon. John W. Smith, former ambassador to Upper Slobovia, and Elizabeth Jones, SFS, Georgetown University
Date: October 15, 1984
Subject: Slobovian Water Dispute Chosen for Case Study

SUMMARY. Since Gloomastan offered negligible opportunities for a significant role by an American ambassador, it was agreed in a conversation with Ambassador John Smith that the Petroland-Upper Slobovia water dispute be studied. It was critical to the latter country's desire to move closer to the Free World.

Having reviewed Ambassador John Smith's extensive experience, both in Washington and as ambassador to Gloomastan and to Upper Slobovia, consideration was given to what issue might be selected as best illustrating what role an ambassador can play in the conduct of American foreign policy. Highlights of the conversation were:

1. *Handicaps in Gloomastan.* Ambassador Smith's three years in Gloomastan were in his view most frustrating. Because of the nature of the regime, there was little that could be done diplomatically on the scene. The ambassador noted that he was seldom allowed to be in contact with any officials other than bureaucrats in the Foreign Office. As a member of a tightly controlled bloc of nations, Gloomastan made very few decisions on its own. About the only thing an embassy could do was to monitor the government-run press and radio, trying to discern policy shifts, if any. What happened in this satellite might help shed some light for Washington on the thrust of the policy of its master. Beyond that, an occasional American visitor would drift through who would ask for briefings. Few government officials found it useful to come.

2. *Upper Slobovia Water Dispute Critical.* While suffering from some of the same authoritarian influence as in Gloomastan, Upper Slobovia, as Ambassador Smith noted, was able to exercise a certain amount of independence. However, its desire to live its own life was adversely affected by historic quarrels with its Free World neighbor, Petroland. A key issue between them was the Easydam River. Although sufficiently wealthy due to oil resources, Petroland took advantage of its position at the Easydam headwaters to take an inordinate share of these water resources. More recently, feeling highly nationalistic, Petroland sought to exploit its position to influence Upper Slobovia's domestic politics. Ambassador Smith quickly realized that if some mutually satisfactory solution could be found to the waters problem, all parties and the Free World would benefit. Working closely with his American colleague in Petroland, a formula for the division of the waters was eventually achieved.

3. *Key Factors in Finding Solution.* Ambassador Smith recommended careful study of all the factors entering into the water dispute. He delineated several. Prior to the next meeting, various sources recommended by the ambassador will be explored.

Tab D

To: All NEA Drafting Officers
From: Deputy Assistant Secretary, NEA
Subject: Drafting Memoranda for Senior U.S. Officials

The Secretary and other top United States officials are very busy men. When sending briefing memoranda or other paperwork to them, it is incumbent upon us to aim for maximum efficiency and effectiveness.

Recommendations:

1. *Subject Matter.* Narrow the subject matter to only that which is essential. If ambassadors are coming in, obtain from their embassies precisely what subjects will be raised.

2. *Background Discussion.* Limit background discussion to the minimum required for a broad understanding of the essentials. If longer explanations are required, append them as "Tabs." Do not repeat thoughts which will be included in "Recommendations."

3. *Recommendations.* Put yourself in the recipient's place. Then set forth succinctly what specific points should be made. Keep each recommendation short and in a numbered series. Underlined subcaptions help.

4. *Broad View.* Remember the world is larger than one country. If the senior official can usefully do some missionary work on some other major international issue, so suggest, noting what point needs particular stress. Also keep in mind the possibility of personal touches.

5. *Distillation.* Above all, be brief. Think. Order your thoughts. Scribble an outline. Draft. Be articulate. Use short sentences. Edit carefully. Redraft as often as necessary. Make it a work of art. Limit yourself to a maximum of two pages.

6. *Promptness.* All memoranda for the topside should be in the Bureau front office two full days in advance. This will permit study and forwarding to the topside one full day in advance.

7. *Check Final Draft.* Check for typos, for misplaced phrases or sentences, for appropriate tabs, for necessary clearances, and final determination that this is your best effort.

A.H. Meyer

Instructor's detailed lecture outlines

I. Diplomacy and Its Changing Nature

A. *Definitions of Diplomacy*
1. Wotton: "honest man sent to lie abroad for his country," a "merriment." Fired by James I. "In retirement we grow wiser."
2. What it is not: a) framing policy; b) international law. Nicolson: It is "executive," not "legislative" conduct.
3. Oxford (Nicolson): "management of international relations by negotiations."
4. Meyer: protection of national interests through negotiations.
B. *Historic Evolution*
1. Theory (Nicolson): Exclusive tribal rights to inclusive common interests. Warrior vs. shopkeeper. Morality factor: religion vs common sense. Nicolson suggests steady progression. Actually, it has been sporadic and oscillatory.
2. Mythology: "Angel's Game"—carry messages between heaven and earth. From Hermes, Zeus's intermediary—imprint of charm, trickery and cunning.
3. Greece. City states—foreigners unwelcome.
   a) Heralds. Trumpet announcements. Homeric period.
   b) Orators. Sent between states to advocate. Ground rules for missions.
   c) Conferences. Ancient tendencies toward Camelot. Amphictyonic (regional) councils, community of interests, covenants. Sparta League vs Athens 432 BC. King Archidam's appeal against war. Cement: enemy. Against Athens, against Persians.
4. Rome. Pax Romana—"habit of peace."
   a) Soldier-conquerors, colonial administrators, laws.
   b) But also "natural law," embryonic human rights.
   c) "Diploun" from Greek "to fold": road documents, treaties, archives.
   d) "Cancellarius": doormen without whom treaties had no sanctity.
5. Byzantines. Justinian, self-interest, ingenuity—trained observers.
   a) Foment rivalries.
   b) Bribe frontier tribes.
   c) Convert to Christianity.
6. Italians. City states, 13th–14th centuries AD, unlike feudal Europe.
   a) First resident diplomat 15th century. Sforza's Milan Ambassador to Genoa.
   b) Rivalries. Refined Byzantine practices. Machiavelli: "The Prince."
   c) Later embassies spread in Europe.

7. Congress of Vienna, 1815. Brought order to ambassadorial jungle.
   a) Four categories of representatives.
   b) Rules of precedence.
8. "Boudoir diplomacy." cf Lord Malmesbury and Empress Catherine.
   a) Absolute monarchies with "sovereign authority."
   b) Concert of Europe—Napoleon the polarizer.
9. Changes: political evolution reflected in diplomatic machinery.
   a) Growing sense of common interests. Motivation of common dangers.
   b) Public opinion more powerful—and exploitable. Authority diffused.
   c) Communications revolution: telegraph, telephone, aircraft, radio, TV, satellites.
   d) Formerly governments, and ambassadors, could be more autocratic.
C. *Democratic Diplomacy*—epitomized by USA Rule: diplomatic apparatus reflects political system and its policies.
   1. Constitutional background—division of powers.
      a) Executive: primary responsibility. Congress: advise and consent.
      b) Senate senior: treaties and ambassadors. Whole Congress: purse and war.
   2. New nation. Normal neutralism. Washington against "entangling alliances," but strong ambassadors for special missions: Franklin, Jefferson, Adams. Cf Monroe sent to help Amb. Livingston in Paris for Louisiana Purchase.
   3. Isolationism. Internal preoccupations. Jackson spoils, little diplomacy. Secretaries of state primary actors. Cf Alaska, "Seward's folly."
   4. Consular service. Inspired by: a) trade, b) protect seamen. Cf Perry/Japan. Political appointees. Minimal remuneration and attention.
   5. 1906 Act of Congress. Milestone. T. Roosevelt organized consular service. Less politics, but salaries still miserly, needed supplementing.
   6. Wilson's idealism. Inspired world: 14 points, open covenants, self-determination. But shaken at Versailles by secret deals. Repudiated at home, Senate.
   7. Rogers Act, 1924. First professional Foreign Service, combined with Consular Service. Small elite corps, a beginning, but still age of isolationism.
   8. Age of FDR. President dominated, enjoyed summitry, dis-

dained Foreign Service. Relied on Hopkins, leaving Secstate Hull to routine matters.
9. Democratic restraints. Make diplomacy more difficult, but more legitimate.
   a) Executive branch: cabinet and bureaucracy intruding roles.
   b) Congress: ratification, purse, consultations, domestic politics.
   c) Public support: ignorance, confusion, morality, cumbersome delays, vagueness and ambiguity = imprecision.
10. Authoritarian regimes, less formidable restraints. Cf USSR, Shah. But can have blowups while democratic diplomacy generates consensus.
D. *Postwar Expansion*
   1. Shrinkage of planet: jet planes, instantaneous communication worldwide.
   2. Problems more global. U.S. plunged into world affairs. Examples: containment, collective security, aid programs, trade and economics.
   3. New set of challenges—transnational in character. Examples: energy, food, environment, terrorism, narcotics, seabeds, space.
   4. Foreign Service expansion: apparatus reflects national policies and attitudes.
      a) FSOs [Foreign Service Officers]: from 350 to 3500, no expansion since 1960. State Department now [1985] circa 15,000 employees, but still the smallest executive department.
      b) Other agencies mushroomed; two-thirds of representation abroad.
   5. New ball game.
      a) From boudoir, to Foreign Offices, to shared decision making.
      b) Coordination of multitude of agencies and actors.

II. Framing Foreign Policy versus Implementation

A. *Foreign Policy Decision Making*
   1. Substance. Tends to be fundamental and continuous. Much inertia.
      a) Based on historic values in which Americans are grounded.
      b) Variation 10%. Difference between campaigning and being in power. Cf perennial rhetoric re foreign aid. Cf Reagan and Red China.

2. Process. Actors who influence policymaking.
   a) President. Chief of State + Head of Government. HST: "Buck stops here."
   b) State Department. Secretary of State should be chief advisor.
      1) "Foggy Bottom," cumbersome, unresponsive. Ball: "fudge factory."
      2) State Table of Organization (from telephone book). Labyrinth.
      3) Trace typical telegram. Action and info copies.
      4) Clearances are exasperatingly time-consuming.
      5) Endless "reorganizations": Hoover, Wriston, Murphy, etc. But Parkinson tends to prevail.
      6) Rusk: "not what you find in textbooks or organization charts. It is how confidence flows down from the President."
   c) Other agencies. Postwar explosion: CIA, DOD, AID, USIA, etc. Inevitable tendency toward bureaucratic politics (Halperin).
   d) Democracy: Congress, special interests, media, public. Tendency toward adversarial relationships.
B. *Presidential Styles.* Each has his own; cf baseball pitchers. None perfect.
   1. Roosevelt: Charisma, brain trust, summits/World War II, Hull secondary. State tiny.
   2. Truman: Unique with urbane Acheson. Decisive, creative. Cf their memoirs. Cf Truman Doctrine, NATO, Point Four. Acheson *Present at the Creation.*
   3. Eisenhower: Military staff work, delegated. State Department "under Dulles' hat." Cf anti-communism crusade, pact-building, Suez and principles.
   4. Kennedy: Open, fast action, can-do. Accent on youth, dynamism. New Frontier. "State to take charge," but White House fountain of activity. Rusk and Bundy.
   5. Johnson: Good instincts, but uncomfortable. Awed by JFK's "awesome foursome." Cf Vietnam (dove yielded to hawks). Cf Iran arms (deferred to McNamara).
   6. Nixon: Familiarity with foreign affairs. With Kissinger disliked bureaucracy. Super secrecy. Few friends. State morale very low. Cf China "shock."
   7. Ford: Mesmerized by Kissinger who took White House role to State. Uneasy re foreign affairs. Tried to improve image, e.g., travel. Difficult. Cf Eastern Europe gaffe in 1976 campaign.

8. Carter: Ideologue buffeted by realities. Nice guys finish last. Cf Iran. Depended on personal relationships. Camp David historic success.
9. Reagan: Board Chairman, great communicator, detachment, teflon existence. Man of convictions, but changeable. Staff role in decision making.
C. *Implementation.* Execution differs from policy formulation.
   1. Unlike army. Orders by headquarters followed by commanders and troops.
      a) Napoleon: "Art of war is simple; all depends on execution."
      b) Eisenhower. Rudely awakened. Truman: "Poor Ike." Prompted Wriston program: "Put all Foreign Service people in same uniform."
      c) Acheson: "Authority fades with distance and speed of light."
   2. Strategy vs tactics. From policy to execution, attempted methods.
      a) NSC (Truman) 1947. Aim: control, coordination of postwar agencies. Palestine issue was one of the first. Not a success.
      b) OCB (Eisenhower). NSC not enough. Assign responsibility.
         1) Poor Herter: agenda, eternal meetings, bureaucratic wrangling.
         2) Dulles ignored machinery: Preferred policy over operations. Ousted USAID and USIA.
      c) Task Forces (JFK). Abolished Ike's committees. Merged policy and operations. Cf task forces on Iran, Laos, Cuban missile crisis.
      d) Interdepartmental Regional Groups and Senior Interdepartmental Groups (LBJ). To handle problems systematically. Formalities, but key decisions made by "awesome foursome."
      e) Options (RMN). JFK too haphazard. Need: "conceptualization"/control.
         1) In theory, distinction between policy and operations restored.
         2) In fact, RMN and Kissinger monopolized key issues.
         3) State spun wheels on NSSMs (National Security Study Memoranda). Generating "options" all but one of which were nonsense.
         4) White House issued NSDMs (Natl Security Decision Memoranda). As Kissinger desired, via SRG (Senior Review Group) or via WASAG (Washington Special Action Group), e.g., covert activities.
         5) Kissinger was king of the hill. State Department frustration.

6) Pluses: Imposition of a) authority, b) coordination, cf Okinawa.
7) Minuses: Morale, government-wide and public support eroded.
   f) Collegialism (Carter). Deep personal involvement. Invites vulnerability. Innocence, diffusion, noncrystallization. Vance vs Brzezinski.
   g) Business approach (Reagan). Fine for chairman, but hard on management, CEOs. Shultz has to fend for himself, without clout of president's backing.
3. Planning. Shape future, not be reactive. Idealistic. Futurology is risky.
   a) Long-range view has value. Cf reversion of Okinawa, U.S.–Japan cement.
   b) But unpredictability. Cf Gemayel assassination and U.S. (Israel) plans.
   c) Unenvisionable opportunities. Cf Nagoya table tennis in PRC relations.
4. Perils. Reasons Kissinger preferred "lone ranger" tactics.
   a) Ignorance. Not many close to president, aware of new initiatives. Cf Laird using "no change" line in Tokyo when Kissinger in Beijing.
   b) Insurmountable difficulties. Cf aborted "strategic consensus" in Middle East.
   c) Resistance. Various forms: disregard, leaks, delays, overzealous, open. Cf MacArthur vs Truman in Korea. Cf State vs Israel in 1948.
D. *Field Indispensability*
   1. Diplomacy is process, not one-shot affair. Requires continual on-scene aid. Ball: "Show biz" diplomacy is undermining diplomatic institutions.
   2. Professional touch is needed, e.g., doctor. "How" more than "what."
   3. Avoiding mistakes often more important than brilliance. Like playing bridge. Horseshoe nail syndrome. Small mistakes lead to major crises.

III. The Functions of an Embassy

A. *Classic.* Two-way street—enlighten host and home countries.
   1. Reporting. Trained observers—Byzantine origin.
      a) Before wire services. News needed. For U.S., isolationist detachment.
      b) Items of home interest: international moves, trade, internal policies, consular problems.

    c) Sources: officialdom, other diplomats, press, ins more than outs.
2. Representation. Present official line, show presence—Greek orator origin.
    a) Official functions, ceremonies. Striped pants, decorations. Still image.
    b) Government-to-government emphasis. Concern for diplomatic perquisites.
3. Negotiation. Tended to be formal, await instructions, messenger.
4. Protection. Safety of citizens. Commercial and other interests. Cf Commodore Perry's Black Ships. Open consulates in Japan.

B. *Post–World War II.* Explosion of interests, shrinkage of planet, more complex world, more active diplomacy.
1. Assessment. More than classic reporting.
    a) Depth, breadth: editorial vs. newsreel. Analysis of options, responses.
    b) Wide sources: whole staff, broad contacts, outs, ins, diplomats, press, business, labor, agriculture, et al.
    c) Accuracy. Nicolson: diplomacy as "written art." Unembroidered truth. Use of notes. Witticisms without distortion.
    d) Selectivity. Quality, not quantity. Cf strategic vs mass bombing. Problem: meeting home front requests, which are excessive.
    e) Distillation. Succinctness. Cf Harriman, read draft several times. Value of summaries. Appreciated by busy senior officials.
    f) Format. From stilted dispatches to airgrams and telegrams. Signature: chief of mission. Problem of drafting credit.
2. Representation. Special emissaries, shuttle bureaucrats, swarms of visitors.
    a) Embassy still paramount but often overloaded with logistics. Hospitality expected, low funds. Cf Congress and constituents.
    b) Imbalance. Reciprocity is lacking for foreign visitors to Washington.
3. Negotiations. More abundant, more complex, more technical.
    a) Preparation. Get facts, define problems, arguments, forces at work. Home front imperatives cannot be disregarded. Cf Vietnam war.
    b) Tactics. Put self in other's shoes. What is possible, what is not. Seek common ground. Value for both sides more lasting.

c) Style. Patience and charm, but hang tough. Fallback position.
d) Flank attacks. Can be useful. Cf ping pong diplomacy with PRC.
e) Resolution: 1. negotiable, 2. impossible, 3. massaged, 4. fuzzy. Cf Panama,"strategic consensus," SALT, UN Resolution 242.
4. Protection. Vastly expanded.
a) Normal functions: passport validations, visa loads, protection cases.
b) New challenges: narcotics, child custody, demonstrations, terrorism.
5. Operations. New responsibility, coordinate plethora of agencies. Especially CIA, USIA, AID and DOD.
a) Murphy Report: oversight and management function (see Unit IV).
b) But ambassador must be more than manager. Remains president's voice.
6. Can-do spirit. Engendered by WWII. Skyrocketed with JFK administration.
a) Talleyrand's "pas trop de zéle" fundamental, but overworked.
b) Excessive anxiety equally bad. Cf Iran hostage debacle.
C. *Philosophy of Negotiations.* Art of the possible, persuasion.
1. Ancient conflicting approaches.
a) Old Testament. Eye for eye, tooth for tooth.
b) New Testament. Golden Rule. "Do unto others..."
2. Nicolson's concepts.
a) Warrior. Desk pounding, threats, ultimata, military action, victory. Cf Operation Peace for Galilee.
b) Shopkeeper. Well-mannered, conciliatory, dialogue, bargaining and compromise. Cf Japanese Peace Treaty. But also Chamberlain at Munich.
3. Golden mean: a blend. Both OT and NT are in Bible. Carrot and stick.
D. *Sense of Mission.* New dimension altogether.
1. What should be accomplished during any given assignment?
a) Country plans are fine, set broad objectives.
b) But critical are personal view and motivation.
2. Diplomat must be an actor, not merely a messenger.
3. Quiet diplomacy rather than "loud mouth" diplomacy or "victories."
a) Patient behind-the-scenes endeavor. Not much glory. "Faceless."

b) Publicity usually when things go wrong. Cf Lebanon.

c) Satisfaction in quiet accomplishment, and less dangerous world.

IV. Structure and Control of a Modern American Mission

A. *Ambassador*

1. Representative of President (not State Department)

    a) Appointment, resignation, as president wishes. Senate confirmation.

    b) In practice, normally deals with secretary of state, not NSC. Cf dilemma during Rogers-Kissinger period.

2. "Ambassador Extraordinary and Plenipotentiary" (AEP)

    a) Theoretically, full power, president's spokesman.

    b) In practice, competing channels, e.g."back channel." VIP visitors. Cf Fulbright question: "Why be an ambassador these days?"

3. JFK landmark directive: Ambassador in full charge of all U.S. Government activities.

    a) Recognized problem of competing agency representatives.

    b) Has been reaffirmed. Unchallengeable, but frequently not respected.

4. Ambassadors have own styles. Like baseball pitchers. Each can be effective.

5. Careerists. Advantage of professional skills, familiarity with system, experience, and contacts. Cf Israel: asks for careerist; feels politicos are discounted in Washington.

6. Noncareerists. Appointments have a variety of motivations.

    a) Advantages: procedurally less encumbered, often pipeline to president.

    b) New blood has value. Questions re qualifications. Bunkers vs Glucks.

7. Selection. Process varies. Tug-of-war between White House and State Department.

    a) Carter's committee approach. "Academy" approach, like Bar Association.

    b) Regardless of administrations, ratio averages out 2/3 careerists.

    c) Choice of careerists: 1. record, 2. chance.

B. *State Department Component* (Consult State Department Foreign Service brochure)

1. Ambassador's office. Aide, secretary, interpreter, social secretary. Security. Host country has basic responsibility.

2. DCM (Deputy Chief of Mission). Ambassador's alter ego, chief-of-staff. Manager of mission. Chargé d'affaires a. i. when ambassador is absent.
3. POL (political section). Heart of the embassy.
   a) Monitors political developments, trends, both internal and external.
   b) Negotiating as well as reporting. Cf Chinese representation issue.
4. ECON (economic section). Of great importance.
   a) Internal: monitor local economy. "Foreign Economic Trends" compilation.
   b) External: monitor international relationships, impact on U.S. interests.
5. POL/MIL (political-military affairs). Liaison with U.S. military. Example: harmonizing U.S. activities under treaty arrangements with local government.
6. CON (consular section). Heavy workload. Importance of local nationals: a) citizenship, b) protection, welfare, c) passports, visas. Hazards.
7. ADMIN (administration). For total mission, not just State component.
   a) B&F (budget and fiscal). Payroll and other financial affairs.
   b) GS (general services). Property, housing, transportation, shipping.
   c) PER (personnel). Handling records and problems of all personnel.
   d) SY (security). Protection of embassy and its personnel. Marines.
   e) COM (communications). Handling all traffic, ciphering, pouches, etc.
   f) Others such as dispensary, information systems, etc.
C. *Other Agencies.* Most activated after World War II (no longer isolationist).
   1. FCS (Foreign Commercial Service). Formerly in State, now Department of Commerce.
      a) Promotion of American trade interests. Assist American businessmen.
      b) Close cooperation with ECON. Formerly manned by FSOs, still some.
   2. USIA (U.S. Information Agency). People-to-people, not just government-to-government.
      a) Outgrowth of OWI (Office of War Information). In and out of State.

b) Truman aim: "present full and fair picture" of U.S.
c) Two basic branches: 1) cultural 2) informational.
d) FSIOs (Foreign Service Information Officers). Take exams like FSOs.
3. CIA (Central Intelligence Agency). Duties Foreign Service does not do.
a) Outgrowth of OSS (Office of Strategic Services), wartime agency. Reference: Allen Dulles's *Craft of Intelligence.*
b) Primarily: 1) collection of clandestine information 2) against potential adversaries, e. g., Communist countries.
c) Supersecret monitoring programs. Collaboration with NSA (National Security Agency).
d) Covert operations. Small component but highly controversial. Much exaggeration. Cf Iran in 1953. Support of foreign media.
4. AID (Agency for International Development). Help those who help themselves.
a) Launched in Truman 1949 Inaugural Address. Whipping boy: "give-away."
b) Rationale: 1) humanitarian, 2) mutual security, 3) self-interest.
c) Many achievements, but media focus on shortcomings.
5. DOD (Department of Defense). Enhance Free World collective security.
a) Attachés. Obtain military information, e.g., order of battle, capabilities.
b) MAAGs (Military Assistance Advisory Groups). Provide training, advice, equipment.
c) MAPs (Military Assistance Program). Handle equipment sales.
d) Generals. Where U.S. troops are stationed pursuant to treaties.
6. Many others. Cf Treasury (financial and monetary reports), Agriculture (promote agricultural sales), National Science Foundation, Department of Health and Human Services, Department of Energy, Maritime Commission, FBIS (Foreign Broadcast Information Service), Geographic Attachés, Customs, Federal Aviation Administration, Bureau of Narcotics and Dangerous Drugs, even IRS.
7. Overseas representation excessive. Each agency considers it a status symbol. Ambassadors try to hold the line. Cf Briggs and Tuthill.
D. *Control.* Management of operations, emphasized by Murphy Commission.

1. State Department personnel. Under ambassador's direct command.
    a) Tools include Foreign Service Manual, efficiency reports, system.
    b) Problem of loyalty and dissent. Arguing from within is preferable. Cf. frequent dissenter who benefits embassy's end product.
2. Personnel of other agencies. Despite JFK directive, bread is buttered by parent agencies.
    a) Tend toward heroics for their home offices.
    b) But team playing is best. Ambassador can help, harm their careers.

E. *Format for Meetings.* Fairly typical, although many variations.
    1. "Command Post." Daily morning conference of nucleus officers.
        a) Includes DCM, POL, ECON, POL–MIL section chiefs, CIA, USIA reps.
        b) Discuss telegrams, news, issues of day. Agree on who does what.
        c) Meyer's law: Effectiveness of meeting inversely proportional to number attending.
    2. "Country Team." Weekly gathering of top reps of all sections and agencies.
        a) Embassy officers explain key current issues and embassy policies.
        b) Agency heads report on key subjects with which they are dealing.

F. *Typical Day*
    7:00 Breakfast. Read local English language papers, listen to VOA, BBC.
    8:00 Embassy. Read incoming telegrams, vernacular press summary.
    9:00 "Command Post" meeting.
    10:00 Appointments with local officialdom, or U.S. VIPs. (Everyone must see the ambassador!)
    12:30 Lunch. Often business-oriented. At residence or local host.
    2:00 More appointments, embassy paperwork, individual staff, e.g., CIA rep.
    5:00 "Bull sessions." Informal, invaluable with news reps, academics, businessmen, politicos. Weekly clusters of visiting Americans.
    6:30 Cocktail parties. Business receptions, national days. Informal chats.

8:30 Dinners (nightshift). Officials more informal and talkative.
11:30 Midnight paperwork. Good advice: "Never leave a scrap of
   paper in the in-box."
Plus travel, at least once per month into countryside.
G. *Size of Missions*
   1. Small. Family camaraderie. Big fish in small pond.
   2. Medium. Some coagulation into groups. Still camaraderie,
      American community.
   3. Large. a) Sense of participation in major history-making institu-
      tion. b) But management problems, impersonality, and some-
      times poor morale.

V. Loci of Implementation

A. *Changing Nature*
   1. Classic: Embassy X to Government Y, reciprocated. Each em-
      bassy represents sovereign. Shades of Greek orators.
   2. Changes due to communications revolution, explosion of na-
      tions, complexity of problems.
   3. Conditioning factors re locus today.
      a) Power relationships. Diplomatic resources, influence, eager-
         ness.
      b) Where is it more effective. Cf dealing with Shah in Iran, as
         against dealing with Israelis in Washington.
      c) Nature of issue. Routine matters usually field responsibility.
         Tendency for good news to be handled by home office; bad
         news left to field.
      d) Personal interests. Cf Undersecretary Johnson's Japan
         specialization.
B. *Washington Venue* (Cf Japanese textile wrangle—Meyer VI,
   Destler).
   1. Issues with powerful domestic interest.
      a) Need for political purposes to demonstrate government is
         taking action.
      b) Trade problems often fall into this category.
   2. Advantages: more expeditious, decision makers immediately in-
      volved. Get results.
   3. Basic problems, not taken into account by home-front actors.
      a) Inordinate domestic influences, one-sidedness.
      b) Clash of decision-making processes in negotiating countries.
         Cf Japan. Prime Minister must depend on developing "con-
         sensus." Often too many chefs in the kitchen, various agen-
         cy officials.

C. *Field Venue* (Okinawa reversion negotiations—Meyer II).
   1. Advantages: Single channel, embassy serves as buffer, more thorough and systematic consideration, tactical tough stances to drive harder bargain, awareness of what is possible, what is not, lower levels of irritation, better chances of precise understandings, more durable results.
   2. Disadvantages: Less opportunity for heroics, more time-consuming, tendency toward excessive compromising.
D. *Personal Diplomacy*
   1. Summitry. Camp David is an excellent example.
      a) Pros: loci come together, dramatic impact, improved atmosphere and rapport among summiteers, speedy results, domestic political value.
      b) Cons: (Nicolson: "Honors excite vanity but bewilder judgement.").
         1) Deliberations inadequate, time pressures, damaging concessions. Cf Yalta.
         2) Imprecise conversations lead to misunderstandings. Cf Camp David.
         3) Unreal expectations, potential disasters. Cf Munich.
         4) Decision making suffers at home. Cf Carter away for 13 days.
         5) Normal channels atrophy, credibility of embassies diminish.
      c) Preparations are sine qua non for success. Also limited objectives. Cf Sato/Nixon communiqué re Okinawa vs JFK/Khrushchev Vienna meeting.
   2. Shuttle Diplomacy. Glamorized by Kissinger, but here to stay.
      a) Similar considerations as with summitry.
      b) Can be productive. Cf Kissinger role after 1973 Arab-Israeli war.
      c) Yet, while virtuoso is fine, an orchestra is better.
E. *Role of Embassy*
   1. Provide vital information on continuing basis for decision makers and shuttlers.
   2. Conduct missionary work, before and after summits and blitz visits. Cf role of Ambassador Eilts vis-a-vis Sadat after Camp David.
   3. Pick up pieces. Repair misunderstandings. Cf "China shock" in Japan.
   4. Maintain mission's credentials. If total spectrum of embassy's work is to be effective, ambassador must be knowledgeable on all key issues. Should participate in summit meetings. Exclusion undermines credentials.

5. Assure full coordination of its government's policies. Cf Ambassador Grew's critique of U.S.-Japan pre-Pearl Harbor relations: A car "must operate on all cylinders."

VI. Perspectives

A. *Expertise*
  1. Need. In isolationism period, disinterest in foreign language and cultures.
     a) World War II demonstrated dearth of experts. Used professors and missionaries.
     b) Postwar explosion of interests. Public outcry for more expertise.
  2. Responses. Promotion of language and area studies.
     a) National Defense Education Act (NDEA). Encouraged schools.
     b) Foreign Service Institute (FSI) founded.
        1) Incentives: salary increments, plus mark in efficiency reports.
        2) Rare language programs—Japanese (Yokohama), Arabic (Beirut).
  3. Values: interpreting, sensing nuances, sounder analyses. Cf Ruth Benedict's *Chrysanthemum and the Sword,* e.g., Japanese "on."
  4. Drawbacks.
     a) Interruption in careers. Removal from professional mainstream.
     b) Restricted assignments. Cf Japanese—posts only in one country.
B. *"Localitis"*—"client advocacy"
  1. Socrates: To know all is to forgive all.
  2. Tendency to become more Catholic than the Pope. Also unwarranted arrogance.
  3. Political appointees at least as susceptible as careerists. Cf Bowles in India.
  4. Various degrees: from reflexive caution to rank emotionalism.
  5. GLOP (Global Outlook Program). Kissinger's annoyance with "localitis." Mandatory assignments outside field of expertise to develop perspective.
C. *Washington Insensitivities*
  1. Powerful domestic forces often distort international policies. Cf U.S.-Japan trade protectionism. Also Arab-Israel dispute.
  2. Eagerness of administrations to "do something." "Loudmouth" diplomacy.

a) Antagonizes countries with which we are trying to deal.
b) They, like us, also have powerful domestic political constraints.
3. Dissociating from foreign policy not possible. Cf lack of support for Vietnam war.
4. Question not one of deliberate malice, but insensitivity. Cf Nixon "shokku."
5. Often failure to understand that "how" can be more important than "what." Cf unwise use of such words as "pressure," "demands," "strings."

D. *Need for Balance*
1. Balance of interests and sensitivities: possible vs impossible.
2. Proper balance of sympathy and cynicism. Excess of either is bad.
3. Major example: Arab-Israel emotionalism. Need to visit, see both sides.

VII. Need for Adequate Guidance

A. *"Linkage" between government and its diplomats*
1. Murphy Report.
   a) Fabulous communications facilities.
   b) But chronic lack of understanding between Washington and field.
   c) Better "linkage" strongly recommended.
2. Halperin.
   a) Government is vast. Few see or know the president or top advisors.
   b) Difficult for implementors of policy to be fully in tune.
3. George Kennan: "Policies can be correctly and effectively implemented only by people who understand the entire philosophy and thoughts of those who make them."

B. *General Directives and Past Precedents*
1. Value. Provide: a) main objectives, b) safety, e.g., "As the President said..." Cf Carter's "human rights" policies, Reagan's Free World vs Communists.
2. Perils: a) imprecise detail, b) inertia—It is always relatively safe to say, "There is no change in policy." Cf Laird in Tokyo when Kissinger in Beijing.

C. *NSSMs (National Security Study Memoranda) and Other Policy Planning*
1. Value: a) focus on specific issue, b) common understanding, c) coordinated implementation. Cf May 1969 NSSM re negotiating return of Okinawa.

2. Perils: a) Compromise language, meaning different things to different people. b) Unpredictable events—coups, assassinations. Cf fall of Shah.

D. *Instructions from Washington*
   1. Value: classical source, specific issue, cleared widely, signed by SecState.
   2. Drawbacks: Lowest common denominator (when in doubt, don't), vague wording. Skeletal: no feeling for forces behind the decisions.

E. *Blackout of Information*
   1. All administrations tend to distrust the bureaucracy.
   2. Kissinger's theory
      a) Any policy change, bureaucracy will 1) resist, or 2) show off.
      b) Ergo, maximum secrecy. Cf China breakthrough. Even Secretary Rogers in the dark.
   3. Disadvantages:
      a) Intensifies resistance and leakage. Jack Anderson's chief sources.
      b) Discourages morale, loyalty and support. Sows more distrust. Cf Pentagon's spying in Kissinger's office.
      c) Invites cross-purposes. Cf Laird in Tokyo while Kissinger in China.
      d) Unnecessary adverse consequences. Cf impact on Japan of U.S. move re PRC.
      e) Undermines credentials of normal channels, the total mission.
   4. "Need to know" policy is often the best course.

F. *Deductive Reasoning.* Ascertaining true policy with all its nuances.
   1. Instinct. Fly by seat of pants. Cf giving OK to ping pong diplomacy.
   2. Public pronouncements. Usually much rhetoric, but they do give direction. Cf Presidential news conferences and other Wireless Bulletin materials.
   3. Official information. Cf telegrams or memcons reporting Washington talks.
   4. Backgrounders. "Senior official" briefings. Cf Kissinger regularly re Vietnam.
   5. Press reports. Scotty Reston's "leaks" to the State Department!
   6. Visiting officials. Bring their impressions of latest Washington thinking.
   7. Frequent visits home. Strongly recommended by Murphy Commission.

8. Foreign Office officials. What they are hearing from their Washington embassies.
9. Official-informal letters. Especially from Country Director.
   a) Provide background information re forces at work in Washington decision making.
   b) Invaluable in guiding embassy's reporting and other ministrations.

VIII. Policy Input

A. *Ultimate Decision-Making Responsibility: President*
  1. Foreign Service expertise can make important contributions.
     a) That is a main reason for home assignments.
     b) Wriston reorganization: mandatory interchange of home/abroad expertise.
     c) Cf JFK's handling of Cuban crisis. ("Missiles of October"). Careerists Bohlen and Thompson on JFK's Task Force.
  2. Value: a) better understanding, b) greater wisdom, c) broader support.
  3. Note of realism when new administration has urge to "do something."
B. *Input from Missions Abroad*
  1. "Man in field." Input often welcome, if he has respect and is persuasive.
     a) Sometimes solicited. When Washington in doubt, passes the buck.
     b) Major function is advice, beyond assessment.
     c) Recommended action/language is often more easily cleared back home.
     d) Regional conferences—loudest talker sometimes prevails over wisdom.
  2. Seldom acknowledged: a) clearance problem, b) preemption by home officials. Cf Grew's postmortem on Pearl Harbor: Tokyo reporting "like pebbles in a pond," never even allowed "to see the ripples."
  3. Often ignored:
     a) Overriding domestic considerations. Cf Truman and Palestine issue.
     b) Passion for secrecy, particularly during Nixon-Kissinger years.
     c) Contrary to preconceptions. Cf Haig and "strategic consensus."

4. Indirect maneuvers.
   a) Use of host country representatives to soften Washington. Cf encouraging VIP visits to Shah, who was very persuasive.
   b) Get message through via third-country representatives and their governments.
   c) Needle Washington via news media. Galbraith model practitioner. (Easier for political appointees than careerists.)
   d) Congressional visitors much more attentive than when in busy Washington.
5. Direct appeals.
   a) Messages direct to secretary of state or even president.
   b) Return home to present case to top officials.

C. *Loyalty and Dissent*
   1. Transition tensions. New administration feels need for innovation.
      a) Previous wisdom does not necessarily change on inauguration day.
      b) Cf Dulles's stirring up East German anti-Communists; backfired.
   2. Best advice is often overruled, but soldiers normally accept decisions. Cf efforts of Foreign Service to prevent 1947–48 Mideast predictions coming true.
   3. Recent years' emphasis on independent thinking and creativity.
      a) Restlessness of youth, peaked during Vietnam era.
      b) "Dissent channel" established. Also "Secretary's Open Forum."
         1) Since channel's creation, only about one dissent per month.
         2) Some officers fear harm to their careers.
         3) Others prefer to work from within for changes they seek.
      c) Confidentiality is an important factor.
   4. Depersonalization of differences.
      a) Too often personal antagonisms develop, backbiting, undermining.
      b) Separate person from ideas. Difference does not mean disloyalty.
      c) Conflicting views inevitably lead to a better end product. Cf Amb Martin Herz—chronic dissenter but invaluable officer.
   5. Resignation is always an available recourse.

IX. Initiatives and Techniques

A. *Decision Making on the Scene*
  1. Routine. Political/economic contacts, management, protection and visa issues.
  2. Crisis situations. Cf Lebanon 1958 (Thayer I–III).
    a) Preservation of American lives and property.
      1) Evacuation plans for whole American community—3 phases. Cf wardens, communications facilities, burn/ shred papers.
      2) Operations centers/task forces: Washington and the field.
      3) Upsurge of terroristic acts. Cf Khartoum, Tehran, Beirut.
      4) Importance of intelligence, precaution, contingency planning.
    b) Political role: fostering American interests.
      1) Reporting, contacts, recommendations, handling of press.
      2) Crucial decisions, e.g., ambassador vs U.S. military.
      3) Political solutions. Use of trouble-shooting emissary.
  3. Issues taboo for Washington. Instructions unclearable.
    a) Chronic problems, unyielding via formal channels.
    b) Behind-scenes diplomacy, based on enjoying the confidence of conflicting parties.
    c) Informal suggestions as to possible road to solution.
    d) Usually with full knowledge of head of government.
    e) Best if parties adopt solution as having been their own idea.
    f) Forego kudos as hero, invite description as "faceless diplomat."
    g) Can be risky, if role becomes public knowledge. Can backfire.
B. *Techniques*
  1. Direct approaches to centers of power.
    a) Varies with nature of host government.
      1) Easy with autocrats like Shah. Aides sycophants, useless.
      2) Less easy with countries whose leaders are not all-powerful.
      3) Difficult with large democracies. Cf need for Japan "consensus."
      4) Communists more autocratic, deals possible. Cf Cuba.

    b) Value of quiet diplomacy. Cf Kissinger/Soviets re Jewish emigration.

    c) Informal rather than formal negotiations. Cf Nixon China breakthrough.

    d) *Bout de papier* vs *aide mémoire.* For precision and to encourage action.

2. Indirect approaches.

    a) Close confidants. Cf Amb. Hare working thru journalist Heikel to Nasser.

    b) Use of opposition. In Free World countries, assist in bridge-building.

    c) Visiting firemen, esp. congressmen. Can reinforce U.S. position.

    d) Others such as scholars and newsmen. Cf AP's Scali in Cuban crisis.

3. Public diplomacy.

    a) Direct pronouncements designed to affect policy. Cf Amb. Allen in 1945 Azerbaijan crisis, strengthened Shah's resolve.

    b) Press backgrounders, rather than public artillery blasts.

    c) USIA: Formal information and cultural programs.

        1) Information: press releases, movies, TV support, etc.

        2) Cultural: libraries, exchange programs, e.g. Fulbright.

    d) Diversions, e.g. baseball and amateur radio in Japan. Access to large apolitical communities.

    e) But basic policies are still 90% of the challenge. Cannot be papered over by public relations or propaganda.

4. Importance of timing.

    a) Strategic targeting is much preferable to mass bombing.

    b) Dulles: "When to go to the brink is the necessary art." Cf Cuba crisis.

X. Multilateral Diplomacy

A. *Community of Interests* (Nicolson theory)

    1. Traditional issues. Expanded bilateralism. More complexity.

    a) Political. Balkanization of the world. Regionalization tendencies. Cf European Community as successor to Concert of Europe.

    b) Security. Collective action, spurred by two world wars, pact-building. Cf NATO, Warsaw, etc.

    c) Economic. Great depression. Postwar trade and monetary

  problems, role of the dollar. Cf Bretton Woods, GATT, OECD, Summits, North-South.
2. Nontraditional issues. Shrinkage of planet.
  a) Global challenges: food, energy, environment, seas, outer space.
  b) Need for specialists, special emissaries, often competing channels.
    1) No one can be expert on everything, e.g., from nuclear fission to whales.
    2) Still role for diplomats: political contexts, negotiating skills. Cf UNESCO, ILO, IAEA votes with injection of Palestine issue.
B. *Conference Diplomacy.* U.S. Government attends over 700 conferences per year!
  1. Institutionalized groups. HQ organizations, regular meetings. Rusk: too many. Cf NATO, OAS, OECD, Japan–U.S. ministerial meetings.
  2. Ad hoc conclaves. Special issues, deliberations seem desirable. Cf arms control, Helsinki, Stockholm (environment), Law of Sea, whaling.
  3. Logistical considerations.
    a) Participation. Jealousies re attendance/absence for political reasons.
      1) Institutional. Cf NATO (Greece/Turkey/Spain).
      2) Ad hoc. Cf jockeying at nonaligned conferences, PLO in Mideast peace.
    b) Composition of delegations: chiefs, seniors, agencies, spear carriers.
    c) Preparations—by far the most important aspect.
      1) Standing committees, working groups. Formally set up.
      2) Missionary work: homework, shuttles, quiet diplomacy, embassy role. Cf full-time office preparing for Economic Summit.
    d) Top-level finales. Ratification of communiqués, pomp and ceremony. Helsinki, NATO ministerial meetings.
  4. Pros and cons.
    a) Defuse crises, progress, community of interests, appearance of motion.
    b) Fixed positions, posturing, ambiguous communiqés. Cf Helsinki-Madrid, Arab League meetings, Geneva arms talks.
  5. Need for procedural wisdom—complexity of organizing voting strategy.

a) Knowledge of political and procedural intricacies.
b) Bloc voting prospects, nose counting.
c) Corridor missionary work, particularly with undecided.
d) No substitute for experience.

C. *United Nations*
1. Its evolution.
   a) History. Ill-fated League of Nations. FDR-Hull-Welles-Pasvolsky architects. Charter San Francisco 1945.
   b) U.S. dominance in early years. Cf Iran, Israel, Chinese representation, Korea.
   c) Cold War period. Soviet vetoes. U.S. "Uniting for Peace" resolution.
   d) Emerging Third World—"neutralism." Nehru, Tito, Nasser.
      1) In theory "plague on both your houses."
      2) In practice, castigate U.S., placate USSR.
      3) Dulles: free vs slave world. "Who is not for us is against us."
      4) Khrushchev shoe-pounding. Abortive effort re "troika"/dominance.
      5) Kennedy: attempt to work with Third World but firm against troika.
   e) U.S. disillusionment. U.S. being steamrollered.
      1) In part reaction to early dominance. Herd instinct.
      2) Small nations demonstrate "independence." Play to gallery.
      3) Bloc voting and log-rolling. Scratch each others' backs.
      4) Resultant U.S. antipathy. LBJ and Nixon began process of bypassing.
   f) Deterioration of Security Council, UNGA and their resolutions.
2. Realistic expectations.
   a) Not world government. Involves sovereign sensitivities.
   b) Exploitable for home consumption.
   c) Safety valve. Cf Palestine, Congo, Cyprus. Imperfect but of some value.
   d) UNGA corridor diplomacy. On occasion, useful channels of communication.
   e) Auxiliary agencies. Their usefulness not always appreciated.
3. Auxiliary agencies.
   a) ICAO. Aircraft procedures for safe travel.
   b) ITU. Regulate international radio frequency spectrum. Bedlam otherwise.

    c) IMF–World Bank. More subjective, but still valuable for development.

    d) Host of others: ILO, WHO, FAO, UNCTAD, UNDP, UNESCO, IAEA, UNICEF, UNEP, etc.

E. *Embassy Role*

  1. Recognize this is new world. Nontraditional fora will continue.

  2. Front-line reporting and support. More than housekeeping.

  3. Maintain credibility of embassy's overall mission.

XI. Personal Skills and Qualities

A. *Qualities.* Foreign Service Officers (FSOs). FSO exams test knowledge and intelligence: obvious requisites. But success depends on personal character: confidence, not cunning.

  1. *Integrity* and *truthfulness* (Nicolson).

    a) U. S. value system: Declaration, Constitution, Bill of Rights, Lincoln. Fundamental to our policies. Freedom is the engine.

    b) Cause is just, motives honorable, basically nothing to hide.

    c) Honesty is best policy. Even patriotic lie is dubious.

  2. *Energy.* Dawes: "easy on the head, hard on the feet."

    a) Secretary Marshall insisted only 9 to 5, but in field diplomats work 15–18 hour day. Drive, dedication, reliability and completed action are essential.

    b) Three-platoon system: day shift, night shift, handling visitors. Even cocktail parties valuable opportunities for informal exchanges.

  3. *Elasticity.* Tendency to grow inward and know answers reflexively.

    a) Rigidity of spirit, subculture, rut. Change of scenery good thing.

    b) Imagination must be exercised to exploit opportunities.

  4. *Self-control.* Calmness. Talleyrand: "Surtout pas trop de zèle."

    a) Good temper. Don't get excited/emotional.

    b) Difference between firmness and histrionics, table pounding. Patience.

  5. *Modesty.* Danger is personal vanity, abetted by sycophants.

    a) Leads to boasting, grandstanding, eagerness for triumphs and illusion that officer's post is center of the world.

    b) Better: private accomplishment. Host officials resent image of defeat.

    c) Admit error. "Moments of truth" when drafting telegrams.

    d) Language show-offs. Even Amb. Reischauer used interpreter.
6. *Loyalty.* Conflicts between post and home office, as well as ego concerns.

    a) Report honestly, not what superiors might like to hear. Cf Vietnam.

    b) But carry out home decision, even if disagree.

B. *Skills*

1. *Assessment* (reporting)—Assiduous investigation; drafting abilities.

    a) Get facts: Cultivate sources of information as widely as possible. Initiative.

    b) Precision: written vs oral—to government, to staff. Note-taking.

    c) Analysis: eye on future, forces at work, pressure points, trends, options.

    d) Prophecy: avoid waffling, also heroics.

2. *Persuasion* (negotiating). How to bring other person to your viewpoint.

    a) College debating fine training for sifting persuasive arguments.

    b) Salesmanship. Put self in other's shoes. Desirable course of action. If you can't sell yourself, you can't sell your product.

3. *Management.* Postwar importance (previously discussed). Murphy report.

C. *U.S. Foreign Service*

1. Qualifications: broad general background, esp re American studies: history, political science, humanities, and culture.

    a) Cross section. No longer Ivy League. 30+ states each year.

    b) Emphasis: women, minorities, postgrads, average age mid-20s.

    c) Many have had previous experience, military, Peace Corps.

2. Entrance formalities.

    a) Application by October. Usually around 20,000+

    b) Written exams. First Sat. in December. Circa 13,000 take, 900+ pass. Composition changes, e.g., general, functional, *verbal.* FSO cones, USIA, Commerce—specialization rankings.

    c) Orals. Perhaps 700+ take, circa 400 pass, 200 + become FSOs. Board seeks to assess personality. Group therapy. In-basket ordeal.

    d) Language. Not sine qua non. But must take later and pass hurdles.

    e) Other: Medical and security clearances.
  3. Register. All survivors on rank-order list; some may have to repeat.
  4. Post-entrance. Junior Officer Training. Like boot camp. Four-year probation.
  5. First assignments and cones established. Future depends on the FSO.
  6. Career ladder. Frequent changes. Senior FSO system (SFS) has some problems.
D. *Diplomatic Life*
  1. Protocol. Procedural codifications dating back to Congress of Vienna.
    a) Complicated but systematizes relationships, e.g., seating at dinners.
    b) Role of wives. Recent controversy, e.g., assisting at embassy functions.
    c) Basically, protocol is question of good manners.
  2. Amenities.
    a) Salaries. Adequate, never get rich, taxable.
    b) Travel expenses, including household effects.
    c) Housing. Quarters or allowances.
    d) Hardship allowances at particularly difficult posts.
    e) Representational allowances. Usually inadequate.
    f) Retirement system. Was very good, but is undergoing change.
    g) Medical care. At FS posts, backed by the State Department.
    h) Diplomatic immunity.
  3. Hardships.
    a) Terrorism. A new scourge. USG no ransom policy.
    b) Transplantation. Affects whole family frequently. Hard on youngsters.
    c) Cultural shock on retirement. Less glamor, fewer friends and amenities.
  4. Satisfactions.
    a) Fascinating work. No clock-watching.
    b) Feeling of involvement in matters of historic importance.
  5. Philosophy of Loy W. Henderson, "Mr. Foreign Service."
    a) "Do the best job you know how each day, and the promotions will take care of themselves."
    b) "In the Foreign Service you will have your ups and your downs, but in the end it will be fair."

4

International Policy Implementation

David D. Newsom

ILLUSTRATIVE OF THE interwoven character of policy and diplomacy is David D. Newsom's two-semester graduate course on "International Policy Implementation," which combines the making and implementation of foreign policy. With the second semester devoted to the perceptions and functioning of an embassy abroad, the course represents a fusion of the Simpson/Cross/Pacy and Meyer approaches. Through simulation exercises in the substantive and operational elements of foreign policy, the student is introduced experientially to the processes and problems of diplomacy and shown how policymaking and implementation are interrelated, with processes and problems viewed from different perspectives according to one's vantage point.

While the first semester's readings and lectures focus on policymaking, simulation exercises involve policy implementation and follow-up decision making in the context of real-world diplomatic problems and events. In each semester the simulation exercises concentrate on a particular country. In the 1983–84 academic year illustrated here, the fall semester exercises involved Poland, the spring semester, the Philippines.

Organization of syllabi

First Semester

95

International Policy Implementation

David D. Newsom

Georgetown University
Master of Science in Foreign Service Program
1983–1984

FIRST SEMESTER

Course objectives

The purpose of this two-semester workshop is to introduce the student to the political perceptions, the exercise of power, and bureaucratic skills essential to effective understanding of and participation in the *making* and the *implementation* of decisions on international problems in both the official and the private sectors. The problem will be viewed not only from the perspective of the United States but from that of another country as well.

The first semester of the workshop is devoted to the process of decision making. The second semester will concentrate on the skills and perceptions important to the implementation of decisions through communicating and negotiating with corresponding sectors in foreign countries.

Organization of the course

The workshop seeks through lectures, reading, outside assignments, and class exercises to combine two interrelated tracks, operational and substantive. There is a heavy emphasis on the ability to write and to present orally the essentials of foreign policy problems.

The course will begin with a look at the nature of power within a democratic foreign policy structure, concentrating on those significant personal and institutional relationships that lie at the heart of the policy process. There will be an examination of the respective roles of the Executive, the Congress, the public, and the media.

The simulated exercises in the first semester will concentrate on U.S.-Polish relations in the years 1980-81. For the purpose of the exercises, the class will be divided into teams and given specific assignments within an American government and a Polish regime framework. The objective will be to introduce the student as realistically as possible to the forces, alternatives, and problems that beset the policymaker in both countries. On the Polish side, students or pairs of students will be assigned to adhere to the particular points of view of the army, the communist party, the financial authorities, the agricultural authorities, the Polish church, and the representative of the Soviet Union. In the United States team, students will be assigned to represent the interests and points of view of the National Security Council, the State Department, the Department of Defense, the Joint Chiefs of Staff, the Treasury Department, the CIA, and the domestic side of the White House.

Policy is never made in a vacuum. Each class session will be opened, therefore, by briefings by students alerting the class to major international and domestic developments bearing upon the consideration of policy toward Poland in the period under review.

There will be one session devoted to an understanding of the media and policymaking. Prominent representatives of both the print and television media will be present.

There will be two term projects. The final paper will be a draft of an official speech on policy toward Poland. The final week will be devoted to oral final examinations on the process of decision making.

Reading assignments will cover both the major elements of decision making, supplementing the lectures, and more specific information relating to the Polish exercise. There will be five writing assignments in addition to the final paper. Given the volume of reading and writing necessary for a student to take full advantage of the course, every effort should be made to keep up with the required deadlines.

Grades will be determined one-third on the basis of class participation, one-third on the basis of writing including the final term paper, and one-third on the basis of the oral final.

Required reading

Available at University Book Store:
Destler, I.M. *Presidents, Bureaucrats and Foreign Policy.* Princeton, 1974.
Hunter, Robert E. *Presidential Control of Foreign Policy.* The Washington Papers, #91, CSIS, 1982.
Kegley, C.W. and N.R. Wittkopf. *American Foreign Policy: Pattern and Process.* St. Martin's Press, 1979.
Machiavelli, N. *The Prince,* Penguin Books, 1961.

On Reserve:
Bennet, Douglas. "Congress in Foreign Affairs." *Foreign Affairs,* Fall 1978.
Burns, James MacGregor. *Leadership.* Harper & Row, 1978.
Christopher, Warren. "Cease-Fire between the Branches: A Compact in Foreign Affairs." *Foreign Affairs,* Summer 1982.
Grieder, William. "The Education of David Stockman." *The Atlantic Monthly,* December 1981.
Heginbotham, Stanley J. "Dateline Washington: The Rules of the Games," *Foreign Policy,* Winter 1983–84 [from a paper entitled "Congressional-Executive Consultation on Foreign Policy: What Works"].
Mathias, Charles McC. "Ethnic Groups and Foreign Policy." *Foreign Affairs,* Summer 1981.
National Security and Freedom of the Press. Transcript of Columbia School of Journalism T.V. Forum.
Newsom, David D. *The Soviet Brigade in Cuba.* Indiana University Press, 1987.
Porter, Roger B. *Presidential Decision Making.* Cambridge University Press, 1982.
Price, Don K., ed. *The Secretary of State.* Books for Libraries Press, 1970.
Shaplan, Robert. "The Eye of the Storm." *The New Yorker,* June 16, 1980.
Sigal, Leon. *Reporters and Officials.* D.C. Heath, 1973.
Tower, John G. "Congress vs. the President." *Foreign Affairs,* Winter 1981/82.
Additional reading material will be provided in class.

Fall 1983 course outline

[Each session consists of two or three separate components, which are set forth across the top for each new session in the outline that follows.]

I	II	III

Session 1

| Initial Exercise (To be provided in class) | Introduction to the Course | Lecture: The Tools of Decision Making |

Writing Assignment:
On Machiavelli: relevance for today.

Reading Assignment:
Machiavelli, *The Prince.*
Burns, *Leadership,* pp. 105–37.

Session 2

| Introduction to Policy Exercise | Lecture and Discussion: The Nature of Political Power |

Writing Assignment:
In the course of the next four sessions, class members will be participating in presentations of the functions and perspectives of elements of the decision-making process in two countries. Each is to select one issue and to prepare a policy memorandum for the Head of State, setting forth the issue from the point of view of his/her assigned role and making recommendations. Memoranda are not to exceed four double-spaced pages. They will be due at the beginning of session 7.

Reading Assignment:
Required:
Kegley & Wittkopf, pp. 352–91; 452–54.
Destler, *Presidents, Bureaucrats and Foreign Policy,* pp. 5–82.
Readings for policy exercise to be given out in class.
Recommended:
Burns, pp. 295–302; 369–97.

Session 3

| Briefing | Policy Presentation I | Lecture: Bureaucratic Power |

Reading Assignment:
Destler, Chapter V, pp. 95–153.

Kegley & Wittkopf, pp. 315–44; 350–51.
Hunter, *Presidential Control of Foreign Policy.*
"How Reagan Decides," *Time,* December 13, 1982, pp. 12–17.

Session 4
Briefing   Policy Presentation II   Lecture: The Role of the
                                             President
Reading Assignment:
Acheson, "The President and the Secretary of State" in Don Price,
The Secretary of State, pp. 27–50.
Selected reprints to be distributed in class.

Session 5
Briefing   Policy Presentation III   Lecture: The Role of the
                                             Secretary
Reading Assignment:
Porter, *Presidential Decision Making,* pp. 123–56.
Kegley & Wittkopf, pp. 344–50.

Session 6
Briefing   Policy Presentation IV   Lecture: Economic Power
                                             (Erland Heginbotham)
Reading Assignment:
Grieder, "The Education of David Stockman," pp. 27–54.
Christopher, "Cease-Fire between the Branches: A Compact in
Foreign Affairs."

Hand in writing assignment at next session.

Session 7
Briefing   Problem I: Debt   Lecture: The Tools of
                 (group meetings)   Public Expression
Writing Assignment:
Response to congressional letter.

Reading Assignment:
Tower, "Congress vs. the President."
Sigal, *Reporters and Officials,* pp. 131–96.
Kegley & Wittkopf: pp. 242–432.
Optional:
Bennet, "Congress in Foreign Affairs."
National Security and Freedom of the Press.
John P. Wallach, "I'll Give It to You on Background," *Washington
Quarterly,* Spring 1982.

Special Session: The Media and Policymaking

Session 8
Briefing   Problem I   Lecture: Congressional
                 (Presentation)   Power (Douglas Bennet)
Writing Assignment:
    Response to letter from private interest group.

Reading Assignment:
    Heginbotham, "Dateline Washington: The Rules of the Games."
    Mathias, "Ethnic Groups and Foreign Policy."

Session 9
Briefing   Problem II: Internal   Lecture: Public Power;
                 Developments   Interest Groups
                 (separate meetings)
Writing Assignment:
    Prepare press release and questions and answers.

Reading Assignment:
    Newsom, *Soviet Brigade in Cuba.*
    Optional:
    Shaplan, "The Eye of the Storm."

Session 10
Briefing   Problem II   Lecture: Crisis
                 (presentation)   Management
Writing Assignment:
    Presidential Speech Draft (due session 12)

Session 11
Briefing   Problem III: Crisis Management
                 (separate meetings
                 and presentation)

Session 12   Oral Finals

Simulation exercise I

To members of the class:
    Following is a scenario for Problem I. This will involve separate
meetings of the Polish group and the U.S. group at session 7. The class
will assemble as usual and divide up at midpoint.

The separate meetings will be for the purposes of:

1. Choosing someone on each side to be the principal spokesperson for the second phase, the bilateral discussion.

2. Reviewing the proposed papers, deciding whether these fit your conception of the issues to be discussed, and then parceling out responsibilities for the brief talking papers.

3. Reviewing what should be said on each issue, to determine whether there is agreement. In this review, each participant should represent the point of view of the element presented in the initial presentation (armed forces, church, party, etc.).

4. Seeking to predict what the other side may raise and making certain that you are prepared to respond.

The following week, the two sides will meet for a discussion of the issues through the respective spokespersons (Foreign Minister and Secretary of State).

Scenario for Meeting between
U.S. Secretary of State and
Polish Foreign Minister
December 15, 1980

The U.S. and Poland have expressed interest in a bilateral foreign ministers meeting.

The U.S. has stressed that, in a period of transition between two administrations, the outgoing administration cannot in any sense commit the incoming. The basic U.S. purpose in a meeting of foreign ministers would be to seek high-level Polish government views on the prospects in Poland, and to convey American concerns, believed to be shared by President-elect Reagan's group, over Polish events.

The principal concern is that Poland should be able to settle its own affairs itself, free from outside interference. President Carter and senior administration officials have made this point publicly on several occasions. By outside interference is meant Soviet (or Warsaw Pact) military action, similar to that taken in Hungary in 1956 and in Czechoslovakia in 1968. Such action in Poland now would be disastrous not only for Poland itself, but also for international relations generally. The danger of wider East-West repercussions from Soviet (or Warsaw Pact) intervention in Poland should not be underestimated.

U.S. concerns also extend to the internal situation within Poland. There is certainly no desire on the U.S. side to interfere in Polish domestic affairs, which are a matter for Poles to settle themselves. At the same time, the U.S. government, the Congress, and the public attach great importance to continuation of the process of seeking peaceful settlement of problems through negotiation and compromise on the part of the Polish government, the new trade unions, and the church. U.S. economic aid measures reflect the sympathy that recent Polish events have evoked in Americans. They also presuppose that the Polish authorities are firmly committed to continue on the path of peaceful negotiation. The Polish side should be aware that any use of force by the authorities to suppress the new trade unions would make it impossible for the U.S. to continue economic aid measures.

The Secretary of State would be prepared to use a meeting with the Polish Foreign Minister for the purpose of giving the incoming administration an up-to-date briefing on Poland.

The Polish side for its part has welcomed the meeting as an opportunity to make its views known, both on the Polish domestic situation and on its international implications, to the present U.S. administration and, through it, to the president-elect. It hopes in this way to overcome the normal gap that occurs when a new administration takes over. The urgency and possible dangers of the Polish situation warrant a meeting between the Secretary and the Minister with these objectives in view.

The Polish government has noted with satisfaction public statements by high-level U.S. officials that Poland should settle its own internal problems, free from outside interference. It is also grateful for U.S. economic assistance measures, notably the $670 million in CCC credit guarantees of last September. Nevertheless, U.S. official statements and actions concerning Poland seem ambivalent and cause concern. At a time when it is essential to maintain calm in Poland and concerning Poland, frequent U.S. official statements concerning military movements near the Polish borders have the unfortunate effect of increasing tension. The Polish side also notes the airing of a "the-worse-the-better" approach to Poland by influential sections of the right-wing American establishment. Such views are inconsistent with U.S. protestations of noninterference. So is the financial aid given to the Solidarity trade union by the AFL–CIO.

Unfortunately, that is not all. The Polish side is most concerned by the irresponsible, tendentious, and inciting radio broadcasts to Poland emanating from Radio Free Europe. Far from showing calm and dispassion in regard to Poland's difficult, complicated domestic situation, RFE broadcasts take a clear, pro-Solidarity line. In some cases, RFE has actually broadcast instructions to Solidarity members from local union officials. The Polish government regards such actions by RFE as blatant interference in Polish domestic affairs, and clearly in contradiction with U.S. government policy, at least as reflected in public statements.

* * *

The first two weeks of December 1980 saw a number of important developments concerning Poland:

Internal

At the December 1–2 plenum of the PUWP Central Committee, First Secretary Kania stated that the process of renewal is irreversible. At the same time, he warned Solidarity not to abuse the strike weapon, and said the Party will not tolerate two centers of power. There were extensive high-level personnel changes at the Plenum. The Plenum showed evidence of serious divisions in the Party leadership.

Following the Plenum, the Central Committee issued an appeal to the country to preserve order. The Military Council of the Ministry of Defense met and expressed concern that the situation in the country could adversely affect Poland's defense potential, and it "specified tasks facing the armed forces."

The National Coordinating Commission of Solidarity stressed on December 5 that there were no strikes going on in Poland, and none were planned.

The Joint Government-Church Commission called on December 8 for national unity to maintain a secure existence for Poland.

On December 10, the Solidarity national leadership rejected charges that Solidarity is responsible for Poland's economic situation, called for a "broad social alliance" to solve the country's problems, and announced the establishment of a committee to work for the release of political prisoners.

On December 12, the Polish Roman Catholic Episcopal Conference called on Poles to create the conditions necessary to implement the agreements reached between the government and society. The episcopate spokesman made clear that the church supports renewal within the existing constitutional framework.

On December 14, Polish private farmers set up their own labor union, Rural Solidarity, and announced their intention to apply for its formal registration.

Also on December 14, Cardinal Wyszynski led prayers said throughout Poland for national unity to insure that the state remained secure and that national sovereignty was not threatened.

International

Following media coverage of western intelligence reports concerning Warsaw Pact troop movements near Poland's borders, the White House, on December 2, issued a statement that Soviet military intervention in Poland would have serious consequences for East-West relations. The statement warned that it would be a mistake to believe the U.S. government lacked either the will or the ability to respond in a period of transition between administrations.

The European Economic Community issued a statement on the importance of Poland in East-West relations. The EEC responded favorably to Polish requests to buy grain, butter, and meat.

President Carter and Secretary of State Muskie, in separate statements on December 3, referred to the unprecedented buildup of Soviet forces on Poland's borders and warned the U.S.S.R. against military intervention.

National Security Adviser Brzezinski, on December 14, called on Polish workers, the Polish government, and the Catholic church to exercise restraint and to seek compromise.

At a December 5 meeting in Moscow, the Warsaw Pact countries expressed confidence that Poland could settle its problems itself, and added that Poland could count on the fraternal support of its allies.

Soviet/Eastern European media attacks on "counter-revolution" in Poland and on Solidarity rose sharply December 6–8.

The White House stated on December 7 that the U.S.S.R. appeared to have completed preparations for possible military intervention in Poland, and again warned against intervention.

Soviet Defense Minister Ustinov, speaking about Poland on December 10, called for increased vigilance against aggressive imperialist forces.

NATO defense ministers issued a statement December 10 that Warsaw Pact intervention in Poland would threaten European security and stability.

The U.S. Defense Department announced on December 10 that four AWACS (radar surveillance) aircraft had been sent to West Germany to help protect America's allies in the event the Polish crisis spilled over into Western Europe.

The NATO Council communiqué of December 12 stated that Soviet military intervention in Poland would destroy workable East-West relations.

The U.S. Senate on December 13 unanimously approved a resolution supporting President Carter's position on Soviet intervention in Poland.

CPSU Central Committee member Falin, in an interview with the West German magazine *Der Spiegel* published December 14, said that the U.S.S.R. had no intention of intervening in Poland, and that it trusted the Polish government to solve its problems on its own.

* * *

Against the background of developments described above, the following background/talking memoranda should be prepared for the use of the principals in the December 15 meeting:

I. U.S. Secretary of State
   Background Papers:
   1. Polish internal situation:
      a. Political
      b. Economic
         This paper should discuss opportunities, costs, and risks for the United States.
   2. International reaction:
      a. Western Allies (to include differences from U.S. views)
      b. Soviet/East European
      c. Nonaligned
      d. U.N. aspects
   Talking Papers:
   3. U.S. policy toward U.S.S.R. and Eastern Europe
   4. Human rights in Poland
   5. Economic (including aid) issues
   6. Polish agriculture
II. Polish Foreign Minister
    Talking Papers:
    1. U.S. treatment of the Soviet intervention "threat"
    2. Western (including U.S.) interference in Polish internal affairs
    3. Human rights situation in Poland
    4. Polish economic and financial issues
    5. Request for U.S. economic assistance

Addendum to Scenario
For December 15, 1980 Meeting
Between U.S. Secretary of State
and Polish Foreign Minister

On December 14, at 2:30 p.m., the Polish security services detained Colonel Wayne Peters and Warrant Officer Robert Poplawski, Office of the Defense Attaché, U.S. Embassy Warsaw, near a Soviet Army training area south of Liegnice. Col. Peters and Warrant Officer Poplawski were kept under guard in separate rooms by Polish security for ten hours before being released. During this time, they were questioned

108 DAVID D. NEWSOM

repeatedly about their visit to the Liegnice area. They asked several times to be put in touch with the Embassy, but their requests were denied. When they returned to their vehicle, they found that its contents, which included official U.S. government property as well as personal items, had been ransacked and, in some cases, removed. Polish security did not respond when Colonel Peters asked that the missing property be returned immediately.

Also on December 14, a CBS-TV team, holding valid Polish visas issued by the Polish Embassy, Washington, D.C., was refused entry when it arrived at Warsaw airport on an Austrian Airlines flight from Vienna at 4:30 p.m. The CBS team was held incommunicado in the terminal building for two hours until the departure of the Austrian Airlines flight for Vienna, when the team was put on board the aircraft by Polish border guard troops.

Simulation exercise II

Professor Paul Yablonsky, fifty years of age, was born in Poland and emigrated to the United States as a displaced person after World War II.

After obtaining a Ph.D. at Columbia, he joined the faculty of the University of Chicago. He is the author of two books and numerous articles on Poland and Eastern Europe. He has been active in anti-Soviet causes, including speaking at "Captive Nations Week" events and openly sponsoring Soviet and Polish defectors. He has a brother and sister who live in Krakow.

In September 1980, he sought to return on a visit to Poland, but was initially refused a visa. Under strong pressure from members of the Polish community in Chicago, the State Department made official representations to permit him to return to give three lectures at Krakow University. It was understood these would be on American institutions and would be nonpolitical in character.

He went to Poland in December 1980. He delivered one lecture on "Free Institutions in the United States" which Polish authorities found offensive by innuendo. During the days before the lecture, he made special and successful efforts to meet with Solidarity leaders and dissident Polish intellectuals.

In late December, he was arrested. Polish authorities have refused to discuss the case with the American Embassy on grounds that Yablonsky is still a Polish citizen. Publicity and political pressures for "strong action" are mounting in the United States.

Class will meet separately in the Polish and U.S. groups. Each group should decide on what is at stake in this problem and how it should be handled. Each will choose one person to present a recommended solution in the next class.

Simulation exercise III

HYPOTHETICAL CRISIS EXERCISE

It is January 1984. General Jaruzelski has been replaced by a hard-line general determined to crush Solidarity once and for all. He clearly has strong Soviet support.

The new general has ordered the arrest of Lech Walesa and Walesa has gone into hiding.

You are a member of a task force in the State Department Operations Center established to monitor the developing crisis in Poland. You have just received a message from the American Embassy in Poland that Walesa has sent word through an intermediary that he wishes to come secretly and take refuge in the Embassy.

You should draft a reply to the Embassy suggesting how they should deal with the request from Walesa.

Do not be surprised if, as you deliberate, there are further developments.

[This Is an Exercise Document]

SECRET

Action: SECSTATE WASHDC FLASH
Warsaw 0267
Ref:Warsaw 0232

1. Father Jankowski, Walesa's advisor, came to the residence unannounced at 20:30 hours local, January 14, and asked to see me. We met for half an hour. Jankowski brought an urgent message from Mrs. Walesa to the President. There was no written text. According to Jankowski, Mrs. Walesa requests the President to act favorably, and immediately, on Walesa's request for refuge in the Embassy. Jankowski said Mrs. Walesa believes—he tended to share her belief—that Walesa's life is in danger from the security authorities. She is highly distraught, Jankowski said, and Western media representatives are in direct touch with her at the family apartment in Gdansk. Jankowski thought she might raise the request for refuge with the media if we do not respond quickly.

2. I told Jankowski we have Walesa's request under urgent consideration at the highest levels in Washington. I urged him to do all in his power to dissuade Mrs. Walesa from discussing the request with anyone, repeat anyone. Jankowski agreed to do so, but noted that Mrs. Walesa is both independent and outspoken.

3. Request instructions FLASH. Jankowski will await our reply at the Primate's residence. His visit to my residence will have been noted by Polish security.

Davis

[This Is an Exercise Document]

MEMCON: January 14, 1984
          3:55 p.m.

The press office (Murray) phoned at 3:50 p.m. to say that NBC has told them it will run item on evening news (7:00 p.m.) that Walesa has requested asylum in American Embassy, Warsaw. NBC says it got the information from completely reliable underground Solidarity sources in the Gdansk area.

NBC asked press officer for Department's comments. Murray said he would look into it and call them back. Press office needs guidance for public statement A.S.A.P.

John Werthmann

[This Is an Exercise Document]

MEMCON: January 14, 1984
          4:25 p.m.

NSC (Waller) phoned at 4:20. NSC advisor Herlihy wants to clear personally reply to Warsaw 0267. Herlihy wants to see our draft text A.S.A.P., that is within the next 15 minutes.

[This Is an Exercise Document]

January 14, 1984

Dear Mr. President:

We, the undersigned members of the Senate and the House, have learned from sources we consider reliable that Lech Walesa, leader of

Polish Solidarity, has requested refuge in the U.S. Embassy, Warsaw. Mr. Walesa has made the request as a step of last resort because General Molczyk, the new head of the Polish junta, has ordered his arrest. There are well-grounded fears that Walesa's life may actually be in danger.

In these circumstances, Mr. President, we believe—and we are sure the American people will share this belief—that we have a clear moral responsibility to come to the aid of Mr. Walesa. We, therefore, strongly urge that you respond affirmatively, and on a most urgent basis, to Mr. Walesa's request.

We look forward to your early reply.

Sincerely,
11 Senators
23 House members

[This Is an Exercise Document]

SECRET

ACTION: SECSTATE WASHDC FLASH
Warsaw 0270
Ref: Warsaw 0267

1. Polish security set up heavy security around Embassy at 2100 hours local and is now screening all persons, including Americans, entering or leaving premises. Screening so far is polite but quite thorough, with close scrutiny of identification documents.

2. I believe we have to assume the security people are on to Walesa's request for refuge. If he shows up, they will undoubtedly arrest him (evening TV news carried item that arrest warrant has been issued).

3. As I left residence to come into Embassy to send this message, normal security guard team, in fixed location, was being reinforced by foot patrols, presumably in expectation, following Jankowski visit, that Walesa might head for residence rather than Embassy.

4. Even if Walesa access to residence and Embassy is blocked, he might still be able to make it into any one of a number of Embassy officers' houses around town. With this eventuality in mind, I have given instructions that on no account is Walesa to be turned away.

5. Request instructions FLASH.

Davis

[This Is an Exercise Document]
SECRET
ACTION: SECSTATE WASHDC FLASH
Warsaw 0272
Ref: Warsaw 0270

1. I have just (2235 local) received a telephone request to come immediately to MFA to meet with Deputy Foreign Minister Dobrosielski on "grave and urgent matter." (Dobrosielski's aide to Embassy officer who took message).
2. Assume subject is Walesa. If Dobrosielski asks do we intend to give Walesa refuge in Embassy, I intend to say that this is a hypothetical question on which I am not authorized to speculate.

First semester oral examination

1. Looked at from the standpoint of the U.S. executive, what are some of the principal considerations that must go into the making of foreign policy decisions?
2. Looking at the U.S. government from outside, where would you say the primary power lay in the foreign policy decision-making process? Does that change with issues or with time?
3. On the basis of our look at Poland, where would you say the primary power lay in the developments in that country in 1980–81?
4. What are the primary constraints on the exercise of power in the United States? In Poland?
5. What are some of the international economic issues that require high-level decisions? What are the elements of government that participate in these decisions?
6. If you were a U.S. government official this week, how would you respond to the question, "Why don't we negotiate with Syria?"
7. How would you describe the role of the press and TV in the making of U.S. foreign policy?
8. What are some of the ways that outside private pressures are brought to bear on government decisions? Are these measures appropriate to a democracy?
9. What were some of the other issues that U.S. policymakers faced internationally during the developments in Poland in 1980–81?
10. If you were in a government position and were overruled on a major issue and you believed the decision was not in the best interests of the country, what would you do?

SECOND SEMESTER

Course organization and texts

The second semester of this MSFS workshop will concentrate on the perceptions and functions of an embassy abroad. Student work will use the present situation in the Philippines as a case study with particular emphasis on two current policy issues:

How does the United States deal with a friendly leader in another country when that leader is under strong opposition pressure?

How does the United States reconcile its security needs (including bases) in an area with the realities of local politics?

These diplomatic issues will serve as a backdrop for an examination of the practice of diplomacy and the functions of an embassy. Writing and class assignments will introduce the student to the forms of diplomatic communication, both written and oral, and to the basic elements of negotiation. Building on the work of the first semester, students will be encouraged to demonstrate how domestic considerations in the United States affect U.S. diplomacy in a country such as the Philippines.

This course will be conducted during a period [i.e., early 1984] when the situation in the Philippines is extremely fragile. Changes in class assignments may be made necessary by unforeseen developments.

Each session will be divided into:

1. An initial briefing of not more than five minutes on the current developments in the Philippines;
2. A presentation of not more than ten minutes on one aspect of the Philippine scene;
3. An exercise or outside speaker related to the Philippines; and
4. A lecture on a general aspect of diplomacy or the functions of an embassy.

There will be one term assignment: a paper of not more than ten double-spaced pages recommending how the United States should deal with problems of political transition in countries where the U.S. has major interests. Any nation, including the Philippines, may be taken for this case presentation.

There will be a take-home final on the tools and practice of diplomacy.

The texts for the course will be:

Modern Diplomacy: The Art and the Artisans, edited by Elmer Plischke

Diplomacy, by Sir Harold Nicolson
Contacts with the Opposition—A Symposium, edited by Martin F. Herz
Conference Diplomacy—A Case Study: The World Food Conference, Rome, 1974, by Edwin M. Martin
The Philippines, by David J. Steinberg
Other material will be placed on reserve or given to the class as required.

Spring 1984 course outline

I	II	III
Session 1		
Lecture: Function of an Embassy	Introduction to the Course	The Present Situation in the Philippines

Writing Assignment: Reporting telegram (expression of concern over local situation)

Reading Assignment:
Diplomacy, Nicolson
Modern Diplomacy, Plischke, ed.
  The New Diplomacy, pp. 54–72
  A Day with the Ambassador, pp. 337–45
The Crisis in American Diplomacy, by Smith Simpson, pp. 5–67
The Philippines, Steinberg, pp. 1–6

To be given out in class:
  Statement of Admiral Long before Solarz Subcommittee
  Testimony and statement of Benigno Aquino
  Collection of current clippings on the Philippines

For Reference: Hearings before the Subcommittee on Foreign Affairs, June 17, 23, 28, 1983

Session 2		
Current Briefing Background Briefing: The Constitutional Situation The Filipino View of the U.S.	Exercise: Critique of Reporting Telegram	Lecture: Forms of Communication with Foreign Governments

Writing Assignment: Note to a Foreign Office

Reading Assignment:
  Gulliver's Troubles, by Stanley Hoffman, pp. 87–125
  Plischke:
    Diplomacy—Contemporary Practice, pp. 3–18
    Diplomacy—Political Technique, pp.19–23
  Steinberg, chapter 3, pp. 17–33

Session 3

Current Briefing	Exercise:	Lecture: U.S.
Background Briefing:	Simulated	Diplomatic Style
The Marcoses	Embassy Staff	
ASEAN	Meeting	

Writing Assignment: Talking points for conversation with Foreign Minister

Reading Assignment:
  Diplomat, by Charles Thayer, pp. 64–68
  Plischke: Transition from the Old to New Diplomacy, pp. 43–53
    Contemporary Diplomacy at Work, pp. 43–53
    Advice for Diplomats, pp. 223–36
  Steinberg, chapter 4, pp. 33–63

Session 4

Current Briefing	Exercise:	Lecture: Congress
Background Briefing:	Demarche to	and Diplomacy
The Political	a Government	
Opposition in		
the Philippines		
Economic Situation		
in the Philippines		

Writing Assignment: Memorandum of Conversation

Reading Assignment:
  Plischke:
    Requisite Success for Modern Diplomacy, pp. 102–108
    Quiet vs. Unquiet Diplomacy, pp. 115–35
    Secret vs. Open Diplomacy, pp. 124–35
  Congressional Travel Handbook, Department of State Office of
    Congressional Relations (1968)
  Steinberg, chapter 7, pp. 99–131

Session 5

Current Briefing	Exercise: Planning	Lecture: Relations
Background	a Congressional	with the Media Abroad
Briefing:	Visit	(by a Foreign
The Military		Correspondent)
Role in the		
Philippines		

Writing Assignment: Briefing for a congressional delegation

Reading Assignment:
The Foreign Correspondents, by Theodore E. Kruglak, chapter VII, pp. 98–105
Coups and Earthquakes, by Mort Rosenblum, pp. 1–53; 157–63
Contacts with the Opposition, Martin F. Herz (ed.)

Session 6

Current Briefing	Exercise: Resource	Lecture: Foreign
Background	Allocation	Assistance (by a
Briefing:		former AID official)
The U.S. Bases in		
the Philippines		

Writing Assignment: Response to a note of protest

Reading Assignment:
Inside Foreign Aid, by Judith Tendler, pp. 54–72
The Practical Negotiator, by I. W. Zartman and M. R. Berman, chapters 2 and 3, pp. 16–81

Session 7

Current Briefing	Exercise: Planning	Lecture: Official
Background	for a Negotiation	Information
Briefing:		Abroad
The Business		
Sector in the		
Philippines		

Writing Assignment: Recommendation on VOA treatment of Philippines

Reading Assignment:
Report of the United States Advisory Commission on Public Diplomacy
Plischke: Diplomacy vs. Propaganda, pp. 111–14
Zartman and Berman, chapter 4, pp. 87–147

Session 8

Current Briefing   Exercise: Lecture: Diplomacy
Background Briefing: Negotiating   and the Private
  The Aquino   Session   Sector
  Case

Writing Assignment: Response to a letter from a businessman

Reading Assignment:
Zartman and Berman, chapters 5 and 6, pp. 147–231

Session 9

Current Briefing   Exercise: Crisis   Lecture: The Consul
Background Briefing: Abroad   and Diplomacy
  The Role of the Church
  in the Philippines

Writing Assignment: Visa denial message

Reading Assignment:
American Consular and Diplomatic Practice, by Graham H. Stuart, pp.
  302–91

Session 10

Current Briefing   Exercise: Lecture:
Background Briefing: Multilateral   Multilateral
  The Muslim Revolt   Diplomacy   Diplomacy

Writing Assignment: Statement for Security Council meeting

Reading Assignment:
Plischke:
  Multilateralism, pp. 188–98
  Negotiating Effectively, pp. 364–72, or Negotiating and Bargain-
    ing in the Modern World, pp. 373–80
  Conference Diplomacy: The World Food Conference, Rome 1974, by
    Edwin M. Martin

Session 11

Current Briefing   Exercise: Negotiation   Lecture: Visit
Background Briefing: of a Communiqué   Diplomacy
  The New
  Peoples' Army

Writing Assignment: Arrival statement for President in Manila

Reading Assignment:
Plischke:
Ministerial Diplomacy—Secretary of State Abroad, pp. 153–68
Summit Diplomacy—Diplomat in Chief, pp. 169–87
"Vienna Summit," *Selected Documents,* No. 13, Department of State
Bureau of Public Affairs, 1979.

Session 12
Current Briefing. Discussion of U.S. diplomatic and policy options in
the Philippines.

Introduction to the second semester of the course
(presented at session 1)

The syllabus describes what we hope to do in the class and how.
Perspective and emphasis will be from the point of view of the field, in
contrast to our earlier look at how things are done in the capital. In this
case, the perspective will be that of the U.S. Embassy in Manila.

This is not a course on the Philippines. Like diplomats who serve for
a few years at a post, you need to know only that which relates directly
to the relationship with the United States. This may, in reality, require a
profound knowledge. We will have to get by on less.

This is a course in a diplomatic problem: how to deal with present or
potential internal crises where the United States has major interests.
This is not unique to the Philippines. It has happened in Iraq, Libya,
Ethiopia, Nicaragua, and can happen elsewhere.

Why the Philippines? Many elements common to other situations:
   1. Authoritarian rule losing support.
      —Protection of power.
      —Protection of family and friends (dynasty).
      —Inadequate arrangements for succession.
      —Protection of security services.
   2. Corruption.
   3. Disparity between wealth and poverty.
   4. Military is a key player in national life.
   5. An incipient guerilla movement exists.
   6. A minority (religious) is in revolt.
   7. Identifiable opposition is potentially accessible to neighbors,
      but regime may not wish to encourage such contacts.
   8. The country is plagued with debts and economic troubles.
   9. It possesses the sensitivity of a Third World country and a love/
      hate relationship with former colonial power.
  10. It is sensitive about ambivalent attitude of other countries be-
      cause it possesses U.S. bases. (Nonaligned Movement.)

From the United States' point of view (all common to other situations):

1. Country is recipient of both military and economic aid.
2. U.S. bases.
3. We are involved in country's internal life, whether we want to be or not.
4. We are identified with the Philippines in the minds of others.
5. Congressional doubts exist about our policies.
6. Immigrant communities in the U.S. keep political issues before the American people.
7. The U.S. president is involved.

We are examining not just the Philippines but how nations do business with one another—diplomacy.

Congressional visit exercise
(for session 5)

For this exercise, you will constitute yourselves into two teams and address the following problem:

The embassy in Manila has just received word that a delegation of fifteen members of the House Foreign Affairs Committee, led by the chairman, will visit Manila, arriving by USAF aircraft at 11 a.m., March 10 and departing at 5 p.m., March 12. The fifteen committee members are accompanied by five wives, six staff members, two secretaries, and the editor of the hometown newspaper of one of the committee members.

The group has declared its primary interests to be human rights in the Philippines, the U.S. bases, and the economy. The group as a whole wishes to call on President Marcos and to visit the U.S. bases. Individual members have filed requests with the Department of State to have the embassy arrange:

—a visit to Mrs. Aquino
—a visit to the anti-American political leader, Diokno
—a visit to the Manila slums
—a talk with representative opposition business leaders in Makati
—a meeting with Cardinal Sin

Wives and some staff members wish to be provided with transportation for shopping and sightseeing.

President Marcos, hearing of the visit, has invited the group to a banquet at Malacanang Palace on March 10 and to spend the next day, March 11, with Mrs. Marcos and himself on the presidential yacht.

Teams A and B will meet separately for half an hour to address the following questions after which they will report their answers to the full class:

1. Would you recommend that the group accept one or both of the Marcos' invitations? What will you do if some of the members refuse to go?

2. What will you do if the President's office says the President will see only the chairman and the ranking minority leader?

3. How would you handle a request from the hometown editor for an exclusive interview with President Marcos? Or an exclusive interview with one of the opposition leaders?

4. How would you handle the requests by individual members to see Mrs. Aquino, Diokno, and the slums? What would you do if the Philippine government suggested strongly that such visits in the present moment were inappropriate?

5. How would you handle a request from one of the members, strongly opposed to the Philippine government, to give a press conference in the embassy?

6. If time permits, structure roughly the schedule you would propose for the group during their stay.

Resource allocation exercise
(for session 6)

For this exercise, you will constitute yourselves into two teams. Each team will, for one half-hour, address the following problem and report back its solution for the full class discussion:

The embassy has proposed to Washington the following breakdown of the allocation for economic assistance for the Fiscal Year 1985 (beginning October 1, 1984):

Rural electrification (second year of five-year program)	$25 million
Community development in Visayan-speaking areas	10 million
Assistance to population program	5 million
Science laboratory at University of the Philippines	15 million
Training for ten Filipino officials in the U.S. for one year:	3 million
agricultural techniques (2)	
air traffic control (1)	
agricultural credit (2)	
rural health services (2)	
public administration (3)	
Farm-to-market road project in northern Luzon	5 million
Dam and irrigation project in Mindanao	10 million
Support for staff of AID (23 persons)	3 million
Community development around U.S. bases	20 million
TOTAL	$96 million

The embassy has now received an urgent message stating that the allocation for FY1985 has been cut to $50 million because of congressional cuts in the overall AID appropriation. The embassy is requested immediately to advise Washington on what should be eliminated from the above list in order to bring the program within available funds.

Exercise: Protest note response

As a writing assignment due at session 7, members of the class will draft a diplomatic note in response to the following note received from the Philippine Government:

The Ministry of Foreign Affairs of the Government of the Philippines presents its compliments to the Embassy of the United States of America and has the honor to bring to the attention of the Embassy a report of unacceptable activity on the part of two members of the Embassy staff.

On January 27, two members of the staff of the Embassy, Ms. Lisa Granick and Mr. Steven L. Zelinger, went to polling places on the island of Panay, interrogated election officials and asked questions of voters that cast doubt on the good faith of the election process in the Republic of the Philippines.

Such activity on the part of members of the diplomatic corps is inappropriate to their status in the country and totally unacceptable to the Government of the Philippines. Any further activities of this type could lead to action by the Government of the Philippines in accordance with understood principles of international law.

Writing assignment on VOA
(due at session 8)

One of the continuing problems of the Voice of America is that of dealing credibly with the problems of political opposition to friendly authoritarian governments. In the case of the Philippines, the government listens carefully to VOA broadcasts and occasionally expresses its displeasure with news and commentary that talks candidly about the policies of the Marcos regime. On the other hand, VOA is criticized by some in Congress for avoiding forthright commentary on the problems of constitutional manipulation and offenses against human rights.

The director of VOA has asked that an editorial be prepared pegged to the release of the human rights report on the Philippines (see *New York Times* for February 11, 1984). In response to this request you are to prepare a commentary to be broadcast on human rights in the Philippines that will be credible to critics in the Congress and, at the same time, cause the minimum of diplomatic problems in the Philippines.

The commentary, to fit the time requirement for broadcasting, should be between 475 and 500 words.

Class exercise
(session 9)

The Consolidated Communications Corporation of Wilmington, Delaware signed a contract with the Government of the Philippines in 1979 to install a telephone system in one of the island provinces. That system has now been installed and the company wishes to bid on another similar installation contract. No U.S. Government grants, licenses, or loans are involved in the previous contract.

Two of the employees of the company, James Whitworth and Arnold Smith, have been unable to get exit permits to leave the Philippines because they have not paid Philippine income tax. Their contract said that all activities of *the company* would be exempt from Philippine taxes; nothing was said about the employees. The company, further, has been unable to obtain the certificate of satisfactory completion of the project from the Philippine government which they need to bid on a new project.

A representative of the company from Wilmington, William Bradford, executive vice president, has met with the American consul general and has asked the intervention of the embassy in obtaining the exit permits for the two employees and the certificate of completion. Given the fact that the company is facing strong competition from Japanese bidders, the representative has also asked that the embassy intervene on behalf of Consolidated's bid. While he has no basis for his view, he suspects that the fact that the company has spurned demands from the governor of the province for a handsome gift may be a factor in the difficulties they are encountering with the national government.

Draft a telegram from the consul general to the Department of State outlining the problem and recommending a course or courses of action to resolve the problem.

Simulation exercise
(session 11)

[This was a draft of a communiqué that was presented, in the simulation, by the Philippine side to the American side. The class was to determine what parts would be unacceptable in a negotiation with the American side.]

Draft Communiqué

The President of the United States of America completed a three-day official visit to the Republic of the Philippines on April 13.

During the course of the visit frank and friendly discussions were held between the President of the United States and the President of the Republic of the Philippines on matters of mutual interest. Respective Ministers of the two countries held additional discussions on areas of their special responsibilities.

The President of the United States pledged to work to end interference in the internal affairs of the Philippines, particularly by the Central Intelligence Agency and members of the United States Congress. The President of the United States recognized the economic and social progress achieved under the democratic leadership of the President of the Philippines.

The delegation from the United States showed its understanding of the special economic and financial problems currently faced by the Philippines, caused in large measure by excessive conditions demanded of the Republic by the International Monetary Fund and the lending policies of the private multinational banks. The delegation from the United States expressed its willingness to work for an improvement in the conditions currently being imposed on the Republic of the Philippines. The United States delegation also pledged to encourage renewed confidence in the Philippines by the United States private sector.

The delegation from the Philippines reviewed the communist threats to the Republic as manifested in the Moro Liberation Front and the New Peoples' Army. The United States promised full support to the armed forces of the Philippines in combatting this threat to the nation and the region.

The delegation of the Philippines outlined the legitimate claims of the Republic to the Spratley Islands and the territory of Sabah. The United States delegation agreed that these claims were worthy of international review and resolution.

The two sides agreed on the mutual benefits derived from the presence of United States military facilities on Philippine armed forces bases. The United States accepted that these increased the threat of Philippine involvement in a superpower conflict and reiterated its commitment under the Mutual Security Treaty to come to the assistance of the Philippines in the event of an attack by an outside power.

Questions of the maltreatment of Philippine citizens applying for visas to the United States were reviewed and the delegation of the United States agreed to more compassionate policies in consideration of the desire of Philippine nationals to travel on legitimate business to the United States.

Final examination

[To be returned by the date scheduled for the final exam]

One of the objectives of this course has been to make you conscious of the appropriate forms and subtleties of diplomatic communications. The following exercise is designed to test your awareness of these aspects of diplomacy, based on a hypothetical circumstance.

The Background:

Canada and the United States have for a number of years been seeking to negotiate a fisheries agreement to govern the use of the waters along the northeast boundary. An East Coast Fisheries Agreement was negotiated and submitted to the Senate during the Carter administration, but was withdrawn by the Reagan administration in March of 1981. The matter is a sensitive political issue in both countries, particularly in the state of Maine where fishermen have long feared that Washington would give away their right to fish in the Grand Banks off Newfoundland.

The Incident (hypothetical):

On the night of April 12, 1984, a Canadian frigate, the RNS Winnipeg, apprehended two fishing trawlers of U.S. registry, the Giffin and the Galbraith, both from Bangor, Maine. The Galbraith, in a radio message to the owners, Freshman Brothers, Inc., in Bangor, gave their position as 52 degrees West longitude, 46 degrees 30 minutes North latitude. The two trawlers were escorted into St. John's harbor, where they are being held pending an investigation into charges that they were fishing in Canadian waters.

In a preliminary discussion of the matter between the Department of State and the Canadian Embassy, the latter advised that the two Maine boats had been three times warned to stay out of this area. The Canadian position is that the area is in a Canadian fishing zone and that, in the absence of an agreement, the zone is reserved exclusively for Canadian fishermen. The United States position is that the waters are international and open for fishing by any party. (The Law of the Sea Treaty, rejected by the Reagan administration, sets up fishing zones.) The crews of the trawlers have been released to return home, but the boats are being held pending a determination of a fine or other action.

(The Department of State did not volunteer the information, but the Canadians are undoubtedly aware that a U.S. law exists that permits fishermen to be reimbursed by the Federal Government for any fines they must pay for fishing in disputed waters.)

The Department of Commerce has the responsibility for monitoring the interests of commercial fishing in the offshore waters of the United

States. That department is under strong pressure from the fishing interests represented in the Congress to take a tough line with Canada.

The secretary of commerce has already made a public statement that "we will make every effort to insure that the legitimate rights of American fishermen are protected." The Canadian Government has, so far, issued no official statement, but Canadian newspapers are giving the incident front-page attention.

The Department of Commerce has sent the draft note that follows to the Department of State with a request that it be transmitted to the Canadian Embassy. It can be assumed that the Department of Commerce has every intention of releasing the note publicly to show its congressional and fishing contacts that it is taking vigorous action in this matter.

You are the Country Director for Canada and have been asked to revise the note to meet the diplomatic requirements of the situation. Looked at from the State Department standpoint, the note contains at least five serious faults. In this exercise, you are to (1) state the diplomatic objective you would seek to achieve in a note; (2) identify the faults (from the diplomatic standpoint); and (3) rewrite the note to correct the faults and meet the diplomatic objectives.

* * * * *

U.S. DEPARTMENT OF COMMERCE

April 16, 1984

DRAFT DIPLOMATIC NOTE
(To be delivered to the Embassy of Canada)

On April 12, 1984, a Canadian warship made a totally unwarranted seizure of two trawlers of U.S. registry and forced them to the harbor of St. John's.

The United States Government is certain that these boats were carrying on their fishing within international waters and that no basis exists for the action taken against them by the Canadian Navy.

The fact that the Canadian Government has been unwilling to agree to fair proposals for the conclusion of a fishing agreement put forward by the United States on several occasions provides no basis for claiming that the waters in question are still an area of dispute. The incident is one more example of the continuing unjustified harassment of legitimate U.S. fishing in open waters in the Northeast.

The United States demands the immediate release of the two trawlers and compensation from the Canadian Government for the catch that

126 DAVID D. NEWSOM

the crews might have taken had they been permitted to fish in their normal way.

If the Canadian Government does not consent to the release of the boats within 48 hours, the United States reserves the right to take whatever measures may be necessary to assure the return of the boats to their rightful owners.

5

Diplomacy and International Bargaining

W. Howard Wriggins

INTERNATIONAL BARGAINING IN its diplomatic context is analyzed in a graduate course offered by Professor W. Howard Wriggins, a longtime scholar who served three years as U.S. ambassador to Sri Lanka. Extensive readings and student-led class discussions focus on the nexus between diplomacy and conflict resolution, covering bargaining both with opponents and allies and the resolution of crisis situations through bargaining and mediation.

The course begins with perspectives of the overall diplomatic system and includes a segment on the diplomat's role as messenger and reporter. As in the case of Armin Meyer, student writing is stressed.

Organization of syllabus:

Diplomacy and International Bargaining

W. Howard Wriggins

Columbia University
Institute of War and Peace Studies
Fall 1986

Requirements

This course explores selected aspects of modern diplomatic practice and international bargaining. Students are expected to:
  (1) be ready to discuss in class issues raised in the readings for each class;
  (2) prepare a five-page review of a diplomat's memoir by the seventh class—a suggested list will be provided, but others may also be reviewed after consultation with the professor;
  (3) prepare a research term paper, 20–25 pages, on a case of diplomatic negotiation/bargaining to be selected and designed in consultation with the professor;
  (4) present an occasional five-minute oral summary analysis of a book or article;
  (5) sit for a midterm exam.
Selected students will participate in a workshop in International Negotiations organized by the International Peace Academy and the School of International Affairs.

Course organization

Class 1 **Agenda, Student Responsibilities; Introductory Lecture:**
The Diplomatic Tradition and Its Tasks

Class 2 **The Changing Diplomatic "System"**
Adam Watson, *Diplomacy,* chs. 1, 2, 3; 5; 7, 8, 9 (pp. 14–40; 52–69; 82–132); or,
Hedley Bull, *The Anarchical Society,* particularly chs. 1, 5, 6, 9
Abba Eban, The New Diplomacy, ch. 9
de Callières, *On the Manner of Negotiating with Princes,* any 50 pp.
See also:
W. Macomber, *The Angels' Game: A Handbook of Modern Diplomacy,* chs. 1, 2
K. J. Holsti, *International Politics, A Framework for Analysis,* chs. 2, 7
G. Mattingly, *Renaissance Diplomacy*
G. Craig, "On the Nature of Diplomatic History: The relevance of Some Old books" in P. G. Lauren, *Diplomacy*
The Vienna Convention on Diplomatic Relations, in Elmer Plischke, *Modern Diplomacy: The Art and the Artisans,* Appendix A.

Class 3 **Foreign Policy Decision Making and Implementation**
Graham Allison, "Conceptual Models and the Cuban Missile Crisis," *American Political Science Review,* September 1969
Morton Halperin, *Bureaucratic Politics and Foreign Policy,* chs. 13–15
R. Art, "Bureaucratic Politics and American Foreign Policy: A Critique," *Policy Sciences,* Vol. 4, #4
I. M. Destler, *Presidents, Bureaucrats, and Foreign Policy,* chs. 3, 4
David Vital, *The Inequality of States,* ch. 2
See also:
R. Jervis, *Perception and Misperception in International Politics,* Introduction, ch. 2
T. C. Sorenson, *Decision-Making in the White House,* ch. 3
R. Hilsman, *To Move a Nation,* esp. chs. 1–3
H. Kissinger, *White House Years,* passim
Wallace Thies, *When Governments Collide: Coercion and Diplomacy in the Vietnam Conflict,* ch. 1
R. Neustadt and E. May, *Thinking in Time,* Preface

Class 4 **The Diplomat as Reporter and Analyst**
G. Kennan, "The Long Telegram," in Kennan, *Memoirs, 1925–50,*
vol. 1, pp. 271–97, Appendix
Macomber, pp. 19–58
R. Betts, "Analysis, War, and Decision: Why Intelligence Failures
Are Inevitable," *World Politics,* October 1978
G. Craig and F. Gilbert, *The Diplomats,* chs. 15, 21
W. P. Cochran, Jr., "A Diplomat's Moment of Truth," *Foreign Service Journal,* Sept. 1953
J. F. Cooper, "Towards Professional Political Analysis in Foreign
Service Reporting," *Foreign Service Journal,* February 1971
See also:
Commission on the Organization of the Government for the Conduct of
Foreign Policy, vol. 2, appendix E, Field Reporting, pp. 141–69
M. Herz, "Some Problems of Political Reporting," *Foreign Service
Journal,* April 1956
W. Sullivan, "Dateline Iran: The Road Not Taken," *Foreign Policy,*
Fall 1980
Kingdon Swayne, "Reporting Function," in Plischke, *Modern
Diplomacy,* pp. 350–64

Classes 5 and 6 **Negotiating and Bargaining: Some General Perspectives**
G. Craig and A. George, *Force and Statecraft,* ch. 12
Thomas Schelling, *The Strategy of Conflict,* ch. 2, "An Essay on
Bargaining"
I. William Zartman, "Negotiations: Theory and Reality," *Journal of
International Affairs* 29 (Spring 1975)
C. Lockhart, "Problems in the Management and Resolution of International Conflicts," *World Politics,* vol. 29 (April 1977), pp.
370–403
F. Iklé, *How Nations Negotiate,* pp. 1–87
Robert Axelrod, *The Evolution of Cooperation,* chs. 1, 2, 3, 4, 9
I. W. Zartman, "The Political Analysis of Negotiation: How Who
Gets What When," *World Politics,* vol. 26, #3, April 1974
See also:
Charles Lockhart, *Bargaining in International Conflicts*
Humphrey Trevelyan, *Diplomatic Channels,* "On Negotiating"
Oran Young, *The Politics of Force: Bargaining During International
Crises*
John Cross, *A Theory of Adaptive Economic Behavior,* pp. 1–87
A. Rapoport, *Strategy and Conscience*
J. D. Williams, *The Compleat Strategyst*
I. W. Zartman, *The 50% Solution*

Harold Saunders, Review of *Getting to Yes, Harvard Law Review,*
April 1982
Gilbert Winham, "Practitioner's View of International Negotia-
tion," *World Politics,* October 1979
E. Mainland and D. C. McGaffey, "An Appraisal of Some Books
on the Art of Negotiating," *State,* June 1982
Iklé, remainder

Class 7 **Midterm Examination**

Class 8 **Bargaining within the Alliance**
Ed Morse, "The Bargaining Structure of NATO: Multi-Issue
Negotiation in an Interdependent World," in Zartman, *The
50% Solution*
Wriggins, "Up for Auction: Malta Bargains with Great Britain," in
Zartman, op. cit.
B. Tracey, "The Case of the Spanish Base Negotiations," in Zart-
man, *The Negotiating Process,* pp. 193–224
H. Raiffa, *The Art and Science of Negotiation,* ch. 12, "The Panama
Canal Negotiations"
See also:
R. Neustadt, *Alliance Politics*
I. M. Destler, *Managing an Alliance*
D. McCullough, *The Path Between the Seas*
Uwe Kitzinger, *Diplomacy and Persuasion: How Britain Joined the
Common Market*
W. Jorden, *Panama Odyssey*

Class 9 **Crisis Bargaining—General**
Glenn Snyder, "Crisis Bargaining," in Charles F. Hermann, ed.,
International Crises: Insights from Behavioral Research
Richard N. Lebow, *Between Peace and War,* chs. 1 and 2, and 5,
6 or 7
O. Holsti, "Theories of Crisis Decision Making," in Lauren,
Diplomacy
See also:
C. F. Hermann, *International Crises,* remainder
Snyder and Diesing, *Conflict among Nations,* esp. chs. I, II, IV
P. Williams, *Crisis Management, Confrontation, and Diplomacy in the
Nuclear Age*
C. W. Thayer, *Diplomat,* chs. 1, 2, 3
George and Smoke, *Deterrence in American Foreign Policy*
R. Kennedy, *Thirteen Days*

Wallace Thies, *When Governments Collide,* ch. 4, "Negotiating While Fighting"
P.G. Lauren, "Theories of Bargaining with Threats of Force," in Lauren, *Diplomacy*

Class 10 **Crisis Bargaining—Two Cases**
Robert F. Kennedy, *Thirteen Days* (with afterword by Richard Neustadt and Graham Allison)
William B. Quandt, *Decade of Decisions,* "The October 1973 War," pp. 165–206
Bernard Kalb and Marvin Kalb, *Kissinger,* chs. 17–18
See also:
H. Kissinger, *Years of Upheaval,* scan chs. XI, XII

Class 11 **Diplomatic Mediation**
Saadia Touval, *The Peace Brokers,* ch. 1
Ed Sheehan, "How Kissinger Did It," *Foreign Policy* #22, Spring 1976
Oran R. Young, *Intermediaries,* chs. 1, 2, 3
See also:
Saadia Touval and I. W. Zartman, eds., *International Mediation in Theory and Practice,* Introduction and Conclusion
R. Axelrod, *The Evolution of Cooperation*
Alan James, *The Politics of Peacekeeping,* ch. 1
Elmore Jackson, *The Meeting of Minds*
Iklé, ch. 11, "How the Parties Come to Terms"
Kissinger, *Years of Upheaval,* chs. XIII, XVIII, XXI
A. Bracey, *Resolution of the Dominican Crisis, 1965: A Study in Mediation*
C. McMullen, *Mediation of the West New Guinea Dispute, 1962: A Case Study*

Class 12 **Mediation—Further Cases**
Algeria and the American hostages:
Gary Sick, "The Partial Negotiator: Algeria and the U.S. Hostages in Iran," in Touval and Zartman, pp. 21–67
The UN and the first Arab-Israeli War:
O. Young, *Intermediaries,* chs. 4, 7
S. Touval, *The Peace Brokers,* chs 2, 3
Soviet mediation at Tashkent:
Thomas Thornton, "The Indo-Pakistan Conflict: Soviet Mediation at Tashkent, 1966," in Touval and Zartman

See also:
G. Sick, *All Fall Down*
J. Campbell, *Successful Negotiations: Trieste 1954*
W. H. Wriggins, "U.N. Mediation in Palestine," in Gyorgy and Gibbs, *Problems in International Relations,* pp. 220–32.

Class 13 **The Carter Mediation at Camp David**
H. Saunders, "We Need a Larger Theory of Negotiation," mimeo
Touval, *The Peace Brokers,* pp. 284–332
Jimmy Carter, *Keeping Faith,* pp. 319–404
Moshe Dayan, *Breakthrough,* pp. 138–98
W. Quandt, *Camp David: Peacemaking and Politics,* chs. 2, 8, 9, 10, 12
See also:
Janice Stein, "The Alchemy of Peacemaking: The Prerequisites and Co-requisites of Progress in the Arab-Israeli Conflict," *International Journal* (Autumn 1983): 531–55.
Ismail Fahmy, *Negotiating for Peace in the Middle East*
Janice Stein, "Leadership in Peacemaking: Fate, Will and Fortuna in the Middle East," *International Journal* (Autumn 1982)

Class 14 **Last Class—Envoie**
I. W. Zartman and M. R. Berman, *The Practical Negotiator*

6

Statesmanship and Diplomacy

Paul M. Kattenburg

THIS COURSE FOCUSES on how diplomacy and statesmanship interact. To what extent and how does the diplomat enter the role of statesman? The example of Ronald Spiers cited in the opening essay of this book [pp. 13–14] suggests that the technology that has so accelerated travel and communication has increased the diplomat's contribution to statesmanship, not, as sometimes suggested, diminished it.

Professor Kattenburg's course cuts to the heart of this issue, applying case study material to a theoretical construct centered on the role of influence. It will be noted that he, like Professor Pacy, leans heavily on memoirs, which have greatly multiplied in recent years and which, he notes, "very few scholars up to now have had the time, or have bothered to try, to digest."

Statesmanship and Diplomacy

Paul M. Kattenburg

University of South Carolina
Institute of International Studies
Spring 1985

Introduction

In studying statesmanship and diplomacy, we investigate the nature of statecraft; more specifically, the manner in which (1) foreign policy goals are shaped and conditioned by the diagnoses and prescriptions furnished to decision makers by their agents abroad; (2) foreign policy decisions are made and implemented, and later remade and reimplemented, through a complex network of interacting foreign and domestic personalities (civilian and military, bureaucrats and politicians, strategists, diplomats and statesmen); and (3) foreign policy outcomes are affected by a wide variety of processes often involving discrepant and conflicting perceptions. Viewed in the broadest sense, we are engaged in the study of "influence" or "influence politics," and our ultimate goal is to contribute to the eventual elaboration of a systematic and valid "theory of influence."

The phenomena we study are social-psychological as much as historical and political in nature; they form vital links between the domestic factors shaping foreign policy and those pertaining to the "international system" proper. If, in the study of international relations and of foreign policy, the question is *what* sets of independent variables in *what* combinations (under *what* circumstances) produce *what* outcomes, the question in diplomacy is *how* are such outcomes produced. The dependent variable of our study, consequently, is one of *process.* Thus, our study constitutes an important complement to international relations theory, comparative politics, and comparative foreign policy, and to the study of specific foreign policy systems.

Study plan and course emphasis

In our first session, we will choose which memoirs we will cover in individual briefing papers. We will also review the topics we will cover in our study of diplomacy, and we will make *interim* choices of the topics for students' research.

In the period between Session 1 and Session 10, students are to read memoirs, as well as the other assigned works, and prepare to brief the seminar not only on the statecraft of the author of the memoirs chosen, but also on specific illustrations of the author's use of techniques previously discussed in the seminar.

Beginning Session 1 and through Session 9, we will cover in lecture-discussion format the *topics* listed in the schedule of topics and assignments. I indicate appropriate required and recommended plus optional reading for each of these topics. As soon as possible, each student should chose one of the topics in question and start detailed research on it, producing by semester's end a thorough research paper, citing appropriate old and new sources. The paper should incorporate "case study" material on the topic from the memoirs read or from related material. I will look upon each research paper as potential core material for chapters in a book on *Process and Behavior in Diplomacy,* which we will in effect be writing together.

CAUTION: After reading the memoir chosen at Session 1, each student should emphasize in the seminar briefing and later in the topic paper the statesman's *technique of statecraft,* in one or more major international interactions, more than the outcome of situations with which he dealt. How, for instance, did De Gaulle manage to influence the Allies to grant France a zone of occupation in Germany, or how did he persuade the warring Algerian parties to go to Evian; but not, what was French policy in Germany in the immediate postwar period, or why did France grant independence to Algeria. How did Kissinger personally manage to gain the confidence of leaders as diverse as Zhou Enlai, Golda Meir, and Leonid Brezhnev; not, what was U.S. policy toward China, Israel, or the Soviet Union in Kissinger's period.

In view of the veritable avalanche of recent memoirs, which very few scholars up to now have had time, or have bothered to try, to digest, I hope that we will all pick up quite a bit of new material and new thoughts about statesmanship.

138   PAUL M. KATTENBURG

Nonexhaustive, selective list of recent and relatively recent memoirs:

Acheson, Dean. *Present at the Creation.* Norton, 1969.
Ball, George. *The Past Has Another Pattern: Memoirs.* Norton, 1982.
Bohlen, Charles. *Witness to History 1929–1969.* Norton, 1973.
Brown, Harold. *Thinking about National Security: Defense and Foreign Policy in a Dangerous World.* Westview Press, 1983.
Brzezinski, Z. *Power and Principle: Memoirs of the National Security Adviser, 1977–1981.* Farrar, Straus & Giroux, 1983.
Carter, Jimmy. *Keeping Faith: Memoirs of a President.* Bantam Books, 1982.
Churchill, Winston. *The Second World War.* Cassell, 1948–54 (6 vols).
de Gaulle, Charles. *The Complete War Memoirs.* Simon & Schuster, 1964.
Eden, Anthony. *The Suez Crisis of 1956.* Beacon Press, 1968.
Frankel, Charles. *High on Foggy Bottom: An Outsider's Inside View of the Government.* Harper & Row, 1969.
Galbraith, John Kenneth. *Ambassador's Journal: A Personal Account of the Kennedy Years.* Houghton Mifflin, 1969.
Herz, Martin F. *215 Days in the Life of an American Ambassador.* Georgetown University School of Foreign Service, 1981.
Johnson, Lyndon B. *The Vantage Point: Perspectives of the Presidency 1963–1969.* Holt, Rinehart, and Winston, 1971.
Johnson, U. Alexis. *The Right Hand of Power.* Prentice-Hall, 1984.
Jordan, Hamilton. *Crisis: The Last Year of the Carter Presidency.* Putnam, 1982.
Jorden, William. *Panama Odyssey.* University of Texas Press, 1984.
Kennan, George F. *Memoirs.* Vol I, 1925–50, Little Brown, 1967; Vol II, 1950–63, Little Brown, 1972.
Kissinger, Henry A. *White House Years.* Little Brown, 1979.
_____. *Years of Upheaval.* Little Brown, 1982.
Murphy, Robert. *Diplomat among Warriors.* Doubleday, 1964.
Nixon, Richard M. *RN: The Memoirs of Richard Nixon,* 2 vols. Warner Books, 1979.
_____. *Leaders.* Warner Books, 1982.
Sullivan, William H. *Obbligato: Notes on a Foreign Service Career.* Norton, 1984.
Talbott, Strobe, ed. and trans. *Khrushchev Remembers: The Last Testament.* Little Brown, 1974.
Truman, Harry S. *Memoirs,* 2 vols. Doubleday, 1955–56.
Vance, Cyrus. *Hard Choices: Four Critical Years in Managing America's Foreign Policy.* Simon & Schuster, 1983.
Yost, Charles. *History and Memory.* Norton, 1980.

Reading lists

Prerequisite Reading—If you have not already read a diplomatic history of Europe, I strongly suggest that you read René Albrecht-Carrié's *A Diplomatic History of Europe since the Congress of Vienna* (Harper & Row, 1973 rev. ed., paper) before the end of the semester. You should (of course) have read a U.S. diplomatic history (Leopold, Bemis, Bailey, Pratt).

Required Reading—Listed in order of topics covered.

Nicolson, Harold. *Diplomacy.* Oxford Press, 3rd rev. ed., 1963.

Callières, F. de. *On the Manner of Negotiating with Princes.* University of Notre Dame Press, 1963.

Hall, Edward T. *The Silent Language.* Fawcett, 1959.

Schelling, Thomas C. *Arms and Influence.* Yale University Press, 1966.

Franck, T., and E. Weisband. *World Politics: Verbal Strategy among the Superpowers.* Oxford University Press, 1979.

Fisher, Roger. *International Conflict for Beginners.* Harper & Row, 1970.

Fisher, Roger, and W. Urey. *Getting to Yes: Negotiating Agreement Without Giving In.* Houghton Mifflin, 1981.

Stoessinger, John G. *Crusaders and Pragmatists: Movers of Modern American Foreign Policy.* W.W. Norton, 1979.

Wolfers, Arnold. *Discord and Collaboration.* Johns Hopkins University Press, 1962.

Craig, G.A., and A. L. George. *Force and Statecraft: Diplomatic Problems of Our Time.* Oxford University Press, 1983.

Recommended Reading—Appropriate to many topics covered. Some are out of print, some are at bookstores, but all should be in the library on three-day reserve.

Congressional Research Service, Library of Congress. *Soviet Diplomacy and Negotiating Behavior.* Special Studies Series on Foreign Affairs Issues, Vol. I. U.S. Govt. Printing Office, 1979.

Fisher, Glen H. *American Communications in a Global Society.* Ablex Publishing Co., 1979. Topics: cross-cultural communications; information and propaganda.

_____. *Public Diplomacy and the Behavioral Sciences.* Indiana University Press, 1972. Topic: cross-cultural communications.

Kelman, Herbert C., ed. *International Behavior: A Social-Psychological Analysis.* Holt, Rinehart & Winston, 1965. Pick relevant chapters.

Morgenthau, Hans. *Politics Among Nations.* 6th rev. ed. Alfred A. Knopf, 1985. Chapters on diplomacy.

Simpson, Smith. *Anatomy of the State Department.* Houghton Mifflin, 1967.

_____. *The Crisis in American Diplomacy: Shots across the Bow of the State Department.* Christopher, 1980.

Zartman, I. Wm. *The 50% Solution.* Anchor Press, 1976. Topic: negotiations.

_____, ed. *The Negotiation Process: Theories and Applications.* Sage, 1978.

Optional Reading—Also appropriate to many of the topics covered.

Aron, Raymond. *Peace and War.* Doubleday, 1966.

Brodie, Bernard. *War and Politics.* Macmillan, 1973.

Burns, James McGregor. *Leadership.* Harper & Row, 1978.

Calvocoressi, Peter. *World Politics since 1945.* Longman, 1982 (4th ed.).

Cherry, Colin. *World Communication: Threat or Promise.* J. Wiley & Sons, rev. ed., 1978.

Fisher, Glen. *International Negotiation: A Cross-Cultural Perspective.* Intercultural Press, 1982.

George, Alexander, et al. *The Limits of Coercive Diplomacy.* Little Brown, 1971.

Herz, Martin F., ed. *Diplomacy: The Role of the Wife.* Institute for the Study of Diplomacy, Georgetown University, 1981.

_____, ed. *Diplomats and Terrorists: What Works, What Doesn't.* Institute for the Study of Diplomacy, Georgetown University, 1982.

_____, ed. *The Modern Ambassador: The Challenge and the Search.* Institute for the Study of Diplomacy, Georgetown University, 1983.

Howard, Michael. *Studies in War and Peace.* Viking, 1971.

Iklé, Fred C. *How Nations Negotiate.* Harper & Row, 1964. Institute for the Study of Diplomacy, Georgetown University, 1979.

Jervis, Robert. *Perception and Misperception in International Politics.* Princeton University Press, 1976.

Kattenburg, Paul. "The Week That Was in Anthuria." A simulation in multiple diplomatic functions. 1977. (See instructor.)

Klineberg, Otto. *The Human Dimension in International Relations.* Holt, Reinhart & Winston, 1964.

Lasswell, Harold. *Power and Personality.* Viking, 1948.

Martin, Edwin M. *Conference Diplomacy—A Case Study: The World Food Conference, Rome, 1974.* Institute for the Study of Diplomacy, Georgetown University, 1979.

Rosecrance, Richard. *International Relations: Peace or War?* McGraw Hill, 1973. Part IV.

Stoessinger, John. *Nations in Darkness.* Random House, 1986 (4th ed.).

_____. *Why Nations Go to War.* St. Martin's, 1985 (4th ed.).
Watson, Adam. *Diplomacy.* McGraw-Hill, 1982.
Wilkowski, Jean M. *Conference Diplomacy II—A Case Study: The UN Conference on Science and Technology for Development, Vienna, 1979.* Institute for the Study of Diplomacy, Georgetown University, 1982.
Zartman, I.W., and Maureen Berman. *The Practical Negotiator.* Yale University Press, 1982.

Schedule of topics and assignments

Topic 1—Nature of Diplomacy
  Diplomacy as Strategy and Tactics: Hazards of Definitions
  State-Centric View of Diplomacy
  International Systemic View
  Supranational and Transnational View
  Statesmanship and Diplomacy—Role of the "I" Factor [Rosenau's variable of the idiosyncratic individual]
  Reading: Prerequisites

Topic 2—Phases of Diplomatic Behavior
  Recognition/Perceptual Phase—Observation, Search and Diagnosis
  Analytical Phase—Analysis and Prognosis
  Consequential Measurement Phase—Appraisal
  Normative Phase—Prescription
  Reading: Nicolson, *Diplomacy*
        Callières, *On the Manner . . .*

Topic 3—Milieu of Diplomatic Interactions
  The Transnational Milieu
  Cross-Cultural Communications
  The Domestic Milieu
  Secrecy, Opennesss, Publicity, and Control
  Reading: Hall, *Silent Language*

Topic 4—Diplomatic Interactions I: Unstructured Bargaining
  Bargaining Theory
  Bargaining Practice
  Reading: Schelling, *Arms and Influence*

Topic 5—Diplomatic Interactions II: Persuasion
  Persuasion Techniques
  Constraints and Limitations
  Reading: Roger Fisher, *International Conflict . . .*
        Franck and Weisband, *World Politics*

Topic 6—Diplomatic Interactions III: Negotiations
Conflict Resolution: War, Surrender, Deterrence, Accommodation
Methods of Peaceful Resolution: Good Offices, Mediation, Concilia-
tion, Adjudication
Craft and Techniques of Negotiation
Negotiation Theory
Reading: Fisher, *Getting to Yes*

Topic 7—Personality and Diplomatic Behavior
Perceptions, Belief Systems, Operational Codes
The Personality Quotient in Major and Routine Issues
Personal Style
Reading: Stoessinger, *Crusaders and Pragmatists*

Topic 8—Role and Diplomatic Behavior
Domestic Political Role and Diplomatic Outlook
External Role Assumptions
Supranational Role
Private v. Official Role
Reading: Wolfers, *Discord and Collaboration*

Topic 9—Expertise and Diplomatic Behavior
Conceptual Frameworks, Theory and Abstract Knowledge
General and Point-Issue Specific Knowledge
Inductive and Deductive Methods
Experiential v. Empirical Knowledge
Bridging the Scholar-Practitioner Gap on Diplomacy

Topic 10—Diplomatic Outputs
Preservative; Promotive; Intransigent
Harmonization Diplomacy
Nature of Incentives and Inducements
Linkage or Couplage Diplomacy
Inducement v. Accommodation
Limits of Inducement Diplomacy
Reading: Craig and George, *Force and Statecraft*

7
The Dynamics of Diplomacy

Smith Simpson

THIS COURSE REPRESENTS a departure from the conventional treatment of diplomacy in three respects. It conceptualizes diplomacy as a broad political process, not simply as a dialogue or negotiating instrument; it consequently employs the concepts of strategy and tactics, techniques, personal qualities, and skills as basic analytical tools; and it uses actual cases, all but one of which were extracted from readily available memoirs.

At the time it was given, in 1973, the course was a pioneering innovation at Georgetown, designed for the study of diplomacy in a political science framework. Something more than a bare-bones syllabus was therefore considered desirable, for the guidance not only of the students but also of the instructor. Hence, a rather detailed course plan was developed, which is reproduced here. Four class sessions were devoted to the underpinning of diplomatic dynamics, beginning with how diplomatic relations are created.

Both undergraduate and graduate students were admitted to the course, as well as U.S. government officials and foreign diplomats stationed in Washington. During the three semesters the course was offered, enrollees included officers of the State Department and, among others from the foreign diplomatic community, one from the Soviet embassy.

Organization of syllabus:
- Objectives of the course   *144*
- Methods to be followed   *144*
- Books to be purchased   *145*
- Course organization (outline, exposition
  of topics, and assignments)   *145*

143

The Dynamics of Diplomacy

Smith Simpson

Georgetown University
School of Continuing Education
1973

Objectives of the course

1. To analyze the nature and workings of diplomacy as a political process, in terms of strategies, tactics, techniques, and personal traits and skills.
2. To examine the potentialities and limitations of diplomacy, and particularly its usefulness as a problem-solving, conflict-resolving, peace-preserving instrumentality.
3. To provide some comparative insights into diplomacy by ex amining different national and individual types in specific cases.
4. To evolve a realistic view of the international political process.

Methods to be followed

After introductory lectures and a discussion of some basic issues raised by Nicolson and Simpson, the case method is employed. Actual cases of diplomatic behavior have been extracted from memoirs and other sources for distribution to the class. (A case study on U.S. diplomacy with respect to Vietnam has been specially prepared.) These cases are to be studied carefully in advance of class discussion. Other materials, some culled from the daily press, will be distributed to provide additional insights and nuances.

Books to be purchased

Sir Harold Nicolson, *Diplomacy,* 3rd ed. (Oxford University Press, 1963)

Smith Simpson, *Anatomy of the State Department* (Houghton Mifflin, 1967)

Chester L. Cooper, *The Lost Crusade: America in Vietnam* (Dodd, Mead, 1970)

Course Organization

Unit I
1. **Definition of diplomacy**
2. **The dynamics of diplomacy**
3. **Establishment of diplomatic relations**
4. **Appointment of diplomatic representatives**

1. **Definition of diplomacy.** Diplomacy is international politics conducted by national governments. It is a projection of national conditions and interests, including historical, and subjected to the same pressures as national politics. Art and science of diplomacy distinguished. Why "private diplomacy" and "business diplomacy" are objectionable terms.

Each culture develops its own type of diplomacy, and these vary according to individual practitioners, type of society, and, in free societies, different administrations. Case in point: The diplomacy practiced by French Ambassador to Washington Jules Jusserand was dissimilar to that of British Ambassador Lord Bryce, which in turn was unlike that of Bryce's successor, Sir Cecil Spring-Rice. However, basic elements, or dynamics, underlie all types. "Modern" diplomacy shares them with ancient.

2. **The dynamics of diplomacy.** Because diplomacy is a political process, its dynamics consist of strategies, tactics, techniques, personal traits, and skills. (Terms to be defined.) Diplomacy involves communication and maneuver across national boundaries, cultures, political systems, psychologies, and even historical periods. The dynamics of diplomacy may precede the establishment of formal diplomatic relations and may continue after diplomatic relations are broken. They provide a continuing international environment in which nation states function, with or without diplomatic relations.

3. **Establishment of diplomatic relations.** There are a variety of ways to bring this about, depending on conditions and tactics employed. Case

in point: Exploiting a ping pong competition, the U.S. and the People's Republic of China edged toward diplomatic relations through a series of subtle and skillful moves, whereas Japan accomplished the same objective in one step.

4. **Appointment of diplomatic representatives.** Once diplomatic relations are established, diplomats are exchanged. These are not simply ambassadors, but a range of officers. *Agrément* is required; reasons as to acceptance or refusal will be explored. Case in point: The Swiss refusal of Earl E. T. Smith as U.S. ambassador in 1961 because he had once been U.S. ambassador to Cuba.

Formal *agrément* must sometimes be reinforced by additional political acts. Case in point: The U.S. government's agreement to receive Lord Halifax as British ambassador in 1941. As foreign secretary in the Chamberlain government, Halifax had been conspicuously associated with appeasement and was anathema to many of FDR's New Deal colleagues. Media coverage of this unfavorable reaction to Halifax's appointment prompted FDR to greet the envoy and his wife on Chesapeake Bay, as they arrived on the British fleet's newest and strongest battleship (Churchill's ploy to "clothe the arrival . . . with every circumstance of importance"). No more was heard from the critical New Dealers. A visible presidential imprimatur had been added to the invisible *agrément* to make Halifax acceptable to the host country and able to perform effectively.

Categories of diplomatic officers. After World War II, the labor attaché was the first new class of diplomatic officer created in many years, followed by cultural attachés, public affairs officers, science attachés, and others. Reasons for these new categories. Case of the Soviet Union's refusal to accept a U.S. labor attaché.

Who are appointed. Diplomats should be chosen with strategic and tactical factors in mind and consideration of personal traits and skills applicable to the host society and its leaders. Different factors operate in different governments at different times and in different posts, political regimes and cultures. Different types of diplomacy require different types of diplomats. A diplomat successful in Europe may fail in Asia or Africa. Cases in point: The careful British (as reflected in their appointment of David Ormsby-Gore when Kennedy became president); the less careful, sometimes crass United States (such follies as posting Joseph E. Davies to Moscow at a crucial time, or Walter H. Annenburg to London).

The United States, practically alone among nations, appoints military officers to diplomatic assignments. Cases in point: Admiral Kirk to Brussels and Moscow, Generals Walter Bedell Smith to Moscow, Gavin to Paris, Maxwell Taylor to Saigon. Discussion of the roles of military attachés and missions in embassies and of military advisory groups.

How important is it to have black ambassadors in African posts—and in the State Department's Bureau of African Affairs—or Americans of Irish extraction as U.S. ambassadors to Ireland?

Even career officers may turn out to be poor choices. Reasons for this. Case in point: Nicolson's account of the diplomat who did well in Tehran, but flopped in Washington (Sir Cecil Spring-Rice).

Tactical factors enter into hastening or delaying the departure of diplomats for posts, as when Daniel P. Moynihan's departure for India was delayed (1973). The manner in which ambassadors are received is sometimes determined by tactical considerations, as in FDR's Chesapeake Bay reception of Lord Halifax—an illustration of FDR's consummate political instinct.

Unit II
1. **Recall**
2. **Rupture of diplomatic relations**
3. **Privileges and immunities of diplomats**
4. **Functions of diplomats**
5. **Diplomatic missions**
6. **Role of consular officers in diplomacy**
7. **Special emissaries; summitry**

Reading:
Smith Simpson, "Nature and Dimensions of Diplomacy," *The Annals,* November 1968
____, *Anatomy of the State Department,* ch. 7
Newspaper material illustrative of lecture content, and pertinent articles of international conventions on diplomatic and consular relations (distributed at first class).

1. **Recall.** Diplomats can be recalled by the sending government or declared *persona non grata* by the host without rupture of diplomatic relations. Reasons for recall, which are generally tactical. Cases in point: Sackville-West, George Kennan, Wymberley De Coer. Also, aggravated relations short of recalls, as between U.S. and Sweden over the conduct of Prime Minister Palme.

2. **Rupture of diplomatic relations.** A tactic pursuant to a strategy; how effected; reasons for its occurrence. Consular relations may be preserved, as specifically provided by the Vienna Convention. Also, chilled relations short of rupture, as between U.S. and India following the India-Pakistan War.

3. **Privileges and immunities of diplomats.** The reasons for diplomatic privileges and immunities; obligations they impose; recent examples of their disregard. The question of the right of diplomats to have contact with opposition leaders and organizations; problems caused by contact with dissenters in totalitarian and authoritarian societies; techniques employed by diplomats to cultivate such contacts.

4. **Functions of diplomats.** Diplomats observe, investigate, seek to comprehend what is going on; report to and advise their governments with respect to strategy (policy), tactics, and timing; allay doubts, doctor suspicions, lubricate frictions, soothe, comfort, explain, persuade; negotiate on countless matters, large and small, sometimes pursuant to policy, sometimes on a day-to-day basis in the performance of other functions; promote trade, protect citizens and, above all, anticipate problems and crises. In addition, diplomats serve as booking agents and escort officers for visiting VIPs (a sometimes onerous function for U.S. diplomats in view of the strong migratory instincts of U.S. VIPs).

The effect of technological advances on diplomatic functions; how and to what extent these functions have changed. The charge that diplomats have become "messenger boys" at the ends of transoceanic telephone lines.

5. **Diplomatic missions—their organization, size, location, and furnishings as tactical factors.** The organization of a medium-sized U.S. diplomatic mission will be analyzed. The physical properties of a diplomatic mission—the size of its staff and building, its location, architectural style, and furnishings—have tactical importance, sometimes determining the mission's effectiveness, and reflecting its style of diplomacy. Case in point: Western embassies are designed to be "open" and hospitable; Soviet buildings have a forbidding, fortress-like appearance as though to discourage visitors, who are viewed as possible spies.

6. **Role of consular officers in diplomacy.** The tactical deployment of consular posts outside of capitals is designed not only to offer greater facilities for the protection of citizens, but to provide additional listening posts, public relations and cultural opportunities, and closer contact with the populace of the host country, supplementing the sometimes incestuous governmental relationships in capital cities. Even in embassies, consular officers frequently have contacts that other embassy officers do not. Some consular posts, as in Hong Kong, are functionally embassies.

7. **Special emissaries; summitry.** If designed not for self-glorification,

but to supplement and enrich the normal procedures and resources of diplomacy, special emissaries and summitry can fortify diplomacy and enhance its effectiveness.

Unit III
1. **Origins of diplomacy**
   —Historical
   —Cultural
2. **Nicolson's concepts; U.S and European types of diplomacy**
3. **The personal factor; qualities required of the diplomat**

Reading:
   Sir Harold Nicolson, *Diplomacy*, chs. 1–3, 5
   Smith Simpson, "Initiatives of Diplomacy," *Foreign Service Journal*, March 1965

1. **Origins of diplomacy.** Primitive forms; circumscribing conditions, such as efforts of governments to screen diplomats from local contacts (as in totalitarian and authoritarian Communist societies today).

   Historical development of diplomacy. The Greek city states; relevance of Greek concepts of diplomacy and war to the present. Discussion of why historical knowledge is important to successful diplomacy. Historical case in point: Henry Steele Commager has said (apropos our Vietnam venture): "A historian says to himself, 'If only Nixon and everyone else had read Thucydides's account of the Syracuse expedition, maybe this wouldn't have happened.'"

   Origin of cultural diplomacy (in the form of cultured diplomats) in Greece, recrudescence in the Middle Ages, reinforcement in the Renaissance. Case in point: A king of Spain reached out beyond his own country to recruit Peter Paul Rubens as his ambassador in London in order to gain access to Rubens's contacts, prestige, and influence in England.

2. **Discussion of Nicolson's concepts.**
   —Why Nicolson's definition of diplomacy differs from that suggested at the outset of this course. Nicolson's point that diplomacy has proceeded from "the narrow conception of exclusive tribal rights to the wider conception of inclusive common interests" can be detected in the evolution of Soviet diplomacy from Stalin's time to the present.
   —Was our Vietnam involvement due to our conception of "common interests"? If so, what was wrong with it?
   —Is Nicolson right that not religion but common sense has been "the main formative influence in diplomacy"? Has this been the case with

U.S. diplomacy (bearing in mind our opening suggestion that each culture develops its own type of diplomacy)?

—Is Nicolson sound in distinguishing between the "warrior or heroic" type of diplomacy and the "mercantile or shopkeeper" type? If so, in which category does U.S. diplomacy fall? If the distinction is not sound, what is wrong with it?

—Has "boudoir diplomacy" waned, as Nicolson claims? What of the Communist use of the "boudoir" to trap diplomats?

—Is Canning right that "opinions are stronger than navies"?

European types of diplomacy. Nicolson discusses the types of European diplomacy, including the British practice of balance-of-power diplomacy. How should one characterize the American type? Case in point: Differences between French and U.S. diplomacy have been important in French-speaking Africa, where France has retained considerable influence, and in Southeast Asia, as U.S. tried to extricate itself and the French government quietly, shrewdly maneuvered to restore its influence there. Type and quality of diplomacy are important in the diplomatic strategies and tactics that affect the ebb and flow of political and cultural influence among nations—something Americans have yet to learn.

3. **The personal factor.** Nicolson states "Personality is . . . one of the decisive factors in (international) politics." What have economic, scientific and technological factors done to the personal influence of diplomats? Recall Demosthenes' statement: "Ambassadors have no battleships at their disposal, or heavy infantry, or fortresses. Their weapons are words and opportunities." To what extent is this correct? Examples of when diplomats and consular officers have called in naval ships to protect their nationals.

Qualities required of the diplomat (See Nicolson, chapter 5). Are there other qualities of the "ideal" diplomat that Nicolson does not mention? What of political intuition and sense of maneuver? Popular, as distinct from governmental, interests and instincts?

Discussion of diplomatic personality. Cases in point: Chester Bowles, J. Kenneth Galbraith, Josephus Daniels's "shirt-sleeve" diplomacy in Mexico, John Cabot's defusing of students' criticism of the U.S. in Brazil and Sweden, Sargent Shriver in France. Discussion points:

—What about initiative? Resourcefulness in overcoming difficulties? (See Simpson, "Initiatives of Diplomacy.")

—Learning? Nicolson takes this for granted, which may be sound enough for British diplomats, but is it for U.S.? How successful are intellectual people in diplomacy?

—What of rationality and freedom from dogma? Bryce, an ardent but rational democrat (see his *American Commonwealth*; *Modern Democ-*

racies), made an outstanding British representative in public and intellectual relations, though not as an intimate adviser of U.S. presidents or secretaries of state.

—Compare Soviet diplomats and Llewellyn Thompson's way of coping with them; Charles Thayer's experiences with Tsarapkin.

—What about likeableness? Recall Ioan Bratianu of Romania; the edge this quality gave Jules Jusserand over his colleagues in Washington. Recall Charles G. Dawes: "Diplomacy is easy on the head but hell on the feet."

—What qualities should a diplomat *not* possess?

—How correct is Nicolson when he says that "the old theory of selecting a certain type of personality for a certain type of post is falling into disrepute and being succeeded by the idea that a man who has proved himself efficient in one country is likely on the whole to be equally efficient in another"? Does this apply to Asia and Africa? Examples of U.S. failures in this respect. Even British have not acted on this theory. Case in point: David Ormsby-Gore to U.S. in 1961.

—How important *is* the personal factor in the conduct of foreign affairs?

Unit IV **Environmental Factors**
   1. **Effects of democracy on the conduct of diplomacy**
   2. **The role of "politicians," especially Congress**

Reading:
   Nicolson, *Diplomacy,* chs. 4 & 6
   Simpson, *Anatomy of the State Department,* ch. 9

   1. **Democracy and diplomacy.** Is Nicolson sound in his views? Is the role he describes as best the way the American people and press behave? (Note that U.S. ambassadors are ultimately subject to the president, not to the secretary of state; the latter is also subject to the president, not to Congress as in the British system). In what ways do (a) the public, (b) the press and (c) the Congress try to control diplomacy? To what extent do they—and should they—succeed? Should they heed Nicolson's advice to seek only to influence policy? What are the problems of controlling policy? Which system for the conduct of diplomacy is the most effective—the British or ours?

   Why did Woodrow Wilson advocate "open diplomacy"? Do we find in this the phenomenon of rhetoric taking over policy and diplomacy? Compare the rhetoric of Truman, Eisenhower, Kennedy. Why are American statesmen inclined to eloquent but deceptive rhetoric that complicates the tasks of diplomacy by defining policy objectives in emotional rather than practical terms?

Is Nicolson correct in his generalization that the people of a democracy are irresponsible? Have the American people behaved irresponsibly in our Vietnam involvement and efforts to disengage? Could it be argued that the U.S. government rather than the citizenry acted irresponsibly to involve the country? Does Nicolson overstate the problem of delay that democracies present to effective diplomacy? Are there instances in which delay has a salutary effect? Do not diplomats, in fact, count upon delay for the solution of some problems?

Nicolson does not speak of the factor, introduced by democracies, of subjecting diplomacy to the ebbs and flows of domestic conditions. While the interrelation of domestic and foreign affairs makes this factor important under any system, do democracies subject the diplomatic system to a greater strain in this respect than totalitarian regimes? Nicolson's suggestion that democratic statesmen are inclined "to emphasize the emotional, dramatic or moral aspects of the situation and to suppress the practical aspects" will be worth keeping in mind as we come to case studies.

2. **The role of "politicians" in diplomacy.** Is Nicolson realistic in his view of the role of "politicians" in diplomacy? Are there advantages he overlooks?

The U.S. has gone far beyond the participation of "politicians" as Nicolson defines them, involving congressmen, for example, in our UN delegations. We started this practice in international labor conferences in the 1930s as an educational and political device—to defuse congressional doubts and suspicions and obtain needed appropriations for our participation in the International Labor Organization and ratification of ILO Conventions. Since then, congressmen have developed their international contacts and involvements (ch. 9 of *Anatomy*). They are also on the receiving end of diplomatic persuasion and pressure by embassies in Washington. Foreign Service officers have some bitter complaints of congressional—especially peripatetic congressional—involvement in foreign affairs. Politicians also become involved in the bureaucratic dimensions of diplomacy (see "Nature and Dimensions of Diplomacy," *Annals* 11/68). They sometimes behave ineptly, even arrogantly. Case in point: Secretary of the Treasury Connally's behavior that piqued the Japanese to engage in a "tit-for-tat" diplomacy in moving more rapidly than we had expected in establishing diplomatic relations with the People's Republic of China. [Recall discussion in Unit I.]

See also Nicolson's views of the role of "the civil service" in diplomacy. Compare ch. 7 of *Anatomy*.

Unit V
1. **Multilateral diplomacy in international organizations**
2. **Case study in the control of nuclear power: the International Atomic Energy Agency**

Reading:
Henry L. Stimson and McGeorge Bundy, *On Active Service in Peace and War* (New York: Harper, 1947), ch. XXIV, "The Bomb and Peace with Russia"
James J. Wadsworth, "Atoms for Peace," in John G. Stoessinger and Alan F. Westin, eds., *Power and Order*

1. **Multilateral diplomacy in international organizations.** "Diplomacy by conference." Philip C. Jessup calls it "parliamentary diplomacy." International organizations through which this type of diplomacy is practiced: UN systems, regional organizations, and specialized organizations (cf. Wadsworth on formation of the International Atomic Energy Agency). Ad hoc conferences on global issues. Growth in the number and variety of international forums for diplomatic maneuver has added to governments' problems of coordination. Thus, the bureaucratic dimension has been amplified, with tactical planning assuming greater importance.

Organizations and ad hoc conferences provide a different terrain for diplomatic strategies, tactics, techniques and skills. The relative importance of bilateral and multilateral diplomacy is not a particularly profitable subject for extended analysis. Both types are necessary and complement each other. *How* governments maneuver—not *where*—is the basic consideration in any analysis of the dynamics of diplomacy.

2. **Case study in the control of nuclear power: the International Atomic Energy Agency.** As the Stimson-Bundy chapter shows, diplomacy sometimes requires a good deal of patient, persistent probing for ways of raising and presenting problems in the light of the strategies, tactics and qualities of other governments, particularly in the case of "a state dictatorially and repressively governed by a single inscrutable character" [p. 638]. (As we shall see, the U.S. has faced this problem in Vietnam.) It is interesting that it was our military establishment that originally called for an international organization to control the use of atomic energy [640] (which opens up the question of the military's role in the strategies and tactics of diplomacy). To what extent and under what conditions does "trust beget trust" [641]? Was "the final question ... 'one of will and understanding'" or also of diplomatic resources [652]?

Was Eisenhower a key factor in the push for an international atomic energy organization? Relevance of this to the question raised in Unit IV as to the importance of the personal factor in international politics and to the presidential role in the strategies and tactics of diplomacy. Note there was no objective of power (no drive to extend U.S. power) in this move. This was a quest for order, for control.

Wadsworth's case study reveals interesting things about contemporary diplomacy—among them, how complex and careful the preparations must be for many questions affecting national security and international organization; how a multilateral forum can be quickly replaced by intensive bilateral diplomacy, as the U.S. turned to persuading the principal power that held the major key to success (but the UNDC offered a means of continued exposition and pressure); how important to successful diplomacy is "gentle but unremitting pressure" [Wadsworth, 38].

What does the study show about the factor of "surprise" in diplomacy? Recall that Nicolson identified the technique or tactic of surprise as characteristic of the "warrior or heroic" type of diplomacy; is it also employed by what he calls the "mercantile or shopkeeper" type? It characterized the grain negotiation between the U.S. and the Soviet Union. Both by keeping secret how much grain it needed and by commencing purchases before the ink was dry on the agreement, the Soviets scored so great an advantage as to produce a "grain scandal" uproar in the U.S. This impelled the U.S. to move to renegotiate the part of the agreement that dealt with shipping the grain, causing the U.S.S.R. to charge the U.S. with reneging on the agreement.

Compare the rotation of the chairmanship of meetings [40] with Lord Curzon's sharp maneuver at the Lausanne Conference of 1922–23 [Nicolson, 110]. Note tactics of backing off from problems [41] in order to let them "simmer" awhile, of using third states as a "buffer" [43], of combining informal meetings of bilateral and multilateral composition, with "well-publicized debate and argument" [45]. Recall Nicolson's repugnance for "well-publicized" diplomacy. Note importance of procedural problems in multilateral diplomacy; "how difficult communication is" [50]; sensitivity of governments to loss of sovereignty. Note that a negotiated agreement does not terminate diplomacy on a matter; it only introduces a new stage of diplomacy. How relevant, then, does Nicolson's definition of diplomacy seem? Phase Seven ("Will the Senate Agree?"), however, underlines Nicolson's point that our system for the conduct of diplomacy presents serious problems to negotiators [57–61]. What does Phase Eight suggest as to the quality of U.S. diplomacy?

Unit VI
Multilateral Regional Diplomacy: Case Study of Negotiating the Termination of a Protracted War in Latin America

Reading:
Spruille Braden, *Diplomats and Demagogues,* chs. 19–21

Recall chapter 7 of *Anatomy of the State Department* and earlier class discussion of the importance of personal qualities in diplomacy. Braden was a noncareer diplomat, a mining engineer with long experience in Latin America, personal knowledge of Latin American people, leaders, and psychology, married to a Chilean lady with wide family contacts in South America. His experience as chief U.S. representative at the Chaco Peace Conference provides a good case study of the ebb and flow of diplomacy at a multilateral conference through the clash of strategies and tactical maneuver and countermaneuver.

Tactics included those of exciting and allaying suspicion and mistrust, false accusations, intrigue à la Talleyrand, delay, secrecy and publicity, threats and bluff, and appeals to presidents over the heads of their ministers of foreign affairs and war. In addition to tactics, the case brings out the technique of flattery and sarcasm, of ridicule and insult, of using social gatherings to further diplomacy, showing the value of extensive friendships and acquaintances—the personal factor—for the success of multilateral diplomacy. It illustrates some of the problems the diplomat has with his own government, the times when the diplomat must take risks, well aware that his own government may not support him, and hence the strong sense of tactical maneuver the successful diplomat must possess and employ, sometimes daringly.

Unit VII
Case study of bilateral diplomacy in a Communist environment: Czechoslovakia
—Tactics of the Czech government
—Responses of the U.S. embassy
—Government protection of nationals

Reading:
Ellis O. Briggs, *Farewell to Foggy Bottom,* chs. 4 and 5

The case study described by Briggs usefully makes the point that diplomatic relations do not ensure pleasant relations nor are pleasant relations invariably an objective of diplomacy. The results of diplomatic relations depend upon the culture, philosophy, kinds of societies involved, and strategic objectives and values of the governing regimes. The case will be discussed in the context of Communist and U.S. strategies and tactics.

Chapter 4 of Briggs examines the tactics an unfriendly regime can employ against an embassy to make the embassy's life miserable and to humiliate its government. It also describes those tactics by which an embassy can respond so as to persuade the host government to modify its behavior. The case thus illuminates how an embassy is organized, the kinds of officers it has on its staff, its dependence upon local nationals as employees, its manner of functioning as a "country team," the use of couriers, the fraternal spirit in the diplomatic corps in a capital and how this can be capitalized upon in political ways, and even the use of the departure of an expelled diplomat to display his colleagues' solidarity. There are also references to diplomatic immunity and the like which tie the case into earlier class discussions.

The tactics of the Czech government. These included the reduction of the size of the U.S. embassy (from 80 to 13); the arrest of the local employees of the embassy, charging them with espionage; propaganda; spy trials; heavy surveillance of the embassy premises and trailing of embassy officers; interception of visitors to the embassy; establishment of an agency to provide houses, servants, and victuals to foreign diplomats (thereby facilitating the bugging of residences and espionage). The Czech strategy included isolating and intimidating the embassy so as to render it useless; discrediting the U.S. and the West generally; strengthening the Communist regime by elimination of opposition leaders and imprisonment of non-Communist citizenry; and, all the while, scoring propaganda points.

Response of the U.S. embassy. The U.S. responded by delaying the border crossing of Czech officials on trips into Germany; reducing the size of the Czech embassy in Washington and closing all Czech consulates in the U.S., thereby reducing the extraction of huge remittances from Czech-Americans worried about their relatives in Czechoslovakia; publicizing (via the Voice of America) the Czech government's expulsion of embassy staff and the slovenly attire and untidy manners of the secret police who trailed U.S. embassy officers and otherwise ridiculing the Prague regime; ostentatiously photographing the police who surrounded the embassy; flying the U.S. flag on the ambassador's car; using microphones in the government-provided residences to communicate preposterous stories which, when publicized by the Czech government, caused merriment and ridicule abroad; making use of a snow-filled ditch across a Czech road to spoil the Soviet ambassador's plans to meet his foreign minister at the border; and using the Communists' potato bug problem and propaganda to ridicule the regime.

(Note: It was the files of the agricultural attaché on the potato bug that provided the factual and scientific material on which this tactic was based. This oft-overlooked attaché, engaged in studies of "nonpolitical" subjects, provided the material for this political-propaganda maneuver.) In all this, the existence of the Voice of America was a vital medium of communication with the Czech people. To what extent was the embassy's resourcefulness due to Briggs's experience as a career officer?

Government protection of nationals. Chapter 5 of Briggs provides a case study of the protection of nationals, which is one of the functions of diplomatic-consular relations and a friction-filled, even explosive, one when certain types of societies and regimes are involved. It illustrates how the abuse of a foreign national can be undertaken as a tactic designed to humiliate and discredit his country and its values. Techniques used by the Communist regime during the trial of Oatis to make him uncomfortable, create in him a sense of insecurity and helplessness. By resorting to the technique of placing embassy observers in out-of-the-way seats, the Czech regime tried to deprive Oatis of any knowledge of his government's presence. The Czech strategy involved in the trial of a Western journalist.

This case brings out the relationship between journalists and diplomats in their efforts to ferret out the facts of what is going on in another society. The U.S. tactics to obtain Oatis's release included the U.S. president's use of the credentials ceremony to give the Czech ambassador a rough time, as did the secretary of state, so that the ambassador never dared return to the State Department. His usefulness thus terminated, his recall swiftly eventuated, showing how ceremonial (or protocol) occasions can be a useful terrain for diplomatic tactics. Czechoslovakia was declared out-of-bounds for U.S. citizens, the Czech airlines was denied access to the U.S., and various kinds of publicity resorted to.

The usefulness of consular treaties and of a knowledge of inter national law is brought out. What a government can do to protect its citizens abroad is an oft-asked question, to which this case study provides material for discussion and some answers. It demonstrates how the protection function is interlaced with international politics.

Unit VIII
Bilateral diplomacy in a multilateral setting: Vietnam as a case study of nation-building and nation-preserving diplomacy

1. **Vietnam**
   A. **Historical background**
   B. **U.S. politico-military strategies**
   C. **Four main phases of U.S. diplomacy**

2. U.S. diplomacy
   A. Factors affecting effectiveness of U.S. diplomacy
   B. Ambassadors
3. Washington-Saigon relations
   A. Roles of U.S. embassy/Saigon and "Republic of Vietnam" (South
      Vietnamese) embassy in Washington
   B. Role of U.S. and South Vietnamese embassies around the world
   C. Public relations of U.S. government and American public opinion
4. Synthesis—more questions and a few conclusions

Required reading:
Chester Cooper, *The Lost Crusade: America in Vietnam* (New York:
Dodd, Mead, 1970)

Recommended reading:
Richard Critchfield, *The Long Charade* (New York: Harcourt,
Brace, 1968)
David Halberstam, *The Making of a Quagmire* (New York: Random
House, 1965)
——, *The Best and the Brightest* (New York: Random House, 1972)
Edward G. Lansdale, *In the Midst of Wars* (New York: Harper &
Row, 1972)
John Mecklin, *Mission in Torment* (Garden City: Doubleday, 1965)
Robert Shaplen, *The Lost Revolution* (New York: Harper & Row,
1965)

1. Vietnam
   A. Historical background
   The focus is on Vietnam and its different regional, political, and social experiences and divisions, cultures, psychologies, religions, as well
as the shattering effects of French rule.
   B. U.S. politico-military strategies
   Review of concepts and definitions of strategies and tactics, crucial to
any understanding of this exercise in politico-military intervention—
including the role of the military in Washington and in the field. Discussion of how clear these concepts and definitions appear to have
been in the minds of U.S. policy shapers and diplomats. Impact of
rhetoric and slogan-thinking in the evolution of our strategy in Southeast Asia and easing of the U.S. into intervention—"No more Mu-
nichs"; "U.S. strategic interests"; the domino concept propounded by
President Eisenhower; and President Kennedy's inaugural address:
"We shall pay any price, bear any burden, meet any hardship, support
any friend, oppose any foe, to assure the survival and the success of
liberty."

C. **Four main phases of U.S. diplomacy**
   (1) 1945–54, the awakening of U.S. interest
   (2) November 1954–July 1963, deepening U.S. involvement
   (3) 1963–68, massive intervention
   (4) 1968–1975 [1973 in original syllabus—Ed.], culmination of
disenchantment and move toward disengagement.
   Each of these phases had its own diplomatic characteristics and
evolved its own diplomatic personnel, tactics and strategies.

2. **U.S. diplomacy**
   A. **Factors affecting the effectiveness of U.S. diplomacy**
   Recruitment of personnel. Was an effort made to recruit Southeast
Asian experts from outside the diplomatic establishment (as OSS did in
World War II)? Educational background and experience of officers
assigned to South Vietnam; how much in Southeast Asia? Linguistic
competence of officers. Were they equipped, linguistically and other-
wise, to "win the hearts and minds of the people"? Did U.S. have of-
ficers as qualified for work in Saigon as Spruille Braden was at the
Chaco Conference?
   *Personal traits and skills of officers assigned to the "Republic of Vietnam"
below the rank of ambassador.* Age of such officers (bearing in mind that
Asians respect age and maturity). Rotation of officers and the extent to
which this dissipated experience, contacts, friendships and influence.
Did it signal that the U.S. might not be serious and lacked staying
power? Did Saigon leaders exploit the interstices provided by rotation?
Did it adversely affect the influence of Embassy Saigon in Washington? Did it complicate the issue of subordinating the military aspect of
intervention to civilian control? When officers were rotated out of Vietnam were they posted in the State Department or dispersed? To what
extent were they later returned to South Vietnam?
   Training of officers. Not until 1962 did the Foreign Service Institute
(FSI) begin a training process for officers assigned to Southeast Asia
and then it was sparked by someone outside the foreign affairs community (Attorney General Robert F. Kennedy). There is no evidence
that at any point in the early years of Washington's rumination over intervention anyone asked how many experts we had on Southeast Asia
or on Vietnam specifically, and neither the State Department nor the
Foreign Service was adequately staffed in this respect. Was this
symptomatic of a deficient planning sense in the State Department and
the White House? Why was this issue of training not raised by the president's national security adviser, or the secretary of state or his top
associates, or the State Department's Policy Planning Staff, or the
deputy under secretary of state for administration? Who served in these
capacities during the 1950s and 1960s? Were they operators or people of

operational sense who asked "how do we get from here to there" or just "policy formulators"?

Even when the counterinsurgency course materialized at the Foreign Service Institute, it was more of an "exposure" than a training exercise. Nor was the FSI course directed to nation-building, but instead focussed on counterinsurgency. With the U.S. embassy in Saigon involved in a desperate fire brigade operation, overtaken and often suffocated by a constant effort to patch up quarrels and rivalries between the Saigon politicians and generals, how adequate, in such a context, is the concept of "training"? Was not profound education also needed so as to produce diplomatic officers whom the Vietnamese would recognize as thoroughly familiar with their history, culture, and thinking—able to communicate persuasively with them, interest them in governance as well as rice, "talk their language" in all senses, and thus "win hearts and minds?" What training of South Vietnamese civil servants was attempted? Was any "training" of political leaders or potential leaders feasible?

The device of a deputy ambassador. Purpose and actual role.

The device of district and provincial officers. Role; how selected; relations with embassy; impact upon U.S. military in South Vietnam and upon Washington.

B. **Ambassadors**

Factors in selection: Background of those dispatched in each phase; shift from career to political appointees and back to career. Were they rotated to State Department so as to use their experience? Managerial capacity (since CIA, AID, USIA, military staff were involved). Were they comparable to Wadsworth, Braden, Briggs? Embassy presiders or able (through personal qualities) and willing to reach "hearts and minds" of leaders and command their respect and willingness to follow? Were they awaiters of instructions or initiators? In what ways and to what extent did they succeed in reaching the Vietnamese people outside Saigon, learn about the country, and come to grips with its complexity? Were they linguistically equipped?

Relations with Washington. Which ambassadors had access to the secretary of state and the president? Techniques and devices used to get information and advice to the top.

3. **Washington-Saigon relations**

A. **Roles of U.S. embassy in Saigon and "Republic of Vietnam" embassy in Washington**

Background and effectiveness of South Vietnamese ambassador and embassy staff in Washington; how USG and Embassy Saigon communicated with each other; tactics and techniques employed. Discussion of significance of the fact that the U.S. secretary of state did not visit South Vietnam but the secretary of defense did frequently. Did this send a signal to the government of South Vietnam?

  B. **Role of U.S. and "Republic of Vietnam" embassies around the world**
  Extent to which they were used to keep other governments informed and persuaded of the wisdom and developments of intervention.

  C. **Public relations of the U.S. government and American public opinion**
  U.S. public opinion not prepared for nor kept well-informed by U.S. government concerning problems encountered in Vietnam. Emphasis of speeches by top U.S. officials was mostly on our intentions and objectives (e.g., "to make the North Vietnamese stop what they are doing"); American public got a daily dosage of reporting from print and electronic media correspondents stationed in South Vietnam who seemed skeptical and unconvinced that the U.S. should be in South Vietnam, understood the situation, had a well thought-out strategy, or knew what it was doing. First war to be televised, mostly in fragments on the nightly news. Impact of this fragmentary, sometimes emotional coverage, as illustrated by the Tet offensive and by the photo of a Viet Cong being shot by a military officer. There was no Office of War Information to turn out films to inform or inspire public opinion as in World War II, nor a concerted use of State Department and Foreign Service officers to speak before groups around the U.S.

4. Synthesis of the Vietnam experience—more questions and a few conclusions

  • "You say that you are going to shoot men into self-government," said Sir Edward Grey to U.S. Ambassador Walter Hines Page in 1913. "Doesn't that strike you as comical?" Page replied, "It is comical only to the Briton and to others who have associated shooting with subjugation. We associate shooting with freedom." (*Life and Letters of Walter Hines Page*, I, 211). This had to do with Woodrow Wilson's policy vis-a-vis Mexico and Latin America. Does it apply to our effort in Southeast Asia?

  • U.S. decision makers in Washington have been nobly motivated but noble motives and good intentions are not enough for effective diplomacy.

  • As an exercise in nation-building diplomacy, U.S. intervention demanded the most thorough kind of preparation and planning, as the U.S. War Department had engaged in for Cuba and the Philippines after the Spanish-American war, including the use of academic specialists. In the case of Vietnam, not a single top official of the White House or State Department had had any experience either in Southeast Asia or in nation-building. Our nation-building diplomacy in Southeast Asia was approached in catch-as-catch-can fashion, as just another "problem" or "crisis" on the daily plate of the State Department and White House. Hence, we never devised an effective way of rooting our ideas in the Vietnamese masses.

• Does the State Department's failure to create a cadre of specialists in anticipation of intervention suggest that the department needs a diplomacy planning staff to relate personnel and other resources to policies?

• Part of the reason the U.S. public was not prepared for intervention nor kept informed concerning problems: U.S. government officials were themselves not well informed. As Chester Cooper points out, there was a good deal of confusion and misinformation in Washington. Secretary Rusk emphasized that the U.S. "cannot be indifferent to what goes on in the world," but did not note that indifference and intervention are two opposite extremes. There is a middle course. Intervention without advance inventorying and mobilization of diplomatic resources and public opinion is folly.

• The war thus became too much of a president's war. Leveling with Congress was at a minimum. One of the basic issues raised is whether a system of checks and balances offers either an effective congressional check or effective presidential accounting to Congress and the public. The war in Vietnam also raised the issue as to whether our presidential form of government, providing a fixed tenure for the chief executive with no opportunity of a congressional vote of "no confidence," can nurture the kind of close-knit relationship between executive and legislature needed to sustain a prolonged politico-military intervention abroad, or a political leadership flexible enough to adjust to public opinion.

• We came to possess tons of captured enemy documents, interrogated thousands of prisoners, and flew thousands of reconnaissance sorties, but without enough people in our government learned and sophisticated enough about Asians, all of this vast intelligence was not properly evaluated and understood and had no persuasive effect upon the top levels of our government. There is no substitute for education, training, and sophistication at all levels of government if a world power is to act wisely with due regard to its own and others' past experience.

Unit IX

Synthesis of course

What do we infer about diplomacy from our discussion and particularly from the case studies? Is it only negotiation, as Nicolson said, or does it include other things so as to constitute a broad sector of international politics? Are its dynamics indeed strategies and tactics, techniques, personal qualities, and skills? What are the limitations of diplomacy? What is its potentiality as an instrument of international understanding, conflict resolution, negotiation, maneuvering in the interest of peace? What is its potential as a nation-building and human rights instrument?

Is diplomacy based upon the presumption that participants in the international community are governments controlled by rational people? Do diplomats and their governments have to keep in mind that not all participants in diplomacy are rational, truth-seeking, peace-seeking people? What types of people did our case studies show are involved in diplomacy? What maneuvers, pressures, inducements had to be resorted to in order to get certain types to adhere to generally accepted norms of international behavior and enter international agreements? Is the deployment of force and manifest willingness to use it indispensable to successful diplomacy? Is force essentially antithetical to diplomacy?

When diplomacy seems to break down, as in Vietnam, is it diplomacy that breaks down or is it a failure to mobilize all the resources (including education and training) that diplomacy demands? In only one of our cases—Vietnam—do covert and military operations play a part in the total political effort. Were these operations adequately fused with diplomacy? Can the government of a democracy effect such a fusion? As we have seen, the government of a democracy can succeed in a protracted diplomatic effort such as "Atoms for Peace" or the termination of the Chaco War, as in the Marshall Plan and the rebuilding of Germany and Japan after World War II, but what were the special factors accounting for U.S. persistence in these cases?

In close-at-hand, bilateral situations, career officers like Briggs can demonstrate the qualities of diplomatic leadership. How much leadership did they show when it came to Vietnam? Does a diplomatic career tend to breed these qualities? Could a career officer have pulled off Braden's feat in bringing the Chaco War to an end? Norman Armour had been working on it and gotten nowhere. What background and qualities enabled Braden to succeed?

If diplomacy is to work with maximum effectiveness, from what backgrounds should it recruit (1) career officers and (2) noncareer ambassadors? What post-university educational preparation should a diplomatic establishment provide its career officers and noncareer inductees so as to achieve the most effective diplomacy? Does the Vietnam experience suggest that this additional preparation should be provided for all government officials dealing with foreign affairs?

Much is made in some U.S. quarters that we should have a "representative" Foreign Service. Should "representativeness" be the objective? What would have happened if the University of Alabama had pressured Bear Bryant to develop "representative" football teams? Is this a sound analogy? What, from the material we have analyzed, goes into a winning diplomatic team? Do *Anatomy of the State Department* and the case studies suggest that we have the necessary ingredients? Do national governments have a responsibility to the international community to develop the best possible performance rather than a "representative" performance?

Appendix A

The Author and Contributors

SMITH SIMPSON is a retired professor, public servant, and diplomat, long noted as an advocate of measures to improve the practice of diplomacy. He is the author of *Anatomy of the State Department* (1967), *The Crisis in American Diplomacy: Shots across the Bow of the State Department* (1980), *Perspectives on the Study of Diplomacy* (1986), and numerous articles in journals, magazines, and newspapers, and editor of *Instruction in Diplomacy: The Liberal Arts Approach* (1972), and other volumes. He received his B.S. and M.S. from the University of Virginia and LL.B. from Cornell. He is a member of the Virginia Bar, has taught at the University of Pennsylvania and Georgetown University, and has chaired numerous panels on diplomacy at conventions of the International Studies Association and American Political Science Association.

During World War II, he served in the War Shipping Administration (1942–43) and the State Department (1943–45), where he worked on the United Nations charter and assisted in the creation of the labor attaché program in the Foreign Service, becoming one of the pioneer labor attachés. As a Foreign Service officer (1945–62), he served at embassies in Brussels, Athens, and México, and in consular posts in Bombay and Lourenço Marques (now Maputo), Mozambique. He has continued writing, teaching, and lecturing on diplomacy ever since.

MARGERY R. BOICHEL directs the publications program of the Institute for the Study of Diplomacy, which she joined in 1980. Her career as an editor, policy researcher, and administrator has included appointments to the Institute of International Education, the Brookings Institution Governmental Studies Program, the University of Pittsburgh Center for Regional Economic Studies, and the Pittsburgh Commission on Human Relations.

CHARLES T. CROSS is a retired career diplomat who has taught history and international studies at the University of Washington. During his thirty-two-year career in the Foreign Service, which began in 1949, he was an East Asian expert, specializing in Chinese affairs. From 1979 to 1981 he served as the first director of the American Institute in Taiwan, the unofficial body created to conduct U.S. relations with Taiwan. He was U.S. ambassador to Singapore in 1969–72, consul general in Hong Kong, 1974–77, and deputy chief of mission in Nicosia, Cyprus, 1964–67. He also served in Jakarta, Kuala Lumpur, Alexandria, London, Danang, and, in Washington, in the East Asian Bureau, the Policy Planning Staff, and as a senior Foreign Service inspector. He attended the National War College in 1963–64 and taught, in 1972, at the University of Michigan. He served in the U.S. Marine Corps, 1942–46, and earned his B.A. from Carleton College and M.A. from Yale.

PAUL M. KATTENBURG was Charles L. Jacobson Professor of Public Affairs and is now Distinguished Professor Emeritus at the University of South Carolina Institute of International Studies, where he has taught since 1973. He is the author of *The Vietnam Trauma in American Foreign Policy, 1945–75* (1980), as well as numerous articles and studies in international affairs and diplomacy. He served in the U.S. Army Office of Strategic Services in 1943–45, joining the Department of State in 1950 as a research specialist on Southeast Asia. Later he served in the Foreign Service in Saigon, Washington, and Bonn/Frankfurt as a political officer. He also worked on Vietnam and Asian regional affairs, on the Policy Planning Council, and as country director for the Philippines. After serving as deputy chief of mission in Georgetown, Guyana, 1966–69, he was coordinator of political studies at the Foreign Service Institute until his retirement in 1972. Dr. Kattenburg earned his B.S. from the University of North Carolina, M.A. from George Washington University, and Ph.D. from Yale.

ARMIN H. MEYER, adjunct professor of diplomacy at the Georgetown University School of Foreign Service from 1975 to 1986, was a career diplomat for thirty years. He had previously taught at Capital University, Columbus, Ohio (1934–42), South Dakota School of Mines and Technology (1973–74), and American University (1974–75). He served as U.S. ambassador to Lebanon (1961–65), to Iran (1965–69), and to Japan (1969–72), as special assistant to the secretary of state on terrorism and on South Asian affairs (1972–73), and as deputy assistant secretary for Near East/South Asia (1960–61). His earlier posts included political, public affairs, and program direction assignments in Baghdad, Beirut, Kabul, and Washington. He is the author of *Assign-*

ment: Tokyo—An Ambassador's Journal (1974) and a consultant to firms doing business in the Middle East. During 1942–46, he served as a radio engineer in Eritrea and with the office of war information in Cairo and Baghdad. Ambassador Meyer received a B.A. from Capital University, an M.A. from Ohio State University, and five honorary degrees.

DAVID D. NEWSOM is director of the Institute for the Study of Diplomacy and associate dean of the School of Foreign Service at Georgetown University. A career diplomat, he served as U.S. under secretary of state for political affairs from 1978 to 1981, ambassador to the Philippines (1977–78), ambassador to Indonesia (1974–77), assistant secretary of state for African affairs (1969–74), and ambassador to Libya (1965–69). He is president of the American Academy of Diplomacy and a board member of numerous international affairs organizations. Ambassador Newsom is the author of *The Soviet Brigade in Cuba: A Study in Political Diplomacy* (1987), editor of *The Diplomacy of Human Rights* (1986) and *Private Diplomacy with the Soviet Union* (1987), and a frequent contributor to foreign policy journals and the *Christian Science Monitor.* He has a B.A. from the University of California, Berkeley, and an M.S. in journalism from Columbia University.

JAMES S. PACY is associate professor of political science at the University of Vermont, where he teaches diplomacy, international relations, and international organization. Before joining the faculty at Vermont in 1967, Dr. Pacy researched and taught political science at American University and Westminster College. He has published numerous articles in professional journals, in particular on British, Polish, and Hungarian diplomats. Among his multiple professional activities, he chaired an American Political Science Association panel on "Political Scientists Interested in Diplomacy" for several years. He has a B.A. from Lebanon Valley College, Pennsylvania, an M.A. from the University of Missouri, and a Ph.D. from American University.

W. HOWARD WRIGGINS is professor of political science and research associate at the Institute of War and Peace Studies of Columbia University, whose faculty he joined in 1967 as director of the Southern Asian Institute and professor of public law and government. He is the author of *Ceylon: Dilemmas of the New Nation* (1960), *The Ruler's Imperative: Strategies for Political Survival in Africa and Asia* (1969), *Population, Politics, and the Future of Southern Asia* (1973), and numerous other studies and articles; editor of *Pakistan in Transition* (1975); and co-editor of *Pakistan: The Long View* (1976), among others. In 1977–79, he took leave from the university to serve as U.S. ambassador to Sri Lanka and the Maldives. He previously taught and researched at George Washington, Johns Hopkins, Vassar, and Yale, and was a Rhodes Fellow at Oxford. He was chief of the foreign affairs division of the Library of Congress Legislative Reference Service (1958–61) and a member of the Department of State Policy Planning Council (1961–66). Ambassador Wriggins earned his B.A. at Dartmouth and his Ph.D. at Yale.

Appendix B

Other Courses of Related Interest

Following are brief descriptions of other courses, taught in recent years, on the diplomatic process generally or on specific aspects or types of diplomacy. Readers may wish to contact the instructors of these courses directly for further details or for syllabi on those that particularly interest them.

1. THE CONDUCT OF AMERICAN DIPLOMACY, Sidney Sober, School of International Service, American University, Washington, DC:
   Emphasizes the role diplomacy plays in the execution of U.S. foreign policy and the conduct of foreign relations. Examines the goals, instruments, and techniques of diplomacy; the role and life of the diplomat; and "the institutions, machinery, and personpower of the American diplomatic system" in the context of contemporary requirements.

2. THE CONDUCT OF FOREIGN POLICY, Frederick Holborn, School of Advanced International Studies, The Johns Hopkins University, Washington, DC:
   Considers foreign policymaking and implementation from various perspectives, including: the presidential role; the function of the State Department and professional diplomacy; and the roles of the press, the Congress, the military, and the intelligence community. Case studies underpin the course material. Extensive reading list.

3. CONTEMPORARY ISSUES IN INTERNATIONAL LAW, Allan Gerson, School of Advanced International Studies, The Johns Hopkins University, Washington, DC:

Examines in depth U.S. diplomatic "responses to and management of contemporary international crises, with particular emphasis on the interplay between law and foreign policy," especially in the UN context. Topics include: the Lebanon war and the Mideast peace process; South Africa and Namibia; the crisis in Central America; the Falklands dispute; the UN's role in conflict resolution; and U.S. foreign policymaking.

4. CULTURAL DIPLOMACY, Richard T. Arndt, Department of Government and Foreign Affairs, University of Virginia, Charlottesville, VA:

Studies the shaping of foreign perceptions affecting U.S. foreign relations through the cultural impact of generations of overseas Americans of every variety; the modest institutionalization of cultural relations in the State Department in 1938; the new "targeted dynamism" generated by World War II and prolonged by the Cold War; and the transfer of the thrust to an independent agency, USIA, with today's "public diplomacy" reflecting the inherent tensions between culture and power.

5. DIPLOMATIC NEGOTIATION, Leonard Unger, Fletcher School of Law and Diplomacy, Tufts University, Medford, MA:

Diplomatic negotiation is defined and classical diplomacy examined. Negotiating simulation exercises and numerous case histories (e.g., Trieste, Law of the Sea, Camp David, Panama Canal, West Irian, among others) are used to illustrate the diplomatic negotiating process. Extensive reading list.

6. DIPLOMACY, Martin Staniland, Graduate School of Public and International Affairs, University of Pittsburgh, Pittsburgh, PA:

Examines the role of diplomacy in the development and resolution of 20th century international conflicts. Uses case studies to analyze participants' objectives and tactics, the character and viability of negotiation in varying situations, retrospective perceptions of prior conflicts, and the implications of particular cases for negotiation and conflict resolution theories.

7. DIPLOMACY: PROFESSION, FUNCTION, PROCESS, Michael J. Flack [now retired], Graduate School of Public and International Affairs, University of Pittsburgh, Pittsburgh, PA:

Focuses on diplomatic function, roles, policy, and implementation; the people, procedures, and environment; the "potentials for effect and initiative." Through role-playing exercises, stu-

dents "look at alternatives in situations and probe the diplomat's functions, skills, and responsibilities."

8. NEGOTIATIONS, I. William Zartman, School of Advanced International Studies, The Johns Hopkins University, Washington
DC:
Examines the negotiation process in the context of the "paradigm of power"—in international diplomacy and elsewhere—
first, through theoretical approaches and concepts, then by
using these approaches to examine specific cases, such as the
Cuban missile crisis and hostage situations.

9. PROBLEMS IN MULTILATERAL DIPLOMACY, Donald F. McHenry,
School of Foreign Service, Georgetown University, Washington,
DC:
Examines the role in the conduct of a nation's foreign policy of
formal international and regional institutions (e.g., UN,
UNESCO, OAS, OAU, etc.), as well as ad hoc multilateral
bodies (e.g., the Frontline States, the Western Contact Group,
the Contadora Group, the Nonaligned Movement, etc.). Historical and current foreign policy cases are studied, as are the
uses and limitations of multilateral diplomacy.

10. PUBLIC DIPLOMACY: AN INTRODUCTION TO INTERNATIONAL POLITICAL
COMMUNICATION, Hewson A. Ryan, Fletcher School of Law and
Diplomacy, Tufts University, Medford, MA:
Examines useful theories for political communication; public
opinion and public diplomacy; communications in open,
developed societies and in controlled societies; the role of the
media (press, radio, TV and films); "communications and
development in the North/South context"; "the personal equa-
tion in intercultural relations"; and the proliferation of transnational actors.

11. THEORY AND PRACTICE OF INTERNATIONAL NEGOTIATION, Allan E.
Goodman, Masters Program, School of Foreign Service, Georgetown University, Washington, DC:
"A course in applied diplomacy" that focuses on "the development of strategy and the use of tactics in bargaining situations
that arise repeatedly but for which there are no fixed solutions."
Requirements include an original analysis of a selected international negotiation and participation in a simulation of an
interagency working group to develop a U.S. negotiating strat-

egy on a given issue (e.g., arms control, the conflict in Central America) chosen each semester.

12. THE UNITED STATES IN INTERNATIONAL NEGOTIATIONS (Fall 1984 policy conference), Richard H. Ullman, Woodrow Wilson School of Public and International Affairs, Princeton University, Princeton, NJ:

Evaluates the United States as an international negotiator and develops recommendations designed to enhance American negotiators' abilities to achieve desired outcomes. Using case studies and extended policy conference simulations, the course examines characteristics of successful negotiations, how negotiations fit into overall U.S. foreign policy, and the processes involved in negotiation and implementation.

Selected
Bibliography

The following bibliography is culled principally from the outlines and syllabi presented in this monograph. Except as instructors have explored special cases or aspects of diplomacy, the listing emphasizes the overall diplomatic process.

Books

Acheson, Dean. *Meetings at the Summit: A Study in Diplomatic Method.* Durham: University of New Hampshire, 1958.

_____. *Power and Diplomacy.* Cambridge: Harvard University Press, 1958.

_____. *Present at the Creation: My Years in the State Department.* New York: W. W. Norton, 1969.

Albrecht-Carrié, René. *A Diplomatic History of Europe since the Congress of Vienna.* Rev. ed. New York: Harper & Row, 1973.

Allison, Graham T. *Essence of Decision: Explaining the Cuban Missile Crisis.* Boston: Little, Brown, 1971.

Allison, John M. *Ambassador from the Prairie; or Allison Wonderland.* Boston: Houghton Mifflin, 1973.

American Assembly. *Cultural Affairs and Foreign Relations.* Rev. ed. Washington: Columbia Books, 1968.

Aron, Raymond. *Peace and War: A Theory of International Relations.* Translated by Richard Howard and Annette Baker Fox. Garden City, NY: Doubleday; London: Weidenfield and Nicolson, 1966. Rev. ed., Malabar, FL: R. E. Krieger, 1981.

Asencio, Diego, and Nancy Asencio, with Ron Tobias. *Our Man Is Inside.* Boston: Little, Brown, 1983.

Attwood, William. *The Reds and the Blacks.* New York: Harper & Row, 1967.

Axelrod, Robert M. *The Evolution of Cooperation*. New York: Basic Books, 1984.

_____, ed. *The Structure of Decision: The Cognitive Maps of Political Elites*. Princeton: Princeton University Press for the Institute of International Studies, University of California (Berkeley) and the Institute of Public Policy Studies, University of Michigan, 1976.

Bacchus, William I. *Staffing for Foreign Affairs: Personnel Systems for the 1980s and 1990s*. Princeton: Princeton University Press, 1983.

Bailey, Thomas A. *The Art of Diplomacy: The American Experience*. New York: Appleton-Century-Crofts, 1968.

_____. *A Diplomatic History of the American People*. 10th ed. Englewood Cliffs, NJ: Prentice Hall, 1980.

Ball, George W. *The Past Has Another Pattern: Memoirs*. New York: Norton, 1982.

Barnet, Richard J. *The Lean Years: Politics in the Age of Scarcity*. New York: Simon & Schuster, 1980. Paper ed., 1982.

Barnet, Richard J., and Ronald E. Muller. *Global Reach: The Power of the Multinational Corporations*. New York: Simon & Schuster, 1974. Paper ed., 1975.

Bauer, P. T. *Equality, the Third World, and Economic Delusion*. Cambridge: Harvard University Press, 1981.

Baumann, Carol Edler. *The Diplomatic Kidnappings*. The Hague: Martinus Nijhoff, 1973.

Bazna, Elyesa. *I Was Cicero*. New York: Harper & Row, 1962.

Beam, Jacob. *Multiple Exposure: An American Ambassador's Unique Perspective on East-West Issues*. New York: W. W. Norton, 1978.

Beaulac, Willard Leon. *Career Ambassador*. New York: Macmillan, 1951.

_____. *Career Diplomat: A Career in the Foreign Service of the United States*. New York: Macmillan, 1964.

Bendahmane, Diane B., and John W. McDonald, Jr., eds. *International Negotiation, Art and Science: Report of a Conference on International Negotiation, June 9-10, 1983*. Washington, DC: Center for the Study of Foreign Affairs, Foreign Service Institute, U.S. Department of State, 1984.

_____. *Perspectives on Negotiation. Four Case Studies and Interpretations: The Panama Canal Treaties; the Falkland-Malvinas Islands; the Cyprus Dispute; Negotiating Zimbabwe's Independence*. Washington, DC: Center for the Study of Foreign Affairs, Foreign Service Institute, U.S. Department of State, 1986.

Blaker, Michael. *Japanese International Negotiating Style*. New York: Columbia University Press, 1977.

Blancké, W. Wendell. *The Foreign Service of the United States*. New York: Praeger, 1969.

Bohlen, Charles E. *Witness to History: 1929–1969.* New York: W. W. Norton, 1973.

Bowers, Claude Gernade. *Chile through Embassy Windows: 1939–1953.* New York: Simon & Schuster, 1958. Reprint. Westport, CT: Greenwood Press, 1977.

Bowles, Chester. *Ambassador's Report.* New York: Harper & Row, 1954.

_____. *Promises to Keep.* New York: Harper & Row, 1971.

Boyce, Richard Fyfe. *The Diplomat's Wife.* New York: Harper, 1956.

Bracey, Audrey. *Resolution of the Dominican Crisis, 1965: A Study in Mediation.* Washington, DC: Institute for the Study of Diplomacy, Georgetown University, 1980.

Braden, Spruille. *Diplomats and Demagogues: The Memoirs of Spruille Braden.* New Rochelle, NY: Arlington House, 1971.

Braestrup, Peter, ed. *Vietnam as History: Ten Years after the Paris Peace Accords.* A Wilson Center Conference Report. Washington, DC: University Press of America, 1984.

Briggs, Ellis O. *Anatomy of Diplomacy: The Origin and Execution of American Foreign Policy.* New York: D. McKay Company, 1968.

_____. *Farewell to Foggy Bottom: The Recollections of a Career Diplomat.* New York: D. McKay Company, 1964.

Brodie, Bernard. *War and Politics.* New York: Macmillan, 1973. Paper ed., 1974.

Brown, Harold. *Thinking about National Security: Defense and Foreign Policy in a Dangerous World.* Boulder, CO: Westview Press, 1983.

Brown, Lester R., with Erik P. Eckholm. *By Bread Alone.* New York: Praeger for the Overseas Development Council, 1974.

Brzezinski, Zbigniew K. *Power and Principle: Memoirs of the National Security Adviser, 1977–81.* Rev. ed. New York: Farrar, Straus, Giroux, 1985.

Buchanan, Wiley T. *Red Carpet at the White House: Four Years as Chief of Protocol in the Eisenhower Administration.* New York: Dutton, 1964.

Bueno de Mesquita, Bruce. *The War Trap.* New Haven: Yale University Press, 1981.

Bull, Hedley. *The Anarchical Society: A Study of Order in World Politics.* New York: Columbia University Press, 1977.

Bullen, Roger, ed. *The Foreign Office, 1782–1982.* Frederick, MD: University Publications of America, 1984.

Burns, James MacGregor. *Leadership.* New York: Harper & Row, 1978. Paper ed., 1979.

Busk, Sir Douglas L. *The Craft of Diplomacy.* New York: Praeger, 1967.

Byrnes, James F. *Speaking Frankly.* New York: Harper, 1947.

Cabot, John Moors. *First Line of Defense: Forty Years' Experiences of a Career Diplomat.* Washington, DC: School of Foreign Service, Georgetown University, 1979.

Calkin, Homer L. *Women in the Department of State: Their Role in American Foreign Affairs.* Department of State Publication 8951. Washington, DC: Government Printing Office, 1978.

Callières, François de. *On the Manner of Negotiating with Princes.* Paris: M. Brunet, 1716. Translated by A. F. Whyte. South Bend, IN: University of Notre Dame Press, 1963. Reissued, Washington, DC: University Press of America, 1983.

Calvocoressi, Peter. *World Politics since 1945.* 4th ed. London, New York: Longman, 1982.

Campbell, Colin. *Governments under Stress: Political Executives and Key Bureaucrats in Washington, London, and Ottawa.* Toronto, Buffalo: University of Toronto Press, 1983.

Campbell, John C., ed. *Successful Negotiation, Trieste 1954: An Appraisal by the Five Participants.* Princeton: Princeton University Press, 1976.

Caradon, Lord (Hugh Foot), Arthur J. Goldberg, Mohammed H. El-Zayyat, and Abba Eban. *U.N. Security Council Resolution 242: A Case Study in Diplomatic Ambiguity.* Washington, DC: Institute for the Study of Diplomacy, Georgetown University, 1981.

Carroll, John M., and George C. Herring, Jr., eds. *Modern American Diplomacy.* Wilmington, DE: Scholarly Resources, 1986.

Carter, Jimmy. *Keeping Faith: Memoirs of a President.* New York: Bantam Books, 1982. Paper ed., 1983.

Cerruti, Elisabeth (Paulay). *Ambassador's Wife.* London: Allen and Unwin, 1952. New York: MacMillan, 1953.

Chagla, Mahomedali Currim. *An Ambassador Speaks.* New York: Asia Publishing House, 1962.

Cherry, Colin. *World Communication: Threat or Promise? A Socio-Technical Approach.* London: Wiley-Interscience, 1971. Rev. ed., Chichester (U.K.), New York: Wiley, 1978.

Christopher, Warren, et al. *American Hostages in Iran: The Conduct of a Crisis.* New Haven, CT: Yale University Press, 1985. Paper ed., 1986.

Churchill, Winston S. *The Second World War.* 6 vols. London: Cassell; Boston: Houghton Mifflin, 1948–53.

Clark, Eric. *Diplomat: The World of International Diplomacy.* New York: Taplinger, 1974. Originally published as *Corps Diplomatique* (London: Allen Lane, 1973).

Cohen, Herb. *You Can Negotiate Anything.* Secaucus: Lyle Stuart, 1980. Paper ed., New York: Bantam Books, 1982, and Secaucus: Citadel Press, 1983.

Coombs, Philip H. *The Fourth Dimension of Foreign Policy.* New York: Harper and Row, 1964.

Cooper, Chester L. *The Lost Crusade: America in Vietnam.* New York: Dodd, Mead, 1970.

Corbett, Percy E. *Law in Diplomacy.* Princeton: Princeton University Press, 1959.

Crabb, Cecil V., Jr., and Pat M. Holt. *Invitation to Struggle: Congress, The President and Foreign Policy.* 2nd ed. Washington, DC: Congressional Quarterly Press, 1984.

Craig, Gordon A. *War, Politics, and Diplomacy.* New York: Praeger, 1966.

Craig, Gordon A., and Alexander L. George. *Force and Statecraft: Diplomatic Problems of Our Time.* New York: Oxford University Press, 1983.

Craig, Gordon A., and Felix Gilbert, eds. *The Diplomats: 1919 to 1939.* Princeton: Princeton University Press, 1953. Reprint (2 vols.). New York: Atheneum, 1963.

Crocker, Walter R. *Australian Ambassador.* Melbourne: Melbourne University Press, 1971.

Cross, John G. *The Economics of Bargaining.* New York: Basic Books, 1969.

_____. *A Theory of Adaptive Economic Behavior.* Cambridge: Cambridge University Press, 1983.

Darlington, Charles F., and Alice B. Darlington. *African Betrayal.* New York: D. McKay Co., 1968.

Davidow, Jeffrey. *A Peace in Southern Africa: The Lancaster House Conference on Rhodesia, 1979.* Boulder, CO and London: Westview, 1984.

Davis, Nathaniel. *The Last Two Years of Salvador Allende.* Ithaca, NY: Cornell University Press, 1985.

Dayan, Moshe. *Breakthrough: A Personal Account of the Egypt-Israeli Peace Negotiations.* 1st American ed. New York: Knopf, 1981.

de Gaulle, Charles. *The Complete War Memoirs.* Translated by Jonathan Green and Richard Howard. 3 vols. New York: Simon & Schuster, 1955-60.

Deibel, Terry L., and W. R. Roberts. *Culture and Information: Two Foreign Policy Functions.* CSIS Washington Paper No. 40. Beverly Hills: Sage, 1976.

Denet, R., and Joseph E. Johnson, eds. *Negotiating with the Russians.* New York: World Peace Foundation, 1951.

De Santis, Hugh. *Diplomacy of Silence: The American Foreign Service, The Soviet Union, and the Cold War, 1933-1947.* Chicago: University of Chicago Press, 1980. Paper ed., 1983.

Destler, I. M. *Presidents, Bureaucrats, and Foreign Policy: The Politics of Organizational Reform.* Princeton: Princeton University Press, 1972. Paper ed., 1974.

Destler, I. M., et al. *Managing an Alliance: The Politics of U.S.-Japanese Relations.* Washington, DC: Brookings Institution, 1976.

Destler, I. M., Leslie H. Gelb, and Anthony Lake. *Our Own Worst Enemy: The Unmaking of American Foreign Policy.* New York: Simon and Schuster, 1984.

de Tocqueville, Alexis. *Democracy in America.* New York: Modern Library, 1981.

Diehl, Charles. *Byzantium: Greatness and Decline.* New Brunswick: Rutgers University Press, 1957.

Dirksen, Herbert von. *Moscow, Tokyo, London: Twenty Years of German Foreign Policy.* Norman, OK: University of Oklahoma Press, 1952.

Dodd, Lawrence C., and Bruce I. Oppenheimer, eds. *Congress Reconsidered.* 3rd ed. Washington, DC: Congressional Quarterly Press, 1985.

Dougherty, Patricia. *American Diplomats and the Franco-Prussian War: Perceptions from Paris and Berlin.* Washington, DC: Institute for the Study of Diplomacy, Georgetown University, 1980.

Druckman, Daniel. *Human Factors in International Negotiations: Social-Psychological Aspects of International Conflict.* Beverly Hills: Sage Publications, 1973.

Eban, Abba. *An Autobiography.* New York: Random House, 1977.

_____. *The New Diplomacy: International Affairs in the Modern Age.* New York: Random House, 1983.

Eden, Anthony, Sir. *The Memoirs of Anthony Eden, Earl of Avon.* 3 vols. London: Cassell; Boston: Houghton Mifflin, 1960–65.

_____. *The Suez Crisis of 1956.* Boston: Beacon Press, 1968.

Esterline, John H., and Robert B. Black. *Inside Foreign Policy: The Department of State Political System and Its Subsystems.* Palo Alto, CA: Mayfield Publishing Co., 1975.

Estes, Thomas S., and E. Allan Lightner, Jr. *The Department of State.* New York: Praeger, 1976.

Ewart-Biggs, Jane. *Pay, Pack and Follow.* London: Weidenfeld & Nicolson, 1984. Chicago: Academy Chicago, 1986.

Fahmy, Ismail. *Negotiating for Peace in the Middle East.* Baltimore: Johns Hopkins University Press, 1983.

Fallows, James M. *National Defense.* New York: Random House, 1981. Vintage Books, 1982.

Fasulo, Linda M. *Representing America: Experiences of U.S. Diplomats at the U.N.* New York: Praeger, 1984.

Feltham, R. G. *Diplomatic Handbook.* 4th ed. London, New York: Longman, 1982.

Fisher, Glen. *American Communication in a Global Society.* 2nd ed. Norwood, NJ: Ablex, 1986.

_____. *International Negotiation: A Cross-Cultural Perspective.* Yarmouth, ME: Intercultural Press, 1982.

_____. *Public Diplomacy and the Behavioral Sciences.* Bloomington: Indiana University Press, 1972.

Fisher, Roger. *International Conflict for Beginners.* New York: Harper & Row, 1969. Paper ed., 1970. Also published as *Basic Negotiating Strategy: International Conflict for Beginners.* London: Allen Lane, 1971.

Fisher, Roger, and William Ury. *Getting to Yes: Negotiating Agreement Without Giving In.* Boston: Houghton Mifflin, 1981. New York: Penguin Books, 1983.

Fox, Annette Baker. *The Power of Small States: Diplomacy in World War II.* Chicago: University of Chicago Press, 1959.

Franck, Thomas M., and Edward Weisband. *World Politics: Verbal Strategy among the Super Powers.* New York: Oxford University Press, 1979.

François-Poncet, André. *The Fateful Years: Memoirs of a French Ambassador in Berlin, 1931–1938.* Reprint of 1949 ed. New York: Howard Fertig, 1973.

Frankel, Charles. *High on Foggy Bottom: An Outsider's Inside View of the Government.* New York: Harper & Row, 1969.

Fukui, Haruhiro, and Hideo Sato. *The Textile Wrangle: The Conflict in Japanese-American Relations, 1969–1971.* Ithaca: Cornell University Press, 1979.

Galbraith, John Kenneth. *Ambassador's Journal: A Personal Account of the Kennedy Years.* Boston: Houghton Mifflin, 1969.

Garthoff, Raymond L. *Détente and Confrontation: American-Soviet Relations from Nixon to Reagan.* Washington, DC: Brookings, 1985.

Gelb, Leslie, with Richard K. Betts. *The Irony of Vietnam: The System Worked.* Washington, DC: Brookings Institution, 1979.

George, Alexander L., and Richard Smoke. *Deterrence in American Foreign Policy: Theory and Practice.* New York: Columbia University Press, 1974.

George, Alexander L., et al. *The Limits of Coercive Diplomacy: Laos, Cuba, Vietnam.* Boston: Little, Brown, 1971.

Graham, Daniel O. *Shall America Be Defended?* New Rochelle, NY: Arlington House, 1979.

Greene, Graham. *The Quiet American.* New York: Viking, 1956. Viking-Penguin, 1982.

Grew, Joseph C. *Turbulent Era: A Diplomatic Record of Forty Years, 1904–1945.* 2 vols. Walter Johnson, ed. Boston: Houghton Mifflin, 1952. London: Hammond, 1953.

Griffis, Stanton. *Lying in State.* Garden City, NY: Doubleday, 1952.

Griscom, Lloyd C. *Diplomatically Speaking.* Boston: Little, Brown, 1940.

Gulliver, Philip H. *Disputes and Negotiations: A Cross Cultural Perspective.* New York: Academic Press, 1979.

Gyorgy, Andrew, and Hubert S. Gibbs, eds. *Problems in International Relations.* New York: Prentice-Hall, 1955.

Hackett, Sir John. *The Third World War.* London: Sidgwick and Jackson, 1978–1982. New York: Macmillan, 1980–1982.

Hall, Edward T. *The Silent Language.* Greenwich, CT: Fawcett, 1959. Reprint of 1979 ed., Westport, CT: Greenwood, 1980.

Halperin, Morton H., et al. *Bureaucratic Politics and Foreign Policy.* Washington, DC: Brookings Institution, 1974.

Hamilton, Alexander, James Madison, and John Jay. *The Federalist Papers: A Collection of Papers Written in Support of the Constitution.* Baltimore: Johns Hopkins University Press, 1981.

Harmon, Robert B. *The Art and Practice of Diplomacy: A Selected and Annotated Guide.* Metuchen, NJ: Scarecrow Press, 1971.

Harr, John Ensor. *The Professional Diplomat.* Princeton: Princeton University Press, 1969.

Harriman, Averell, and Elie Abel. *Special Envoy to Churchill and Stalin, 1941–1946.* New York: Random House, 1975.

Hayter, Sir William. *The Diplomacy of the Great Powers.* New York: Macmillan, 1961.

_____. *The Kremlin and the Embassy.* New York: Macmillan, 1966.

Heinrichs, Waldo H., Jr. *American Ambassador: Joseph C. Grew and the Development of the United States Diplomatic Tradition.* Boston: Little, Brown, 1966.

Helms, Cynthia. *An Ambassador's Wife in Iran.* New York: Dodd, Mead, 1981.

Henderson, Sir Neville. *Water under the Bridges.* London: Hodder & Stoughton, Ltd., 1945.

Henkin, Louis. *Foreign Affairs and the Constitution.* New York: Norton, 1975.

Henrikson, Alan K., ed. *Negotiating World Order: The Artisanship and Architecture of Global Diplomacy.* Wilmington, DE: Scholarly Resources, 1986.

Hermann, Charles F., ed. *International Crises: Insights from Behavioral Research.* New York: Free Press, 1972.

Herz, Martin F. *Beginnings of the Cold War.* Bloomington & London: Indiana University Press, 1966. Paper ed., New York: McGraw-Hill, 1968.

_____. *David Bruce's "Long Telegram" of July 3, 1951.* Washington, DC: Institute for the Study of Diplomacy, Georgetown University, 1978. Reprint. Lanham, MD: University Press of America, 1986.

_____. *Making the World a Less Dangerous Place: Lessons Learned from a Career in Diplomacy.* Washington, DC: Institute for the Study of Diplomacy, Georgetown University, 1981.

_____. *215 Days in the Life of an American Ambassador (Diary Notes from Sofia, Bulgaria).* Washington, DC: School of Foreign Service, Georgetown University, 1981.

_____. *A View from Tehran: A Diplomatist Looks at the Shah's*

Regime in 1964. Washington, DC: Institute for the Study of Diplomacy, Georgetown University, 1979.

_____, ed. *The Consular Dimension of Diplomacy.* Washington, DC: Institute for the Study of Diplomacy, Georgetown University, 1983. Reprint. Lanham, MD: University Press of America, 1986.

_____, ed. *Contacts with the Opposition—A Symposium.* Washington, DC: Institute for the Study of Diplomacy, Georgetown University, 1979. Reprint. Lanham, MD: University Press of America, 1986.

_____, ed. *Diplomacy: The Role of the Wife.* Washington, DC: Institute for the Study of Diplomacy, Georgetown University, 1981.

_____, ed. *Diplomats and Terrorists: What Works, What Doesn't.* Washington, DC: Institute for the Study of Diplomacy, Georgetown University, 1982.

_____, ed. *The Modern Ambassador: The Challenge and the Search.* Washington, DC: Institute for the Study of Diplomacy, Georgetown University, 1983.

_____, ed. *The Role of Embassies in Promoting Business: A Symposium.* Washington, DC: Institute for the Study of Diplomacy, Georgetown University, 1981.

Hilsman, Roger. *To Move a Nation: The Politics of Foreign Policy in the Administration of John F. Kennedy.* Garden City, NY: Doubleday, 1967.

Hoare, Sir Samuel J. G. *Complacent Dictator.* New York: Knopf, 1947. Originally published as *Ambassador on Special Mission* (London: William Collins, 1946).

Hoffmann, Arthur S., ed. *International Communication and the New Diplomacy.* Bloomington: Indiana University Press, 1968.

Hoffmann, Stanley. *Gulliver's Troubles, or, The Setting of American Foreign Policy.* New York: McGraw Hill for the Council on Foreign Relations, 1968.

Holsti, K. J. *International Politics: A Framework for Analysis.* 3rd ed. Englewood Cliffs, NJ: Prentice-Hall, 1977.

Howard, Michael E. *Studies in War and Peace.* New York: Viking Press, 1971.

Hunter, Robert E. *Presidential Control of Foreign Policy: Management or Mishap?* Washington Papers, #91. New York: Praeger for the Center for Strategic and International Studies, 1982.

Huntington-Wilson, F. M. *Memoirs of an Ex-Diplomat.* Boston: Humphries, 1945.

Iklé, Fred C. *How Nations Negotiate.* New York: Harper & Row, 1964. Republished by the Institute for the Study of Diplomacy, Georgetown University, 1979.

_____. *International Negotiation: American Shortcomings in Negotiating with Communist Powers.* Washington, DC: U. S. Government Printing Office, 1970.

Independent Commission on International Development Issues (Brandt Commission). *North-South: A Programme for Survival. Report of the Independent Commission on International Development Issues.* Cambridge: MIT Press, 1980.

Isaacson, Walter, and Evan Thomas. *The Wise Men. Six Friends and the World They Made: Acheson, Bohlen, Harriman, Kennan, Lovett, McCloy.* New York: Simon & Schuster, 1986.

Jackson, Elmore. *The Meeting of Minds: A Way of Peace through Mediation.* New York: McGraw-Hill, 1952.

Jackson, Henry M. ed. *The Secretary of State and the Ambassador.* New York: Praeger, 1964.

James, Alan. *The Politics of Peacekeeping.* London: Praeger, 1969.

Jervis, Robert. *Perception and Misperception in International Politics.* Harvard Center for International Affairs Series. Princeton: Princeton University Press, 1976.

Johnson, E. A. J., ed. *Dimensions of Diplomacy.* Baltimore: Johns Hopkins University Press, 1964.

Johnson, Lyndon B. *The Vantage Point: Perspectives of the Presidency, 1963–1969.* New York: Holt, Rinehart & Winston, 1971.

Johnson, U. Alexis, with Jef Olivarius McAllister. *The Right Hand of Power.* Englewood Cliffs, NJ: Prentice-Hall, 1984.

Jonsson, Christer. *Soviet Bargaining Behavior: The Nuclear Test Ban Case.* New York: Columbia University Press, 1979.

Jordan, Hamilton. *Crisis: The Last Year of the Carter Presidency.* New York: Putnam, 1982.

Jorden, William J. *Panama Odyssey.* Austin: University of Texas Press, 1984.

Joy, Charles Turner. *How Communists Negotiate.* New York: Macmillan, 1955.

Jusserand, Jean Jules. *What Me Befell: The Reminiscences of J. J. Jusserand.* Boston: Houghton Mifflin, 1933. Reprint ed., Salem, NH: Ayer Co., 1972.

Kahn, E. J., Jr. *The China Hands: America's Foreign Service Officers and What Befell Them.* New York: Viking, 1975.

Kalb, Bernard, and Marvin Kalb. *Kissinger.* Boston: Little, Brown, 1974.

Kalb, Madeleine G. *The Congo Cables: The Cold War in Africa— from Eisenhower to Kennedy.* New York: Macmillan, 1982.

Karass, Chester L. *Give & Take: The Complete Guide to Negotiating Strategies and Tactics.* New York: Crowell, 1974.

Kaufman, John. *Conference Diplomacy.* Dobbs Ferry: Oceana Publications, 1980.

Kaznacheev, Aleksandr Iurevich. *Inside a Soviet Embassy: Experiences of a Russian Diplomat in Burma.* Edited by Simon Wolin. London: Hale, 1963.

Kegley, Charles W., Jr., and Eugene R. Wittkopf. *American Foreign Policy: Pattern and Process.* 2nd ed. New York: St. Martin's, 1982.

Kelman, Herbert C., ed. *International Behavior: A Social-Psychological Analysis.* New York: Holt, Rinehart & Winston, 1965.

Kennan, George F. *American Diplomacy 1900-1950.* Chicago: University of Chicago Press, 1969.

_____. *Memoirs: 1925-50* and *1950-63.* 2 vols. Boston: Little, Brown, 1967-72. Paper ed., New York: Pantheon Books, 1983.

Kennedy, Robert F. *Thirteen Days: A Memoir of the Cuban Missile Crisis.* New York: W. W. Norton, 1969. College ed., with Afterword by Richard E. Neustadt and Graham T. Allison, 1971. Paper ed., 1973.

Kertesz, Stephen D. *The Quest for Peace through Diplomacy.* Englewood Cliffs, NJ: Prentice-Hall, 1967.

Kertesz, Stephen D., and M. A. Fitzsimons, eds. *Diplomacy in a Changing World.* South Bend: University of Notre Dame Press, 1959. Westport, CT: Greenwood Press, 1974.

Khrushchev, Nikita. *Khrushchev Remembers.* Introduction, Commentary, and Notes by Edward Crankshaw. Translated and edited by Strobe Talbott. Boston: Little, Brown, 1970.

_____. *Khrushchev Remembers: The Last Testament.* Translated and edited by Strobe Talbott. Boston: Little, Brown, 1974.

Kincade, William H., and Jeffrey D. Porro, eds. *Negotiating Security: An Arms Control Reader.* Washington: Carnegie Endowment for International Peace, 1979.

Kirk, Lydia. *Postmarked Moscow.* New York: Scribner, 1952.

Kirkpatrick, Jeane J. *Dictatorships and Double Standards: Rationalism and Reason in Politics.* New York: American Enterprise Institute/ Simon & Schuster, 1982.

Kissinger, Henry A. *White House Years.* Boston: Little, Brown, 1979.

_____. *Years of Upheaval.* Boston: Little, Brown, 1982.

Kitzinger, Uwe W. *Diplomacy and Persuasion: How Britain Joined the Common Market.* London: Thames and Hudson, 1973.

Klineberg, Otto. *The Human Dimension in International Relations.* New York: Holt, Rinehart & Winston, 1964.

Knatchbull-Hugessen, Sir Hughe Montgomery. *Diplomat in Peace and War.* London: J. Murray, 1949.

Knorr, Klaus. *Power and Wealth.* New York: Basic Books, 1973.

Krasner, Steven D. *Defending the National Interest: Raw Material Investments and U.S. Foreign Policy.* Princeton: Princeton University Press, 1978.

Kruglak, Theodore E. *The Foreign Correspondents.* Westport, CT: Greenwood Press, 1974.

Lall, Arthur S. *How Communist China Negotiates.* New York: Columbia University Press, 1968.

_____. *Modern International Negotiation: Principles and Practice.* New York: Columbia University Press, 1966.

Lansdale, Edward G. *In the Midst of Wars: An American's Mission to Southeast Asia.* New York: Harper & Row, 1972.

Lasswell, Harold. *Power and Personality.* New York: Viking, 1948. Reprint ed., Westport, CT: Greenwood, 1976.

Lauren, Paul G. *Diplomacy: New Approaches in History, Theory and Policy.* New York: Free Press, 1979.

Lebow, Richard Ned. *Between Peace and War: The Nature of International Crisis.* Baltimore: Johns Hopkins University Press, 1981. Paper ed., 1984.

Lederer, William J., and Eugene Burdick. *The Ugly American.* New York: Norton, 1958. Reprint. New York: Columbia University Press, 1979.

Lockhart, Charles. *Bargaining in International Conflicts.* New York: Columbia University Press, 1979.

Lombard, Helen Cassin. *Washington Waltz: Diplomatic People and Policies.* New York: Knopf, 1941. London: R. Hale, Ltd., 1942.

Machiavelli, Nicolo. *The Prince.* Reprint ed. New York: Penguin Books, 1961.

Macomber, William B. *The Angels' Game: A Handbook of Modern Diplomacy.* New York: Stein & Day, 1975.

Mahoney, Richard D. *JFK: Ordeal in Africa.* New York: Oxford University Press, 1983.

Margiotta, Franklin D., ed. *Evolving Strategic Realities: Implications for U.S. Policymakers.* Washington, DC: National Defense University Press, 1980.

Martin, Edwin M. *Conference Diplomacy—A Case Study: The World Food Conference, Rome, 1974.* Washington, DC: Institute for the Study of Diplomacy, Georgetown University, 1979.

Martin, Edwin W. *Divided Counsel: The Anglo-American Response to Communist Victory in China.* Lexington, KY: University Press of Kentucky, 1986.

Martin, John Bartlow. *Overtaken by Events: The Dominican Crisis from the Fall of Trujillo to the Civil War.* New York: Doubleday, 1966.

Marye, George Thomas. *Nearing the End in Imperial Russia.* Reprint of 1929 Ayer Co. ed. Russia Observed series, no. 1. New York: Arno Press, 1970.

Mattingly, Garrett. *Renaissance Diplomacy.* Boston: Houghton Mifflin; London: Cape, 1955. New York: Russell & Russell, 1970.

May, Gary. *China Scapegoat: The Diplomatic Ordeal of John Carter Vincent.* Washington, DC: New Republic Books, 1979. Prospect Heights, IL: Waveland, 1982.

Mayer, Martin. *The Diplomats.* New York: Doubleday, 1983.

McCamy, James L. *Conduct of the New Diplomacy.* New York: Harper & Row, 1964.

McCullough, David G. *The Path between the Seas: The Creation of the Panama Canal, 1870–1914.* New York: Simon & Schuster, 1977.

McDonald, John W., Jr. *How to Be a Delegate.* Washington, DC: Center for the Study of Foreign Affairs, Foreign Service Institute, Department of State, 1984.

_____. *The North-South Dialogue and the United Nations.* Washington, DC: Institute for the Study of Diplomacy, Georgetown University, 1982.

McGhee, George. *Envoy to the Middle World: Adventures in Diplomacy.* New York: Harper & Row, 1983.

McMullen, Christopher J. *Mediation of the West New Guinea Dispute, 1962: A Case Study.* Washington, DC: Institute for the Study of Diplomacy, Georgetown University, 1981.

_____. *Resolution of the Yemen Crisis, 1963: A Case Study in Mediation.* Washington, DC: Institute for the Study of Diplomacy, Georgetown University, 1980.

Meyer, Armin H. *Assignment: Tokyo; An Ambassador's Journal.* Indianapolis: Bobbs-Merrill, 1974.

Miller, Hope Ridings. *Embassy Row: The Life and Times of Diplomatic Washington.* New York: Holt, Rinehart and Winston, 1969.

Millis, Walter, and Eugene S. Duffield, eds. *The Forrestal Diaries.* New York: Viking Press, 1951.

Mitchell, J. M. *International Cultural Relations.* London: Allen and Unwin, 1986.

Morgenthau, Hans J. *Politics among Nations.* 6th ed. New York: Alfred A. Knopf, 1985.

Morrow, John H. *First American Ambassador to Guinea.* New Brunswick, NJ: Rutgers University Press, 1967.

Mosher, Frederick C., and John E. Harr. *Programming Systems and Foreign Affairs Leadership: An Attempted Innovation.* New York: Oxford University Press, 1970.

Moynihan, Daniel Patrick. *A Dangerous Place.* Boston: Little, Brown, 1978.

Moyzisch, L. C. *Operation Cicero.* Translated from German by Constantine Fitz-Gibbon and Heinrich Frankel. London & New York: Allan Wingate-Baker, 1969.

Murphy, Robert D. *Diplomat among Warriors.* Garden City, NY: Doubleday, 1964. Reprint. Westport, CT: Greenwood, 1976.

Nathan, James A., and James K. Oliver. *Foreign Policy-making and the American Political System.* 2nd ed. Boston: Little, Brown, 1987.

Neustadt, Richard E. *Presidential Power: The Politics of Leadership.* New York, London: John Wiley, 1960; rev. paper ed., 1980.

_____. *Alliance Politics*. New York: Columbia University Press, 1970.

Neustadt, Richard E., and Ernest R. May. *Thinking in Time: The Uses of History for Decision Makers*. New York: Free Press, 1986.

Newhouse, John. *Cold Dawn: The Story of SALT*. New York: Holt, Rinehart and Winston, 1973.

Newsom, David D. *The Soviet Brigade in Cuba: A Study in Political Diplomacy*. Bloomington: Indiana University Press, 1987.

_____, ed. *The Diplomacy of Human Rights*. Washington, DC: Institute for the Study of Diplomacy, Georgetown University, and University Press of America, 1986; paper, 1986.

Nicolson, Sir Harold G. *Diplomacy*. 3rd rev. ed. New York: Oxford University Press, 1963.

_____. *Dwight Morrow*. London: Constable, and New York: Harcourt Brace, 1935.

_____. *The Evolution of Diplomatic Method: The Chichele Lectures Delivered at Oxford, November, 1953*. Reprint of 1954 ed. Westport, CT: Greenwood, 1977.

Ninkovich, Frank A. *The Diplomacy of Ideas: U.S. Foreign Policy and Cultural Relations, 1938–50*. Cambridge: Cambridge University Press, 1981.

Nixon, Richard M. *RN: The Memoirs of Richard Nixon*. New York: Grosset & Dunlap, 1978. Reprint, 2 vols. New York: Warner Books, 1979.

_____. *Leaders*. New York: Warner Books, 1982.

Noble, Harold Joyce. *Embassy at War*. Seattle: University of Washington Press, 1975.

Novak, Michael. *Moral Clarity in the Nuclear Age*. New York: Thomas Nelson, 1983.

Numelin, Ragnar Julius. *The Beginnings of Diplomacy: A Sociological Study of Intertribal and International Relations*. London: Oxford University Press, 1950.

Panikkar, Kavalam Madhava. *In Two Chinas: Memoirs of a Diplomat*. London: G. Allen & Unwin, 1955.

Pearson, Lester B. *Diplomacy in the Nuclear Age*. Cambridge: Harvard University Press, 1959.

Peterson, Sir Maurice Drummond. *Both Sides of the Curtain: An Autobiography*. London: Constable, 1950.

Petrov, Vladimir. *A Study in Diplomacy: The Story of Arthur Bliss Lane*. Chicago: Regnery, 1971.

Pfaltzgraff, Robert, Jr., ed. *Politics and the International System*. 2nd ed. Philadelphia: Lippincott, 1972.

Plischke, Elmer. *Diplomat in Chief: The President at the Summit*. New York: Praeger, 1986.

_____. *U.S. Foreign Relations: A Guide to Information Sources.* Detroit: Gale Research, 1980.

_____, ed. *Modern Diplomacy: The Art and the Artisans.* Washington, DC: American Enterprise Institute, 1979.

Price, Don K., ed. *The Secretary of State.* Englewood Cliffs: Prentice Hall, 1960. Freeport, NY: Books for Libraries Press, 1970.

Quandt, William. *Camp David: Peacemaking and Politics.* Washington: Brookings, 1986.

_____. *Decade of Decisions.* Berkeley: University of California Press, 1977.

Quaroni, Pietro. *Diplomatic Bags: An Ambassador's Memoirs.* Translated and edited by Anthony Rhodes. London: Weidenfeld and Nicolson; New York: D. White, 1966.

Raiffa, Howard. *The Art and Science of Negotiation.* Cambridge: Belknap Press of Harvard University Press, 1982.

Rankin, Karl Lott. *China Assignment.* Seattle: University of Washington Press, 1964.

Rapoport, Anatol. *Strategy and Conscience.* New York: Schocken Books, 1969.

Ravenal, Earl C. *Never Again: Learning from America's Foreign Policy Failures.* 2nd ed. Philadelphia: Temple University Press, 1980.

Roetter, Charles. *The Diplomatic Art: An Informal History of World Diplomacy.* Philadelphia: Macrae Smith, 1963.

Rosecrance, Richard. *International Relations: Peace or War?* New York: McGraw Hill, 1973.

Rosen, Barbara, and Barry Rosen. *The Destined Hour: The Hostage Crisis and One Family's Ordeal.* Garden City, NY: Doubleday, 1982.

Rosenau, James N., ed. *International Politics and Foreign Policy.* 2nd ed. New York: Free Press, 1969.

Rosenblum, Mort. *Coups and Earthquakes: Reporting the World to America.* New York: Harper & Row, 1981.

Sands, William Franklin. *Our Jungle Diplomacy.* Chapel Hill: University of North Carolina Press, 1944.

Satow, Ernest, Sir. *A Guide to Diplomatic Practise.* London: Longmans, Green, 1922. 5th ed. titled *Satow's Guide to Diplomatic Practice.* Edited by Lord Gore-Booth. London, New York: Longmans, 1979.

Savelle, Max, with Margaret Anne Fisher. *The Origins of American Diplomacy: The International History of Angloamerica, 1492–1763.* New York: Macmillan, 1967.

Schell, Jonathan. *The Abolition.* New York: Knopf, 1984.

Schelling, Thomas C. *Arms and Influence.* New Haven: Yale University Press, 1966. Reprint ed., Westport, CT: Greenwood, 1976.

_____. *The Strategy of Conflict.* Cambridge: Harvard University Press, 1960; paper ed., 1980.

Sick, Gary. *All Fall Down: America's Tragic Encounter with Iran.* New York: Random House, 1985.

Sigal, Leon V. *Reporters and Officials: The Organization and Politics of Newsmaking.* Lexington, MA: D. C. Heath Co., 1973.

Simpson, Smith. *Anatomy of the State Department.* Boston: Houghton Mifflin, 1967.

_____. *The Crisis in American Diplomacy: Shots across the Bow of the State Department.* North Quincy, MA: Christopher Publishing House, 1980.

_____. *Perspectives on the Study of Diplomacy.* Occasional Paper. Washington, DC: Institute for the Study of Diplomacy, Georgetown University, 1986.

_____, ed. *Instruction in Diplomacy: The Liberal Arts Approach.* Philadelphia: American Academy of Political and Social Science, 1972.

Singer, Marshall R. *Weak States in a World of Powers: The Dynamics of International Relationships.* New York: Free Press, 1972.

Slater, Jerome. *Intervention and Negotiation: The United States and the Dominican Revolution.* New York: Harper & Row, 1970.

Sloss, Leon, and M. Scott Davis. *A Game for High Stakes: Lessons Learned in Negotiating with the Soviet Union.* New York: Ballinger, 1985.

Smith, Gaddis. *Morality, Reason, and Power: American Diplomacy in the Carter Years.* New York: Hill and Wang, 1986.

Smith, Gerard C. *Doubletalk: The Story of SALT I.* New York: Doubleday, 1980. Reprint. University Press of America, 1985.

Smith, Steve, and Michael Clarke, eds. *Foreign Policy Implementation.* London and Boston: G. Allen & Unwin, 1985.

Smith, Walter Bedell. *My Three Years in Moscow.* Philadelphia: Lippincott, 1950.

Snyder, Glenn H., and Paul Diesing. *Conflict among Nations.* Princeton: Princeton University Press, 1977.

Sorensen, Thomas C. *The Word War: The Story of American Propaganda.* New York: Harper & Row, 1968.

Sorenson, Theodore C. *Decision Making in the White House.* New York: Columbia University Press, 1963.

_____. *A Different Kind of Presidency: A Proposal for Breaking the Political Deadlock.* New York: Harper & Row, 1984.

_____. *Kennedy.* New York: Harper & Row, 1965.

Spaak, Paul-Henri. *The Continuing Battle: Memoirs of a European.* Boston: Little, Brown, 1971.

Spain, James W. *American Diplomacy in Turkey: Memoirs of an Ambassador Extraordinary and Plenipotentiary.* New York: Praeger, 1984.

Spanier, John. *Games Nations Play: Analyzing International Politics.* 5th ed. New York: Holt, Rinehart and Winston, 1984.

Spanier, John, and Joseph Nogee, eds. *Congress, the Presidency and American Foreign Policy.* Elmsford, NY: Pergamon, 1981.

Spiegel, Steven L., and Carol Becker, eds. *At Issue: Politics in the World Arena.* 4th ed. New York: St. Martin's, 1984.

Standley, William H. *Admiral Ambassador to Russia.* Chicago: H. Regnery, 1955.

Steigman, Andrew L. *The Foreign Service of the United States.* Boulder, CO: Westview Press, 1985.

Steinberg, David J. *The Philippines: A Singular and A Plural Place.* Boulder, CO: Westview Press, 1982.

Steiner, Zara, ed. *The Times Survey of the Foreign Ministries of the World.* London: Times Books; Westport, CT: Meckler, 1982.

Stempel, John D. *Inside the Iranian Revolution.* Bloomington, IN: Indiana University Press, 1981.

Stern, Laurence. *The Wrong Horse: The Politics of Intervention and the Failure of American Diplomacy.* New York: Times Books, 1977.

Stimson, Henry L., and McGeorge Bundy. *On Active Service in Peace and War.* New York: Harper Brothers, 1948.

Stoessinger, John G. *Crusaders and Pragmatists: Movers of Modern American Foreign Policy.* New York: W. W. Norton, 1979.

_____. *Nations in Darkness: China, Russia and America.* 4th ed. New York: Random House, 1986.

_____. *Why Nations Go to War.* 4th ed. New York: St. Martin's, 1985.

Stoessinger, John G., and Alan F. Westin, eds. *Power and Order: Six Cases in World Politics.* New York: Harcourt, Brace & World, 1964.

Strang, William, baron. *The Diplomatic Career.* London: A. Deutsch, 1962.

Stuart, Graham H. *American Diplomatic and Consular Practice.* 2nd ed. New York: Appleton-Century-Crofts, 1952.

Sullivan, William H. *Mission to Iran.* New York: Norton, 1981.

_____. *Obbligato: Notes on a Foreign Service Career, 1939–1979.* New York: Norton, 1984.

Sundquist, James L. *The Decline and Resurgence of Congress.* Washington, DC: Brookings Institution, 1981.

Symington, James W. *The Stately Game.* New York: Macmillan, 1971.

Talbott, Strobe. *Deadly Gambits: The Reagan Administration and the Stalemate in Nuclear Arms Control.* New York: Alfred A. Knopf, 1984.

_____. *Endgame: The Inside Story of SALT II.* New York: Harper & Row, 1979.

Taylor, William J., Jr., and Steven A. Maaranen, eds. *The Future of Conflict in the 1980s.* Lexington, MA: Lexington Books, 1983.

Tendler, Judith. *Inside Foreign Aid.* Baltimore: Johns Hopkins University Press, 1977.

Thayer, Charles W. *Diplomat.* New York: Harper, 1959. Reprint. Westport, CT: Greenwood, 1974.

Thies, Wallace J. *When Governments Collide: Coercion and Diplomacy in the Vietnam Conflicts, 1964–1968.* Berkeley: University of California Press, 1980.

Thompson, Kenneth W., ed. *Diplomacy and Its Values: The Life and Works of Stephen Kertesz in Europe and America.* Washington, DC: University Press of America, 1984.

Thompson, W. Scott, ed. *The Third World: Premises of U.S. Policy.* 2nd rev. ed. San Francisco: Institute for Contemporary Studies, 1983.

Thomson, Charles A., and Walter H. C. Laves. *Cultural Relations and U.S. Foreign Policy.* Bloomington: Indiana University Press, 1963.

Tilley, John A. *London to Tokyo.* London: Hutchinson, 1942.

Touval, Saadia. *The Peace Brokers: Mediators in the Arab-Israeli Conflict, 1948–1979.* Princeton: Princeton University Press, 1982.

Touval, Saadia, and I. William Zartman, eds. *International Mediation in Theory and Practice.* Boulder: Westview, 1985.

Trautman, Kathleen. *Spies behind the Pillars, Bandits at the Pass.* New York: McKay, 1972.

Trevelyan, Humphrey. *Diplomatic Channels.* Boston: Gambit; London: Macmillan, 1973.

_____. *Living with the Communists: China 1953–5, Soviet Union 1962–5.* Boston: Gambit, 1971.

Truman, Harry S. *Memoirs.* 2 vols. Garden City, NY: Doubleday, 1955–56; paper, 1986.

Tucker, Robert W. *The Inequality of Nations.* New York: Basic Books, 1979.

Twiggs, Joan E. *The Tokyo Round of Multilateral Trade Negotiations: A Case Study in Building Domestic Support for Diplomacy.* Washington, DC: Institute for the Study of Diplomacy, Georgetown University, and University Press of America, 1987; paper, 1987.

Vance, Cyrus R. *Hard Choices: Four Critical Years in Managing America's Foreign Policy.* New York: Simon & Schuster, 1983.

Varé, Daniele. *Laughing Diplomat.* New York: Doubleday, Doran, 1938.

Villard, Henry S. *Affairs at State.* New York: T. Y. Crowell Co., 1965.

Vital, David. *The Inequality of States: A Study of the Small Power in International Relations.* Oxford: Clarendon Press, 1967.

Watson, Adam. *Diplomacy: Dialogue between States.* New York: McGraw Hill, 1982. Paper ed., Philadelphia: Institute for the Study of Human Issues, 1986.

Weihmiller, Gordon R., and Dusko Doder. *U.S.-Soviet Summits: An Account of East-West Diplomacy at the Top, 1955–1985.* Washington, DC: Institute for the Study of Diplomacy, Georgetown University, and University Press of America, 1986; paper, 1986.

Weintal, Edward, and Charles Bartlett. *Facing the Brink: An Intimate Study of Crisis Diplomacy.* New York: Charles Scribner's Sons, 1967.

West, Rachel. *The Department of State on the Eve of the First World War.* Athens: University of Georgia Press, 1978.

Wilcox, Francis O. *Congress, the Executive, and Foreign Policy.* A Council on Foreign Relations book. New York: Harper & Row, 1971.

Wilkowski, Jean M. *Conference Diplomacy II—A Case Study: The UN Conference on Science and Technology for Development, Vienna, 1979.* Washington, DC: Institute for the Study of Diplomacy, Georgetown University, 1982.

Williams, John D. *The Compleat Strategyst, Being a Primer on the Theory of Games and Strategy.* Rev. ed. New York: McGraw Hill, 1966. Paper ed. New York: Dover, 1986.

Williams, Phil. *Crisis Management: Confrontation and Diplomacy in the Nuclear Age.* London: M. Robertson, 1976.

Wolfers, Arnold. *Discord and Collaboration: Essays on International Politics.* Baltimore: Johns Hopkins University Press, 1962.

Wriston, Henry M. *Diplomacy in a Democracy.* New York: Harpers, 1956.

Yost, Charles W. *The Conduct and Misconduct of Foreign Affairs.* New York: Random House, 1972.

_____. *History and Memory: A Statesman's Perceptions of the Twentieth Century.* New York: W. W. Norton, 1980.

Young, Kenneth T. *Negotiating with the Chinese Communists: The United States Experience 1953-1967.* New York: McGraw-Hill, 1968.

Young, Oran R. *Intermediaries: Third Parties in International Crises.* Princeton: Princeton University Press for the Center for International Studies, 1967.

_____. *The Politics of Force: Bargaining during International Crises.* Princeton: Princeton University Press, 1968.

_____, ed. *Bargaining: Formal Theories of Negotiation.* Urbana, IL: University of Illinois Press, 1975.

Zartman, I. William. *The 50% Solution.* Garden City, NY: Anchor Press, 1976.

_____, ed. *The Negotiation Process: Theories and Applications.* Beverly Hills, CA: Sage, 1978.

Zartman, I. William, and Maureen R. Berman. *The Practical Negotiator.* New Haven: Yale University Press, 1982. Paper ed., 1983.

Articles

Adelman, Kenneth L. "Speaking of America: Public Diplomacy in Our Time." *Foreign Affairs* 59 (Spring 1981):913-36.

Allison, Graham T. "Conceptual Models and the Cuban Missile Crisis." *American Political Science Review* LXIII(September 1969):689-718.

Allison, Graham T., and Morton H. Halperin. "Bureaucratic Politics: A Paradigm and Some Policy Implications." In *Theory and Policy in International Relations*, edited by Richard H. Ullman and Raymond Tanter. Princeton: Princeton University Press, 1972. Brookings Reprint #246.

Art, Robert J. "Bureaucratic Politics and American Foreign Policy: A Critique." *Policy Sciences* 4(December 1973):467-90.

Bacchus, Wilfred A. "The Relationship between Combat and Peace Negotiations: Fighting While Talking in Korea, 1951-53." *Orbis* XVII (Summer 1973):545-74.

Ball, George W. Memorandum to Rusk, McNamara, and McGeorge Bundy (TOP SECRET), reprinted as "Top Secret: The Prophecy the President Rejected. How valid are the assumptions underlying our Viet-Nam policies?" *Atlantic,* July 1972, 36-49.

Bennet, Douglas T., Jr. "Congress in Foreign Policy: Who Needs It?" *Foreign Affairs* 57(Fall 1978):40-50.

Bergsten, C. Fred. "The Threat from the Third World." *Foreign Policy* 11(Summer 1973):753-68.

Betts, Richard K. "Analysis, War, and Decision: Why Intelligence Failures Are Inevitable." *World Politics* XXXI (October 1978):61-89.

Blechman, Barry M., and Janne E. Nolan. "Reorganizing for More Effective Arms Control Negotiations." *Foreign Affairs* 61(Summer 1983): 1157-82. Replies in *Foreign Affairs* 62(Fall 1983): 206-10.

Briggs, Ellis O. "Why Not Give Diplomacy Back to the Diplomats?" *Foreign Service Journal* 46(March 1969): 48-49, 68.

"Britain's Foreign Office." *The Economist,* 27 Nov. 1982.

Brown, Winthrop G. "The Art of Negotiation." *Foreign Service Journal* 45(July 1968): 14-17.

Bundy, McGeorge, George F. Kennan, Robert S. McNamara, and Gerard C. Smith. "Nuclear Weapons and the Atlantic Alliance." *Foreign Affairs* 60(Spring 1982):753-68.

Burrows, William E. "Skywalking with Reagan." *Harper's,* January 1984, 50-57.

Campbell, John C. "Negotiation with the Soviets: Some Lessons of the War Period." *Foreign Affairs* 34(January 1956):305-19.

Carter, Alan. "The State of the Art: Communications and Foreign

Affairs." *Foreign Service Journal* 47(September 1970):31–32, 46–47.

Chace, James. "Is a Foreign Policy Consensus Possible?" *Foreign Affairs* 57(Fall 1978):1–16.

Christopher, Warren. "Ceasefire between the Branches: A Compact in Foreign Affairs." *Foreign Affairs* 60(Summer 1982):989–1005.

Cochran, W. P., Jr. "A Diplomat's Moment of Truth." *Foreign Service Journal* 30(September 1953): 23; 62.

Cooper, James Ford. "Towards Professional Political Analysis in Foreign Service Reporting." *Foreign Service Journal* 48(February 1971): 24–27.

Crocker, Chester A. "South Africa: Strategy for Change." *Foreign Affairs* 59(Winter 1980/1981):323–51.

Curran, R. T. "Diplomat, Heal Thyself." *Foreign Service Journal* 62(May 1985): 23–25.

Cutler, Lloyd N. "To Form a Government." *Foreign Affairs* 59(Fall 1980):126–43.

Davis, Nathaniel. "The Angola Decision of 1975: A Personal Memoir." *Foreign Affairs* 57(Fall 1978):109–24.

_____. "The Foreign Service and Presidential Control of Foreign Policy." *Foreign Service Journal* 57(March 1980):8–14, 38–40.

Destler, I. M. "Country Expertise and U.S. Foreign Policymaking: The Case of Japan." *Pacific Community* 5(July 1974):546–64. Brookings Reprint #298.

_____. "National Security Advice to U.S. Presidents: Some Lessons from Thirty Years." *World Politics* 29(January 1977):143–76.

_____. "The Nixon NSC: Can One Man Do?" *Foreign Policy* 5(Winter 1971/1972):28–40.

Donahue, Gilbert J. "Diplomacy in the Schools: Creating Understanding." *Foreign Service Journal* 62(December 1985):26–28.

Draper, Theodore. "The Dominican Intervention Reconsidered." *Political Science Quarterly* LXXXVI(March 1971):1–36.

Eagleburger, Marlene. " 'Mrs. Foreign Service' Deserves to Be Paid, Too." *Washington Post,* 7 March 1984, A23.

Frankel, Charles. " 'Cultural,' 'Information,' 'Foreign Policy'." *Public Administration Review.* XXIX(November/December 1969):593–600.

Frye, Alton. "Strategic Build-Down: A Context for Restraint." *Foreign Affairs* 62(Winter 1983/1984):293–317.

Gardner, Richard N. "Selling America in the Marketplace of Ideas." *New York Times Magazine,* March 20, 1983, 44, 58–64.

Gedda, George. "Larger Than Life" [Vernon Walters]. *Foreign Service Journal* 61(December 1984):28–31.

George, Alexander L. "The Case for Multiple Advocacy in Making Foreign Policy." *American Political Science Review* 66(September 1972): 751–85.

Gray, Colin S., and Keith Payne. "Under the Nuclear Gun: Victory Is Possible." *Foreign Policy* 39(Summer 1980):14-27.

Grayson, Benson L. "Austria's Diplomats: Numbers Few, Opportunities Numerous." *Foreign Service Journal* 63(March 1986):24-25.

Greider, William. "The Education of David Stockman." *The Atlantic Monthly,* December 1981, 27-54.

Hamilton, Lee H., and Michael H. Van Dusen. "Making the Separation of Powers Work." *Foreign Affairs* 57(Fall 1978):7-39.

Heginbotham, Stanley J. "Dateline Washington: The Rules of the Games." *Foreign Policy* 53(Winter 1983-84):157-72.

Heinrichs, Waldo H., Jr. "Bureaucracy and Professionalism in the Development of American Career Diplomacy." In *Twentieth Century American Foreign Policy,* edited by John Braemen et al. Columbus: Ohio State University Press, 1972.

Herz, Martin F. " 'Prostitution' in the Foreign Service—and What to Do About It." *Foreign Service Journal* 55(August 1978):12-15, 42-43.

_____. "Some Problems of Political Reporting." *Foreign Service Journal* 33(April 1956):20-21, 50-51.

_____. "View from the Top. A Former Ambassador Ponders the Real Goals and Successes of a Foreign Service Career." *Foreign Service Journal* 60(June 1983):26-27, 32-33.

_____. "Who Should Be an American Ambassador?" *Foreign Service Journal* 58(January 1981):23-28, 68.

Hess, Stephen. "The Golden Triangle: The Press at the White House, State, and Defense." *Brookings Review* 1(Summer 1983):14-19.

Hitchcock, David I., Jr. "Publics and Policy." *Foreign Service Journal* 62(April 1985):26-29.

Holland, Harrison M. "The Japanese FSO." *Foreign Service Journal* 60(July/August 1983):18-21.

Huntington, Samuel P. "Transnational Organizations in World Politics." *World Politics* 25(April 1973):333-68.

Jervis, Robert. "Hypotheses on Misperception." *World Politics* 20(April 1968):454-79.

Johnson, U. Alexis. "Diplomacy: The Price of Terror." *Foreign Service Journal* 62(May 1985):18-19.

Joseph, Geri. "Learning to Lead." *Foreign Service Journal* 62(May 1985):34-37.

Kazuo, Ogura. "How the 'Inscrutables' Negotiate with the 'Inscrutables': Chinese Negotiating Tactics vis-a-vis the Japanese." *China Quarterly* 79(September 1979):529-52.

Kellogg, Frank B. "The American Foreign Service as an Instrument for World Peace." *Foreign Service Journal* 7(October 1930):1.

Kennan, George F. "Diplomacy as a Profession." *Foreign Service Journal* 38(May 1961):23–26.

_____. "Foreign Policy and the Professional Diplomat." *Wilson Quarterly* 1(Winter 1977):148–57.

_____. "The Sources of Soviet Conduct." *Foreign Affairs* 25(July 1, 1947):566–82.

Klare, Michael T. "Resource Wars." *Harper's,* January 1981, 20–23.

Leacacos, John P. "The Nixon NSC: Kissinger's Apparat." *Foreign Policy* 5(Winter 1971/1972):3–27.

Leff, Nathaniel H. "The New Economic Order—Bad Economics, Worse Politics." *Foreign Policy* 24(Fall 1976):202–17.

Lever, Harold. "The Debt Won't Be Paid." *New York Review of Books,* June 28, 1984, 3–5.

Lockhart, Charles. "Problems in the Management and Resolution of International Conflicts." *World Politics* 29(April 1977):370–403.

Low, Susan. "Associates of the Service." *Foreign Service Journal* 62(March 1985):24–26.

Luce, Clare Boothe. "The Ambassadorial Issue: Professionals or Amateurs?" *Foreign Affairs*36(October 1957):105–21. Reprinted in *The Modern Ambassador,* edited by Martin F. Herz (1983), qv.

Maechling, Charles, Jr. "Containing Terrorism." *Foreign Service Journal* 61(July/August 1984):33–37.

_____. "Handcuffing Terrorism." *Foreign Service Journal* 64 (January 1987):21–27.

Mainland, Edward A., and David C. McGaffey. "An Appraisal of Some Books on the Art of Negotiating." *State,* June 1982, 36–38.

Malone, Gifford D. "Public Diplomacy: Challenge and Response. Managing Public Diplomacy." *Washington Quarterly* 8(Summer 1985):199–216.

Maresca, John J. "Leaders and Experts." *Foreign Service Journal* 63(March 1986):30–32.

Marks, Edward. "Diplomacy: FSOs or MBAs?" *Foreign Service Journal* 62(December 1985):16–17, and letter of comment by Smith Simpson, idem 63(April 1986).

_____. "Professionalism Is on the Rise in China's Diplomatic Service." *Foreign Service Journal* 61(February 1984):21–23.

Mathias, Charles McC. "Ethnic Groups and Foreign Policy." *Foreign Affairs* 59(Summer 1981):975–98.

McGhee, George C. "The Twilight of Diplomacy." *Foreign Service Journal* 63(April 1986):34–37.

Newsom, David D. "Leaders and Experts." *Foreign Service Journal* 63(June 1986):36–37.

Ninkovich, Frank. "The Currents of Cultural Diplomacy: Art and the State Department, 1938-47." *Diplomatic History* 1(Summer 1977): 215-37.

Nugnes, Paul R. "Crucial Communications" (letter to the editor). *Foreign Service Journal* 62(July/August 1985):7-8.

Odeen, Philip. "Organizing for National Security." *International Security* 5(Summer 1980):111-29.

Pacy, James S. "Subverting Immunity: The Soviet Union and the Iranian Hostage Crisis." *Foreign Service Journal* 61(July/August 1984):32, 43-44.

Piet-Pelon, Nancy J. "A Spouse-less Service." *Foreign Service Journal* 62(March 1985):22-23.

Plischke, Elmer. "Summit Diplomacy: Its Uses and Limitations." *Virginia Quarterly Review* 48(Summer 1972):321-44.

Poullada, Leon B. "Leaders and Experts: The Professional Solution." *Foreign Service Journal* 63(October 1986):24-25.

Pringle, Robert. "Creeping Irrelevance at Foggy Bottom." *Foreign Policy* 29(Winter 1977-78):128-39.

Ravenal, Earl C. "Carter's Year of Human Rights." *Inquiry* 1(January 23, 1978).

_____. "Does Poland Matter?" *Inquiry* 5(August 1982):24-28.

_____. "The Oil-Grab Scenario." *New Republic,* January 18, 1975, 14-16.

_____. "Who Pays for Foreign Policy? A Debate on Consensus: Who Needs It?" *Foreign Policy* 18(Spring 1975):80-91.

Richardson, John, Jr. "Institutional Innovation: Organizing for Better International Relationships." *The Annals* 442(March 1979):117-24.

Roth, Lois W. "Public Diplomacy and the Past: The Search for an American Style of Propaganda (1952-1977)." *Fletcher Forum* 8(Summer 1984):353-91.

Saunders, Harold. Review of *Getting to Yes. Harvard Law Review* 95, No. 6(April 1982):1503-8.

Schlesinger, Arthur M., Jr. "Congress and the Making of American Foreign Policy." *Foreign Affairs* 51(October 1972):78-113.

Scott, Andrew M. "The Department of State: Formal Organization and Informal Culture." *International Studies Quarterly* 13(March 1969):1-18.

Shaplen, Robert. "Profile: Ambassador" [John M. Cabot]. *New Yorker,* March 4, 1961, 39ff.

_____. "Profiles: Eye of the Storm" [David D. Newsom]. *New Yorker,* June 2, 1980, 43ff; June 9, 1980, 48ff; June 16, 1980, 44ff.

Sheehan, Edward F. "How Kissinger Did It: Step by Step in the Middle East." *Foreign Policy* 22(Spring 1976):3-70.

Silberman, Laurence H. "Toward Presidential Control of the State Department." *Foreign Affairs* 57(Spring 1979):872–93. Reprinted in *The Modern Ambassador,* edited by Martin F. Herz (1983), qv.

Simpson, Howard R. "War of the Present." *Foreign Service Journal* 62(October 1985):27–30.

Simpson, Smith. "Adventure in Understanding." *Foreign Service Journal* 28(November 1951):18–19.

_____. "The Frontier in American Diplomacy." *Foreign Service Journal* 57(December 1980):4–8, 39–40.

_____. "Our Faltering Diplomacy." *Foreign Service Journal* 60(September 1983):24–29, 32.

Sowell, Thomas. "Second Thoughts about the Third World." *Harper's,* November 1983, 39–42.

Spiers, Ronald I. "Thinning the Soup." *Foreign Service Journal* 62(March 1985):34–37.

_____(interview). "Managing Adversity: The State of State." *Foreign Service Journal* 64(February 1987):30–35.

Stearns, Monteagle. "Democratic Diplomacy and the Role of Propaganda." *Foreign Service Journal* 30(October 1953):24ff.

Stein, A. "The Politics of Linkage." *World Politics* 33(October 1980):62–81.

Stein, Janice G. "The Alchemy of Peacemaking: The Prerequisites and Corequisites of Progress in the Arab-Israeli Conflict." *International Journal* XXXVIII(Autumn 1983):531–55.

_____. "Leadership in Peacemaking: Fate, Will and Fortuna in the Middle East." *International Journal* XXXVII(Autumn 1982):517–42.

Steiner, Zara. "Foreign Ministries Old and New." *International Journal* XXXVII(Summer 1982):349–77.

Sullivan, William H. "Dateline Iran: The Road Not Taken." *Foreign Policy* 40(Fall 1980):175–86.

Szanton, Peter, and Graham Allison. "Intelligence: Seizing the Opportunity." With Comments by George A. Carver, Jr., and Morton H. Halperin. *Foreign Policy* 22(Spring 1976):183–214.

Tower, John G. "Congress versus the President: The Formulation and Implementation of American Foreign Policy." *Foreign Affairs* 60 (Winter 1981/1982):229–46.

Tucker, Robert W. "A New International Order?" *Commentary,* February 1975, 36–50.

Tuthill, John W. "Operation Topsy." *Foreign Policy* 8(Fall 1972):62–85.

Urquhart, Brian E. "Peacekeeping: A View from the Operational Center." In *Peacekeeping: Appraisals and Proposals,* edited by Henry Wiseman, 161–73. Elmsford, NY: Pergamon, 1983.

Wallach, John P. "A Walk in the Woods." Interview with Paul Nitze, *Washingtonian,* January 1984, 61-77.
_____. "I'll Give It to You on Background." *Washington Quarterly,* Spring 1982, 53-66.
Wang, Robert S. "Talking Turkey with Tokyo." *Foreign Service Journal* 62(November 1985):34-37.
Watzman, Sanford. "The South African Challenge: How Do American Diplomats Fare in the Land of Apartheid?" *State,* October 1986.
Webb, James H., Jr. "Cultural Attaché: Scholar, Propagandist, or Bureaucrat?" *The South Atlantic Quarterly* 71(Summer 1972):352-64.
Winham, Gilbert R. "Practitioner's Views of International Negotiation." *World Politics* 32(October 1979):111-35.
_____. "International Negotiation in an Age of Transition." *International Journal* XXXV(Winter 1979-80):1-20.
Wohlstetter, Roberta. "Cuba and Pearl Harbor: Hindsight and Foresight." *Foreign Affairs* 43(July 1965):691-707.
Wriston, Henry M. "The Secretary of State Abroad." *Foreign Affairs* 34(July 1956):523-40.
Zartman, I. W. "The Political Analysis of Negotiation: How Who Gets What When." *World Politics* 26(April 1974).
_____. "Negotiations: Theory and Reality." *Journal of International Affairs* XXIX(Spring 1975):69-77.

Addresses, Documents, Reports, and Unpublished Manuscripts

Commission on the Organization of Government for the Conduct of Foreign Policy (Murphy Commission). *Report and Appendices on the Organization of Government for the Conduct of Foreign Policy.* 7 vols. Washington, DC: Government Printing Office, 1975.
Kattenburg, Paul M. "The Week That Was in Anthuria." A simulation in multiple diplomatic functions (unpublished). Produced on contract for the Foreign Service Institute, Department of State, 1977.
Kellerman, Henry I. *Cultural Relations as an Instrument of Foreign Policy: The Educational Exchange Program between the United States and Germany, 1945-54.* Washington, DC: Government Printing Office, 1978.
Pastoral Letter on War and Peace (Third Draft). "The Challenge of Peace: God's Promise and Our Response." United States Catholic Conference, 1983.
Spiers, Ronald I. "Diplomacy, the Foreign Service and the Department of State." *Current Policy,* No. 800. U.S. Department of State, Washington, D.C. March 1986.

_____. "Managing the Department of State." *Current Policy,* No. 747. U.S. Department of State, Washington, D.C. October 1985.

_____. "The U.S. Foreign Service: Problems and Prospects." *Current Policy,* No. 699. U.S. Department of State, Washington, D.C. May 1985.

U.S. Advisory Commission on Public Diplomacy, *Annual Report of the United States Advisory Commission on Public Diplomacy.* Washington, DC: Government Printing Office, 1986 *et seq.*

U.S. Congress. House. Committee on Foreign Affairs. *Soviet Diplomacy and Negotiating Behavior: Emerging New Context for U.S. Diplomacy.* Special Studies Series on Foreign Affairs Issues, Vol. I. Study prepared by Joseph G. Whelan, Congressional Research Service, Library of Congress. Washington, DC: Government Printing Office, 1979.

_____. Senate. Committee on Government Operations. Subcommittee on National Security and International Operations. *International Negotiation.* 6 vols. Washington, DC: Government Printing Office, 1969–71.

_____. *Negotiation and Statecraft.* Washington, DC: Government Printing Office, 1970.

_____. *Specialists and Generalists: A Selection of Readings.* Washington, DC: Government Printing Office, 1968.

_____. Subcommittee on National Security Staffing and Operations (Jackson Subcommittee). Eighty-eighth Congress. *S3731. Administration of National Security. Staff Reports and Hearings.* Washington, DC: Government Printing Office, 1965.

U.S. Department of State. *Diplomacy for the '70s: A Program of Management Reform for the Department of State.* Department of State Publication 8551. Washington, DC: Government Printing Office, 1970.

_____. Bureau of Public Affairs. "Vienna Summit." *Selected Documents,* No. 13. Washington, DC: Government Printing Office, 1979.

_____. *"This Worked for me...": Useful Ideas and Techniques for New Ambassadors.* November 1985.

_____. Office of Congressional Relations. *Congressional Travel Handbook.* 1968.

Other Books of Interest from the
Institute for the Study of Diplomacy and University Press of America

CASE STUDIES IN DIPLOMACY

The Diplomacy of Human Rights
edited by David D. Newsom
The Tokyo Round of Multilateral Trade Negotiations: A Case Study in Building
Domestic Support for Diplomacy
by Joan E. Twiggs, with a Foreword by Robert S. Strauss
U.N. Security Council Resolution 242: A Case Study in Diplomatic Ambiguity
by Lord Caradon, Arthur J. Goldberg, Mohamed El-Zayyat and Abba Eban
Resolution of the Dominican Crisis, 1965: A Study in Mediation
by Audrey Bracey, with concluding chapter by Martin F. Herz
Mediation of the West New Guinea Dispute, 1962: A Case Study
by Christopher J. McMullen, with Introduction by George C. McGhee
Resolution of the Yemen Crisis, 1963: A Case Study in Mediation
by Christopher J. McMullen
Conference Diplomacy—A Case Study: The World Food Conference, Rome, 1974
by Edwin McC. Martin
Conference Diplomacy II—A Case Study: The UN Conference on Science and
Technology for Development, Vienna, 1979
by Jean M. Wilkowski, with Foreword by John W. McDonald, Jr.

SYMPOSIA ON PROBLEMS AND PROCESSES OF DIPLOMACY

The Modern Ambassador: The Challenge and the Search
edited by Martin F. Herz, with Introduction by Ellsworth Bunker
Diplomats and Terrorists: What Works, What Doesn't—A Symposium
edited by Martin F. Herz
Private Diplomacy with the Soviet Union
edited by David N. Newsom
Diplomacy for the Future
edited by George C. McGhee
Contacts with the Opposition—A Symposium
edited by Martin F. Herz
The Role of Embassies in Promoting Business—A Symposium
edited by Martin F. Herz, with Overview by Theodore H. Moran
Diplomacy: The Role of the Wife—A Symposium
edited by Martin F. Herz
The Consular Dimension of Diplomacy—A Symposium
edited by Martin F. Herz

EXEMPLARY DIPLOMATIC REPORTING SERIES & OCCASIONAL PAPERS

David Bruce's "Long Telegram" of July 3, 1951
by Martin F. Herz
A View from Tehran: A Diplomatist Looks at the Shah's Regime in 1964
by Martin F. Herz
The North-South Dialogue and the United Nations
by John W. McDonald, Jr.
Making the World a Less Dangerous Place: Lessons Learned from a Career in
Diplomacy
by Martin F. Herz

DIPLOMATIC AND CONTEMPORARY HISTORY

215 Days in the Life of an American Ambassador
by Martin F. Herz
First Line of Defense—Forty Years' Experiences of a Career Diplomat
by John Moors Cabot
The Vietnam War in Retrospect
by Martin F. Herz
U.S.—Soviet Summits: An Account of East-West Diplomacy at the Top, 1955-1985
by Gordon R. Weihmiller and Dusko Doder